First World War
and Army of Occupation
War Diary
France, Belgium and Germany

12 DIVISION
35 Infantry Brigade
Princess Charlotte of Wales's (Royal Berkshire Regiment)
5th Battalion
and Cambridgeshire Regiment
1st Battalion
30 May 1915 - 10 May 1919

WO95/1850

The Naval & Military Press Ltd
www.nmarchive.com
Published in association with The National Archives

Published by

The Naval & Military Press Ltd

Unit 10 Ridgewood Industrial Park,

Uckfield, East Sussex,

TN22 5QE England

Tel: +44 (0) 1825 749494

www.naval-military-press.com

www.nmarchive.com

This diary has been reprinted in facsimile from the original. Any imperfections are inevitably reproduced and the quality may fall short of modern type and cartographic standards.

© **Crown Copyright**
Images reproduced by permission of The National Archives, London, England, 2015.

Contents

Document type	Place/Title	Date From	Date To
Heading	1850/1 5th Battalion Royal Berkshire Regiment		
Heading	12th Division 35th Infy Bde 5th Bn Roy. Berks Regt Jun 1915-Jan 1918 To 36 Bde 12 Div		
Heading	35th Inf. Bde. 12th Div. War Diary 5th Battn. The Royal Berkshire Regiment June (30.5.15 To 20.6.15) 1915 Jan 18		
Heading	War Diary 5th (S) Battn. Royal Berkshire Regiment From 30th May 1915 To (Volume 1)		
War Diary		30/05/1915	20/06/1915
Heading	WO95/1850 5 Berks		
Heading	35th Inf. Bde. 12th Div. War Diary 5th Battn. The Royal Berkshire Regiment July (4.7.15-31.7.15) 1915		
War Diary		04/07/1915	31/07/1915
Heading	35th Inf. Bde. 12th Div. War Diary 5th Battn. The Royal Berkshire Regiment August (3.8.15 To 28.8.15) 1915		
War Diary		03/08/1915	28/08/1915
Heading	35th Inf. Bde. 12th Div. War Diary 5th Battn. The Royal Berkshire Regiment September (3.9.15 To 30.9.15) 1915		
War Diary		03/09/1915	01/10/1915
Heading	35th Inf. Bde. 12th Div. War Diary 5th Battn. The Royal Berkshire Regiment October 1915		
War Diary		01/10/1915	13/10/1915
Map			
War Diary		13/10/1915	31/10/1915
Miscellaneous			
Heading	35th Inf. Bde. 12th Div. War Diary 5th Battn. The Royal Berkshire Regiment November 1915		
War Diary		01/11/1915	30/11/1915
Miscellaneous	3 Maps		
Map	5th Rl Berks Regt		
Map	5th Rl Berkshire Regt		
Heading	35th Inf. Bde. 12th Div. War Diary 5th Battn. The Royal Berkshire Regiment December 1915		
War Diary	Thiennes	01/12/1915	31/12/1915
Miscellaneous	2 Maps		
Map	Map To Illustrate Trenches		
Heading	5th R. Berks Vol 8 Jan		
War Diary		01/01/1916	11/01/1916
Miscellaneous	H.Q. 35th Bgde	31/10/1917	31/10/1917
War Diary		11/01/1916	14/01/1916
Map			
War Diary		15/01/1916	31/01/1916
Heading	War Diary Of 5th Royal Berkshire Regt From 1st February 1916 To 29th February 1916		
War Diary		01/02/1916	29/02/1916
Map			
Heading	War Diary Of 5th Royal Berkshire Regiment From 1st March To 31st March 1916 5 R Berks Vol 10		

War Diary		29/02/1916	31/03/1916
Heading	War Diary Of 5th Royal Berks Regiment From 1st April 1916 To 30th April 1916 Volume 11		
War Diary		01/04/1916	02/04/1916
War Diary	Bethune	03/04/1916	06/04/1916
War Diary	Sailly Labourse	07/04/1916	30/04/1916
Heading	5th R. Berks Vol 9		
Heading	War Diary Of 5th Royal Berkshire Regiment From 1st May 1916 To 31st May 1916 5 Berks Vol 12		
War Diary		01/05/1916	31/05/1916
Heading	War Diary Of 5th Royal Berkshire Regiment From 1st June 1916 To 30th June 1916 Volume 13		
War Diary		01/06/1916	30/06/1916
Heading	5th Bn. Royal Berkshire Regt July 1916		
Miscellaneous	2nd Copy. The Gallipoli Campaign Chapter XIII		
Heading	War Diary 5th Battalion Royal Berkshire Regiment 29-7-16 5 Vol 14		
War Diary		01/07/1916	29/07/1916
Map			
Heading	35th Brigade. 12th Division 1/5th Battalion Royal Berkshire Regiment August 1916		
Heading	War Diary 5th Royal Berkshire Regiment From July 30th/1916-August 30th/1916 5 Vol 15		
War Diary		30/07/1916	30/08/1916
Heading	War Diary Of 5th Royal Berkshire Rgt From September 1st 1916-September 30th		
War Diary		31/08/1916	25/09/1916
Diagram etc	Sketch Shewing Enemy's Parapit and Wire At The Point Where Forpe does Were Exploded		
War Diary		25/09/1916	29/09/1916
Heading	5th Royal Berkshire Rgt Oct. 1916 Vol 17		
War Diary		30/09/1916	30/10/1916
Heading	War Diary November 1916 5th Bn Royal Berkshire Regt Vol 18		
War Diary		31/10/1916	30/11/1916
Heading	War Diary Of 5th Royal Berks Decbr 1916		
Heading	169th Inf. Bde. May 1917		
Miscellaneous	British Salonika Force War Diary		
Heading	War Diary 5th Royal Berks Regt Vol 19		
War Diary		01/12/1916	31/12/1916
Heading	5th (S) Battn R Berkshire Regt. War Diary January 1917 Vol 20		
War Diary		01/01/1917	30/01/1917
Heading	War Diary Of 5th Battn. R. Berks Regt. For Month Feb 1917 Vol 21		
War Diary		31/01/1917	27/02/1917
Heading	5th R. Berks Rgt War Diary March 1917 Vol 22		
War Diary		28/02/1917	30/03/1917
Heading	War Diary 5th Bn Royal Berkshire Regiment 5 R Berks Rgt Vol 23 April 1917		
War Diary		31/03/1917	01/05/1917
Miscellaneous	Account Of Operations East Of Arras April 9th-12th 1917		
Heading	War Diary 5th R Berks Rgt May 1917 Vol 24		
War Diary		02/05/1917	31/05/1917

Heading	War Diary Of 5th (Ser) Bn The Royal Berkshire Regiment For June 1917 Vol 25		
War Diary		01/06/1917	30/06/1917
Heading	War Diary Of 5th (Ser) Bn Royal Berkshire Regt. For July 1917 Vol 26		
War Diary		01/07/1917	30/07/1917
Heading	War Diary For August 1917 5th Bn R. Berks Regt Vol 27		
War Diary		31/07/1917	31/08/1917
Heading	War Diary Of 5th Bn. Royal Berks For September 1917 Vol 28		
War Diary		01/09/1917	30/09/1917
War Diary	Achicourt	01/10/1917	30/10/1917
Operation(al) Order(s)	5th Royal Berkshire Regiment Operation Order No. 3	21/10/1917	21/10/1917
Operation(al) Order(s)	5th Royal Berkshire Regiment Operation Order No. 4	22/10/1917	22/10/1917
Operation(al) Order(s)	5th Royal Berkshire Regiment Operation Order No. 5	24/10/1917	24/10/1917
Operation(al) Order(s)	5th Royal Berkshire Regiment Operation Order No. 6	27/10/1917	27/10/1917
Heading	5 R Berks Regt Vol 30 Nov 17		
War Diary		01/11/1917	30/11/1917
Miscellaneous	Account Of Operations Carried Out On Nov 20th 1917	20/11/1917	20/11/1917
War Diary		02/12/1917	03/12/1917
War Diary		01/12/1917	02/12/1917
Operation(al) Order(s)	5th. Royal Berkshire Regiment Operation Order No. 7	28/10/1917	28/10/1917
Heading	WO95/1850 Plan A Fragment		
Miscellaneous	C Battn. Appendix Tank		
Heading	WO95/1850 Plan A		
Diagram etc	Identification Trace For Use With Artillery Maps		
Map			
Miscellaneous	Message Form		
Map	To Accompany 35th Bde. O. No. 212		
Operation(al) Order(s)	35th Infantry Brigade Order No. 212	23/11/1917	23/11/1917
Miscellaneous			
Miscellaneous	35th Infantry Brigade Instructions No. 3	15/11/1917	15/11/1917
Miscellaneous	Amendment No. 2 To 35th Infantry Brigade Instructions No. 1	17/11/1917	17/11/1917
Miscellaneous	5th Royal Berks Brigade Instruction No. 1	13/11/1917	13/11/1917
Miscellaneous		15/11/1917	15/11/1917
Miscellaneous	Royal Berkshire Regiment Preliminary Instructions		
Miscellaneous	35th Infantry Brigade	24/11/1917	24/11/1917
Map			
Operation(al) Order(s)	Royal Berkshire Regt Order No. 12	23/11/1917	23/11/1917
Miscellaneous	The references Scrip are	24/11/1917	24/11/1917
Diagram etc	Position Of Battalion When Forming Up		
Miscellaneous			
Miscellaneous	Appendix A To Accompany 35th Infantry Brigade Instructions No. 3 Of 15th November 1917		
War Diary		04/12/1917	30/12/1917
Heading	35th Brigade 12th Division 5th Battalion Royal Berkshire Regiment January 1918		
War Diary		31/12/1917	31/01/1918
Miscellaneous	? Re-enforcements During January 1918		
Heading	1850/2 1st Battalion Cambridgeshire Regiment		
Heading	12th Division 35th Infy Bde 1-1st Bn Cambridgeshire Regt May 1918-Mar 1919 From 39 Bn 118 Bde		
Heading	35th Brigade. 12th Division 1/1st Battalion Cambridgeshire Regiment May 1918		

Heading	War Diary 1/1st Cambs May 1918 Absorbed 7 Suffolk 19.5.18 Vol 234		
War Diary	Dickebusch	01/05/1918	03/05/1918
War Diary	Busse Boom	04/05/1918	04/05/1918
War Diary	Popperinghe	05/05/1918	05/05/1918
War Diary	Ruminghem	06/05/1918	09/05/1918
War Diary	Audricques	09/05/1918	09/05/1918
War Diary	Lealvillers	10/05/1918	18/05/1918
War Diary	Acheux	19/05/1918	19/05/1918
War Diary	Mailly-Maillet	20/05/1918	27/05/1918
War Diary	Raincheval	28/05/1918	31/05/1918
Operation(al) Order(s)	1/1st Cambridgeshire Regiment Operation Order No. 77	08/05/1918	08/05/1918
Operation(al) Order(s)	1/1st Cambridgeshire Regiment Operation Order No. 78	12/05/1918	12/05/1918
Operation(al) Order(s)	1/1st Cambridgeshire Regiment Operation Order No. 79	20/05/1918	20/05/1918
Operation(al) Order(s)	1/1st Cambridgeshire Regiment Operation Order No. 80	26/05/1918	26/05/1918
Miscellaneous	1/1st Cambridgeshire Regiment Casualties During May 1918		
Heading	35th Brigade 12th Division 1/1st Battalion Cambridgeshire Regiment June 1918		
Heading	War Diary 1/1st Cambs Regt June 1918 Vol 25		
War Diary	Raincheval	01/06/1918	15/06/1918
War Diary	Hedauville	16/06/1918	01/07/1918
Operation(al) Order(s)	1/1st Cambridgeshire Regiment Operation Order No. 81	15/06/1918	15/06/1918
Operation(al) Order(s)	1/1st Cambridgeshire Regiment Operation Order No. 82	21/06/1918	21/06/1918
Miscellaneous	Reinforcement During June 1918		
Miscellaneous	Casualties During June 1918		
Heading	35th Brigade 12th Division 1/1st Battalion Cambridgeshire Regiment July 1918		
Heading	War Diary For July 1918 1/1st Cambs Regt Vol. 26		
War Diary	Martinsart	01/07/1918	09/07/1918
War Diary	Herissart	10/07/1918	13/07/1918
War Diary	Rumigny	14/07/1918	31/07/1918
Miscellaneous	Appendix I 1/1st Cambridgeshire Regiment Minor Operation	08/07/1918	08/07/1918
Operation(al) Order(s)	1/1st Cambridgeshire Regiment Operation Order No. 88	08/07/1918	08/07/1918
Operation(al) Order(s)	Appendix II 1/1st Cambridgeshire Regiment Operation Order No. 89	13/07/1918	13/07/1918
Operation(al) Order(s)	Appendix III 1/1st Cambridgeshire Regiment Operation Order No. 90	30/07/1918	30/07/1918
Miscellaneous	1/1st Cambridgeshire Regiment Reinforcements During Month Of July 1918	23/07/1918	23/07/1918
Miscellaneous	1/1st Cambridgeshire Regiment Casualties During Month Of July 1918		
Heading	35th Brigade 12th Division 1/1st Battalion Cambridgeshire Regiment August 1918		
Heading	War Diary For August 1918 1/1 Cambridge Vol 27		
War Diary	Canaples	01/08/1918	02/08/1918
War Diary	Ribemont	03/08/1918	07/08/1918
War Diary	Morlancourt	08/08/1918	19/08/1918
War Diary	Ville-S-Ancre	19/08/1918	21/08/1918
War Diary	Morlancourt	22/08/1918	24/08/1918
War Diary	Meault	25/08/1918	25/08/1918
War Diary	Mametz	25/08/1918	26/08/1918
War Diary	Maricourt	27/08/1918	27/08/1918
War Diary	Montauban	28/08/1918	31/08/1918

Miscellaneous	Appendix I 1/1st Cambridgeshire Regiment Report on Operations August 8th 1918	08/08/1918	08/08/1918
Miscellaneous	Appendix II 1/1st Cambridgeshire Regiment Report On Operation 9/8/18	14/08/1918	14/08/1918
Operation(al) Order(s)	1/1st Cambridgeshire Regiment Operation Order No. 91	02/08/1918	02/08/1918
Operation(al) Order(s)	1/1st Cambridgeshire Regiment Operation Order No. 92	07/08/1918	07/08/1918
Operation(al) Order(s)	1/1st Cambridgeshire Regiment Operation Order No. 93	16/08/1918	16/08/1918
Operation(al) Order(s)	1/1st Cambridgeshire Regiment Operation Order No. 94	19/08/1918	19/08/1918
Operation(al) Order(s)	1/1st Cambridgeshire Regiment Operation Order No. 95	21/08/1918	21/08/1918
Miscellaneous	1/1st Cambridgeshire Regiment Reinforcements For August 1918		
Miscellaneous	1/1st Cambridgeshire Regiment Casualties For August 1918	07/08/1918	07/08/1918
Heading	12th Division 35th Brigade 1/1st Cambridge Regiment September 1918		
War Diary	Montauban	01/09/1918	04/09/1918
War Diary	Sailly-Sallisel	04/09/1918	05/09/1918
War Diary	Nurlu	05/09/1918	08/09/1918
War Diary	Riverside Wood (Nurlu)	09/09/1918	17/09/1918
War Diary	Epehy	18/09/1918	30/09/1918
Operation(al) Order(s)	Appendix I 1/1st Cambridgeshire Regiment Operation Order No. 96	17/09/1918	17/09/1918
Miscellaneous	1/1st Cambridgeshire Regiment Supplement To Operation Order No. 95	17/09/1918	17/09/1918
Operation(al) Order(s)	Appendix I 1/1 Cambridgeshire Regt Operation Order No. 97	26/09/1918	26/09/1918
Miscellaneous	1/1st Cambridgeshire Regt Casualties During September 1918		
Miscellaneous	1/1 Cambridgeshire Regt September 1918		
Miscellaneous	1/1st Camb Regt		
Miscellaneous	1/1st Cambridgeshire Regiment Reinforcements During September 1918		
Heading	35th Brigade 12th Division 1/1st Battalion Cambridgeshire Regiment October 1918		
Heading	War Diary 1/1st Camb Regt October 1918 Vol 27		
War Diary	Epehy	30/09/1918	13/10/1918
War Diary	Auby	14/10/1918	15/10/1918
War Diary	Drocourt La Fosse	16/10/1918	20/10/1918
War Diary	Jameon	21/10/1918	21/10/1918
War Diary	Rue Balory (Rusult)	22/10/1918	26/10/1918
War Diary	Coutiches	27/10/1918	27/10/1918
War Diary	Raches	28/10/1918	31/10/1918
Operation(al) Order(s)	Appendix No. 1 1/1st Cambridgeshire Regiment Operation Order No. 100	05/10/1918	05/10/1918
Operation(al) Order(s)	Appendix No. 2 1/1 Cambridgeshire Regiment Operation Order No. 101	05/10/1918	05/10/1918
Operation(al) Order(s)	Appendix No. 3 1/1 Cambridgeshire Regiment Operation Order No.102	06/10/1918	06/10/1918
Operation(al) Order(s)	Appendix No. 4 1/1 Cambridgeshire Regiment Operation Order No. 103	06/10/1918	06/10/1918
Operation(al) Order(s)	Appendix No. 5 1/1st Cambridgeshire Regiment Operation Order No. 104	15/10/1918	15/10/1918
Miscellaneous	Appendix No. 7 1/1st Cambridgeshire Regiment Casualties For October 1918		
Miscellaneous	Appendix No. 6 1/1st Cambridgeshire Regiment Reinforcements For October 1918		

Miscellaneous	Appendix No. 8 1/1st Cambridgeshire Regiment		
Heading	35th Brigade 12th Division 1/1st Battalion Cambridgeshire Regiment November 1918		
Heading	War Diary 1/1st Cambridgeshire Regt Vol 30 November 1918		
War Diary	Raches	01/11/1918	01/11/1918
War Diary	Le Hennoy	05/11/1918	09/11/1918
War Diary	Odomez	10/11/1918	10/11/1918
War Diary	Hergnies	11/11/1918	11/11/1918
War Diary	Bonsecours	12/11/1918	24/11/1918
War Diary	Stamand	25/11/1918	25/11/1918
War Diary	Somain	26/11/1918	30/11/1918
Operation(al) Order(s)	1/1st Cambridgeshire Regiment Operation Order No. 106	04/11/1918	04/11/1918
Operation(al) Order(s)	1/1st Cambridgeshire Regiment Operation Order No. 107	09/11/1918	09/11/1918
Operation(al) Order(s)	1/1st Cambridgeshire Regiment Operation Order No. 108	10/11/1918	10/11/1918
Operation(al) Order(s)	1/1st Cambridgeshire Regiment Operation Order No. 109	12/11/1918	12/11/1918
Operation(al) Order(s)	1/1st Cambridgeshire Regiment Operation Order No. 110	24/11/1918	24/11/1918
Operation(al) Order(s)	1/1st Cambridgeshire Regiment Operation Order No. 111	25/11/1918	25/11/1918
Miscellaneous	1/1st Cambridgeshire Regt Reinforcements During November 1918		
Miscellaneous	1/1st Cambridgeshire Regt Casualties During November 1918		
Heading	War Diary 1/1st Camb Regt November 1918		
Miscellaneous	1st Cambridgeshire Regt Reinforcement During December 1918		
Heading	War Diary 1/1st Camb Regt Decr 1918		
Heading	35th Brigade 12th Division 1/1st Cambridgeshire Regiment December 1918		
Heading	War Diary December 1918 1/1 Camp Regt Vol 31		
War Diary	Somain	01/12/1918	31/12/1918
Heading	War Diary January 1919 1/1st Bn Cambridgeshire Regt Vol 32		
War Diary	Somain	04/01/1919	08/01/1919
War Diary	Auberchicourt	08/01/1919	08/01/1919
War Diary	Pecquencourt	09/01/1919	11/01/1919
War Diary	Somain	12/01/1919	13/01/1919
War Diary	Auberchicourt	13/01/1919	14/01/1919
War Diary	Somain	15/01/1919	31/01/1919
Operation(al) Order(s)	Appendix No. 1 1st Cambridgeshire Regiment Operation Order No. 112	08/01/1919	08/01/1919
Operation(al) Order(s)	Appendix No. 2 1st Cambridgeshire Regiment Operation Order No. 114	14/01/1919	14/01/1919
Miscellaneous	Appendix No. 3 1st Cambridgeshire Regiment Decreases During January 1919		
Heading	War Diary 1/1st Bn Cambridgeshire Regt February 1919 Vol 33		
War Diary	Somain	01/02/1919	28/02/1919
Heading	War Diary 1/1st Camb Regt Feby 1919		
Miscellaneous	1st Cambridgeshire Regiment		

Heading	War Diary 1/1st Cambridgeshire Regiment From 1/3/19 To 31/3/19 Vol 34		
War Diary	Somain	01/03/1919	31/03/1919
Operation(al) Order(s)	Appendix No. 1 1st Cambridgeshire Regiment Operation Order No. 117	13/03/1919	13/03/1919
Miscellaneous	Appendix No. 2 1st Cambridgeshire Regiment Decrease in Strength In During Month Of March 1918	01/04/1919	01/04/1919
Miscellaneous	Appendix No. 3 1st Cambridgeshire Regiment Strength		
Heading	War Diary Of 1/1st Bn. Cambridgeshire Regt April 1919 Vol 35		
War Diary	Somain	02/04/1919	27/04/1919
Miscellaneous	Appendix I 1st Cambridgeshire Regiment	30/04/1919	30/04/1919
Miscellaneous	Appendix II 1st Cambridgeshire Regiment	30/04/1919	30/04/1919
War Diary	Somain	01/05/1919	06/05/1919
War Diary	Dunkerque	07/05/1919	10/05/1919
Operation(al) Order(s)	Sheet 2 Operation Order No.118		

1850/1
5th Battalion
Royal Berkshire
Regiment

12TH DIVISION
36TH INFY BDE

5TH BN ROY. BERKS REGT

JUN 1915 - JAN 1918

To 36 BDE   12 DIV

35th Inf.Bde.
12th Div.

Battn. disembarked
Boulogne from
England. 31.5.15.

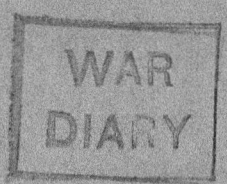

5th BATTN. THE ROYAL BERKSHIRE REGIMENT.

J U N E

(30.5.15 to 20.6.15)

1 9 1 5

Jan '16

INTELLIGENCE SUMMARY.

Confidential

War Diary
of
5th (S) Batn Royal Berkshire Regiment

from 30th May 1915 to

(Volume 1)

INTELLIGENCE SUMMARY.

(Erase heading not required.)

Instructions regarding War Diaries and Intelligence Summaries are contained in F.S. Regs., Part II. and the Staff Manual respectively. Title pages will be prepared in manuscript.

Place	Date	Hour	Summary of Events and Information	Remarks and references to Appendices
	30/5/15	7.25 p.m. 7.50 p.m.	Battn left Aldershot in two trains for FOLKESTONE and crossed to BOULOGNE.	Wrommi
	31/5/15	2 a.m.	Battn arrived at rest camp at BOULOGNE.	werner
	1/6/15	midn.	Battn marched to PONT AU BRIQUES and entrained at 2 a.m. Detrained at LUMBRES and marched to billets with headquarters at ZUDAUSQUES arriving 8 a.m. remaining there till 5th June.	wromm
	5/6/15		Battn marched with Division and went into billets at RENESCURE (14 miles)	wommi
	6/6/15		Battn marched to billets in STRAZEELE. Heat very trying	wromm
	7/6/15		Battn marched to permanent billets in ARMENTIERES (15 miles) remaining there till 14th June. The Battn accommodated in the ground floor of a large three storied cotton factory owned by Mr. Dufour. Officers billeted in private houses	wromm

1577 Wt.W10791/1773 500,000 1/15 D.D.&L. A.D.S.S./Forms/C. 2118.

INTELLIGENCE SUMMARY.

(Erase heading not required.)

Place	Date	Hour	Summary of Events and Information	Remarks and references to Appendices
	14/6/15		Batt marched to Romarin PLUGSTREET WOOD and were attached to the 145th Inf y/Brigade, consisting of 4th Gloster Regt, 4th Oxford Bucks L.I., 1st Bucks L.I. & 4th Berkshire Regt under the command of Bt. General W. K. McClintock, for instruction in trench warfare. 'A' coy, Major Rayley, went into the trenches being attached by platoons to coys of 4th Ox & Bucks L.I. The trenches frontage held by this Batt. is about 2000 yards and the trenches are numbered 37, 38, 39, 40, 61, 62, 63. The MESSINES—ARMENTIÈRES road runs about midway through the frontage & the German trenches are from 300 yards to 400 yards distant.	berma
	15/6/15		'B' coy, Capt G. Hopton relieved 'A' coy being attached in the same manner to the 4th Berkshire Royal Berks Regt who had taken over the section from the 4th Ox & Bucks L.I.	vromes
	16/6/15		'C' coy Capt G. Healy relieved 'B' coy	vernes

Army Form C. 2118.

WAR DIARY
or
INTELLIGENCE SUMMARY.
(Erase heading not required.)

Instructions regarding War Diaries and Intelligence Summaries are contained in F.S. Regs., Part II. and the Staff Manual respectively. Title pages will be prepared in manuscript.

Place	Date	Hour	Summary of Events and Information	Remarks and references to Appendices
	17/6/15		"D" coy. inor'intrustant relieved "C" coy	
	18/6/15		"A" & "B" coys relieved 2 coys of 4th Bⁿ in the trenches. No 7540 Coy Sergt. Maj^r H. COX "B" coy wounded in the arm while shooting at a sniper	
	20/6/15	5am	Batⁿ returned to their former billets in ARMENTIERES and became Divisional Reserve.	

W045/1890

W045/1850 S Reeks

35th Inf.Bde.
12th Div.

5th BATTN. THE ROYAL BERKSHIRE REGIMENT.

J U L Y
(4.7.15 - 31.7.15)
1 9 1 5

5th Battalion The Royal Berkshire Regiment.

July 1915

| 4/7/15 | noon | Battn marched to PLOEGSTEERT WOOD to form Brigade Reserve and to hold the subsidiary line in rear of the Norfolk Regt lines & hitherto taken over from the 7th Bn. The Queens Regt. Battn disposed N as follows. Head Quarters at HANTS FARM |

INTELLIGENCE SUMMARY.

(Erase heading not required.)

Instructions regarding War Diaries and Intelligence Summaries are contained in F. S. Regs., Part II. and the Staff Manual respectively. Title pages will be prepared in manuscript.

Place	Date	Hour	Summary of Events and Information	Remarks and references to Appendices
	6/7/15	9 P.m.	'B' Coy at TOUQUET LE BERTHE Farm, A, C & D Coys in bivouacs in PLOEGSTEERT WOOD	Weather
	7/7/15		No 10682 Pte A. LOVETT 'B' Coy wounded by a stray bullet while in billet	Weather
			No 11075 Pte J. MERCER 'D' Coy killed and No 10302 Pte E. STURGESS 'D' Coy wounded while on working party in neighbourhood of HUNTERS FARM	
	8/7/15		No 7305 Sergt R. Hemmings 'C' Coy accidentally wounded by a revolver	Weather
	9/7/15	11 a.m.	No 16366 Pte F. Meade 'A' Coy killed by a shell while on working party in rear of fire trenches	
		noon	No 10338 Pte A. Nash 'C' Coy wounded by rifle bullet while on working party at LANCASHIRE SUPPORT FARM. No 10509 Pte G. Harrison 'A' Coy wounded by rifle bullet while on working party	

INTELLIGENCE SUMMARY.

(Erase heading not required.)

Instructions regarding War Diaries and Intelligence Summaries are contained in F.S. Regs., Part II. and the Staff Manual respectively. Title pages will be prepared in manuscript.

Place	Date	Hour	Summary of Events and Information	Remarks and references to Appendices
10⁷⁄₁₅	10/7/15	6 a.m.	Battn relieved the 7th North hlf. in the trenches. The trenches are numbered 113 to 120 and commencing with No 120 on the north east corner of PLOEGSTEERT WOOD run in a south westerly direction to the about the S.E. corner. Companies disposed of as follows. "D" wg trenches 119 to 120 with two sections in a supporting point, FORT BOYD. "C" wg trenches 118 to half 116 and "B" wg half 116 to 113. "A" wg in reserve in 3 pokts in HUNTERS AVENUE. The Canadian Division in trenches on the left & the 4th Bn on the right.	
		2.30 a.m		
11⁷⁄₁₅	11/7/15	2.30 a.m	½ hours bombardment of enemy's trenches in the BIRD CAGE by the trench mortar artillery of the Canadian Division and the battn opened rapid fire in co-operation with the infantry.	
		4 p.m.	A battery of our artillery fired 25 rounds of lyddite at 3 new shields in the BIRD CAGE which were thought to be machine gun positions. Parapet knocked about but the shields were intact.	

INTELLIGENCE SUMMARY.

(Erase heading not required.)

Place	Date	Hour	Summary of Events and Information	Remarks and references to Appendices
	11/7/15		2nd Lt A.L. Scott severely wounded by a stray rifle bullet while standing near 'C' Coy H.Q. dugout. Capt. G.M. B. Ware, 2nd Lt. C. Hopford, 2nd Lt Corning N.F.A. No 10367 P/Sgt Graham, No 11246 Sergt Oliver, No 10235 Pte Hepburn all slightly wounded by a high explosive shell which burst about 10 yards in rear of 'C' Coy H.Q. No 9530 Pte F. Harvey "D" Coy accidentally wounded by the discharge of a rifle while in the trenches. Died 12/7/15 A quiet night, a great deal N Work done in repairing parapet and improving fire wire.	
	12/7/15		A quiet day in the trenches.	
	13/7/15		'A' Coy took 'C' Coys place in the trenches. At 9 P.M. a defensive mine was exploded in front of the Canadian line at trench. The explosion was followed by a burst of artillery, rapid infantry & machine gun fire, the "hate" co-operating with the Canadian Division. The enemy responded vigorously and put down German artillery fire, shells falling behind the trenches and in PLOEGSTERT WOOD

INTELLIGENCE SUMMARY.

(Erase heading not required.)

Place	Date	Hour	Summary of Events and Information	Remarks and references to Appendices
	13 7/15	cont.	Duration of fire 35 minutes. Casualties 20/1093 Pte W. Cornelius 'A' Coy killed by a machine gun bullet whilst in the trenches. 2nd Lt 11576 Pte H. Porter 'C' Coy slightly wounded by shell fire.	Warren
	14 7/15		A quiet day & night. 2nd Lt. P.H. Gould fired 12 rifle grenades into the enemy's trenches. 20 were sent back by the enemy—wounded 1 man. 2w 10326 Corpl C. Hillsdon 'B' Coy wounded by a rifle grenade 2w 10643 Pte W. Yarlett 'B' Coy slightly wounded by a rifle bullet 2w 11079 Pte J. Prior 'D' Coy wounded by a shell (not severe) 2w 10985 Pte A. Beale 'D' Coy wounded by a shell (slight)	Warren
	15 7/15		Quiet day & night in the trenches. No casualties.	
	16 7/15		No 10917 Pte J. Gant 'B' Coy slightly wounded by a rifle bullet in the trenches No 11356 Corpl W. Langley 'B' Coy slightly wounded by rifle bullet " No 10838 Pte C. Webber 'B' Coy severely wounded " " No 10309 Pte H. Griffin 'D' Coy severely wounded " " 10544 Pte A. Collins 'B' Coy slightly wounded " "	Warren

INTELLIGENCE SUMMARY.

(Erase heading not required.)

Place	Date	Hour	Summary of Events and Information	Remarks and references to Appendices
	25/7/15		No 11338 L/Corpl W. Tidsdale 'A' Coy slightly wounded by rifle bullet in HUNTERS AVENUE	
	26/7/15		No 10503 L/Corp E. Parkes 'C' wounded by rifle bullet in HUNTERS AVENUE	
	27/7/15		At about 11 P.m. Captain G. W. Hopton and 2nd Lieut A. R. Treherne, Regtal Intelligence Officer, were both mortally wounded by rifle fire while on outside Trench 115. 2nd Lieut Treherne died in a few minutes after being brought back to his trench. Captain Hopton lived for about an hour and died in the journey down to Head Quarters. No 11058 Pte W. Rozetree 'B' Coy dangerously wounded by rifle bullet died 31st day July notwithstanding. No 10503 L/Corp E. Parkes wounded by rifle bullet	

INTELLIGENCE SUMMARY.

(Erase heading not required.)

Instructions regarding War Diaries and Intelligence Summaries are contained in F. S. Regs., Part II. and the Staff Manual respectively. Title pages will be prepared in manuscript.

Place	Date	Hour	Summary of Events and Information	Remarks and references to Appendices
	28/7/15	10 a.m.	Funeral service for Capt G. Hopton 1/2/1st Trenches who were buried in the Cemetery adjoining Rifle House. No 10728 Pte A. Henley slightly wounded in the trenches.	
	29/7/15	10 p.m.	Battn relieved in the trenches by the 7:15th Norfolk Regt and retired to previous billets with H.Q.s as before at HANTS FARM. Total Casualties during term of duty in the trenches.	
				killed wounded
			Officers	2 —
			Other Ranks	— 5
			so slightly wounded 1	
	31/7/15		No 10652 Pte W. Burchell "A" Coy wounded by rifle fire whilst in working party.	Burma

1577 Wt. W10791/1773 500,000 1/15 D. D. & L. A.D.S.S./Forms/C. 2118.

35th Inf.Bde.
12th Div.

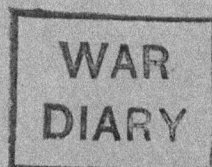

5th BATTN. THE ROYAL BERKSHIRE REGIMENT.

A U G U S T

(3.8.15 to 28.8.15)

1 9 1 5

INTELLIGENCE SUMMARY.

(Erase heading not required.)

Instructions regarding War Diaries and Intelligence Summaries are contained in F. S. Regs., Part II. and the Staff Manual respectively. Title pages will be prepared in manuscript.

Place	Date	Hour	Summary of Events and Information	Remarks and references to Appendices
	3/8/15		No 15676 Pte A. Curtis 'C' Coy, No 9924 Pte W. Cork 'C' Coy wounded by shrapnel whilst in working party	Sussex
	4/8/15		Batln relieved 7th Norfolk Regt in the trenches	Sussex
	6/8/15		No 10461 Sergt Ely Hillier wounded by shrapnel. No 11098 L/Corp A. J. Taylor 'B' Coy killed & No 11135 L/Corp: S. Taylor 'B' Coy & No 10079 Pte G. Neale 'B' Coy wounded by a rifle grenade whilst in the trenches	Sussex
	8/8/15		No 11063 Pte E. Horde 'B' Coy killed by a stray bullet whilst in FORT READING, HUNTERS AVENUE	Sussex
	10/8/15		No 10885 Pte G. Banner 'D' Coy killed by rifle bullet whilst in the trenches. Batln relieved in trenches by 7th Norfolk Regt and returned support	Sussex

1577 Wt.W10791/1773 500,000 1/15 D.D.&L. A.D.S.S./Forms/C. 2118.

INTELLIGENCE SUMMARY.

Instructions regarding War Diaries and Intelligence Summaries are contained in F.S. Regs., Part II. and the Staff Manual respectively. Title pages will be prepared in manuscript.

(Erase heading not required.)

Place	Date	Hour	Summary of Events and Information	Remarks and references to Appendices
	10/8/15		No 11326 L/Cpl: Hern D'Coy, No 11359 Pte H. Gover D'Coy No 11350 Pte J. Burt D'Coy No 15693 Pte A. Cook D'Coy wounded by rifle grenade, in the trenches. Pte Gover died of wounds the same day. Casualties during tour in the trenches 6 officers 0 other ranks Killed 3 Died of wounds 1 Wounded 6	
	13/8/15		No 11800 Pte W. Kennedy D'Coy wounded by shell near HANTS FARM	
	16/8/15		Bn relieved 7th Norfolk Regt. in the trenches	
	18/8/15		A'Coy 13th Bn. K.R.R. attached to the Battn for instruction in trench duties	

INTELLIGENCE SUMMARY.

(Erase heading not required.)

Instructions regarding War Diaries and Intelligence Summaries are contained in F. S. Regs., Part II. and the Staff Manual respectively. Title pages will be prepared in manuscript.

Place	Date	Hour	Summary of Events and Information	Remarks and references to Appendices
	18/8/15		No 11318 Pte C. Trimble 'D' coy killed by a stray rifle bullet while standing outside C.O.s Quarters at RIFLE HOUSE.	Appx
	19/8/15	2.30 p.m.	No 10509 Pte S. Savage 'C' coy slightly wounded by rifle grenade	Appx
	20/8/15		No 10811 Pte P. Dowd 'A' coy severely wounded by a rifle bullet in ear at trench 119	Appx
			No 16581 Pte F. Simpson slightly wounded by rifle bullet in the trenches	Appx
	21/8/15		A draft of 50 N.C.Os & men under Lieut T. L. Reid joined Battalion	
	22/8/15		No 10057 Pte Capper 'D' coy wounded in the finger slightly by surprise but went back in trenches	Appx

Casualties during tour of duty
Officers & other Ranks

Killed   1
Died of wounds   —
Wounded   4 men.

1577 Wt.W10791/1773 500,000 1/15 D. D. & L. A.D.S.S./Forms/C. 2118.

Army Form

WAR DIARY
5th (Serv) Bn Royal Berkshire Regt
INTELLIGENCE SUMMARY.
(Erase heading not required.)

Instructions regarding War Diaries and Intelligence Summaries are contained in F. S. Regs., Part II. and the Staff Manual respectively. Title pages will be prepared in manuscript.

Place	Date	Hour	Summary of Events and Information
	28/8/15		No 10456 Pte C. Smith "D" coy slightly wounded by rifle bullet at HANTS FARM. Batty relieved 7th Norfolk kept in the trenches

35th Inf.Bde.
12th Div.

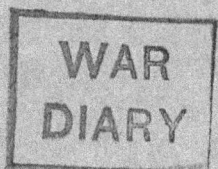

5th BATTN. THE ROYAL BERKSHIRE REGIMENT.

S E P T E M B E R

(3.9.15. to 30.9.15)

1 9 1 5

5th Battalion The Royal Berkshire Regiment.

September 1915
(3.9.15 to 30.9.15)

3/9/15	Batt. relieved by the 7th Norfolk Regt and went back in support
	Casualties during 5 days tour of duty in trenches Nil
9/9/15	Batt. relieved 7th Norfolk Regt in the trenches. Nos 152 36 Pte J. Turner D Coy slightly wounded by rifle bullet
	in support line
10/9/15	Bombardment by Brigade Artillery of Wurtumb opposite trench
	110 for ½ hour

Army Form C. 2118.

WAR DIARY
5th (Ser) Bn Royal Berkshire Regt
INTELLIGENCE SUMMARY.

(Erase heading not required.)

Place	Date	Hour	Summary of Events and Information	Remarks and references to Appendices
	10/9/15		No 17017 L/Cpl W. Carey "D" Coy No 10992 Pte H. Murphy "D" Coy severely wounded & No 11272 Pte S. Wilby "D" Coy slightly wounded by shell fire in Trench 120. No 11709 L/Cpl A. Brown & No 10578 Pte C. Marlow "B" Coy wounded by rifle grenade in Trench 113	wounded
	15/9/15		No 10698 Pte J. Fitzgerald "B" Coy slightly wounded by rifle grenade. Batln relieved by 7th hortsh and went back in support. Casualties during 6-10m of duty in trenches Wounded 7	wounded

5th Bn or Royal Berkshire Regt

INTELLIGENCE SUMMARY.

(Erase heading not required.)

Place	Date	Hour	Summary of Events and Information	Remarks and references to Appendices
	17/9/15		No 10466 Pte J. Middleton D' Coy severely wounded by stray rifle bullet while in bivouac with his Coy.	Evans
	21/9/15		Battn relieved 7' Norfolk Regt in the Trenches	
	24/9/15		Snow fallen upto knees in trenches and soaked with water. Patrols out in own wire preparation made for attack & promised to cooperate with troops on our right	
	25/9/15		Bombardment by our guns began at 5am Some casualties Started at 5.50am. Enemy shortly retaliated & we gave in response German lines also replied with Rifle Fire & artillery many & bad shells 3 men slightly wounded. Capt. B. Mugret in 118120 knocked down. Quiet afternoon. On 2nd G return evening afternoon & bombers in evening. Gaps in wire closed up for	
	26/9/15		Quiet morning. Relieved by 15' Batt Londons and Div at 9pm Marched to bill 6 at WESTHOF for the night	
	27/9/15		Marched at 1.30pm to MERRIS	

Army Form C. 2118.

5th (Ser) Bn Royal Berkshire Regt
WAR DIARY
INTELLIGENCE SUMMARY.
(Erase heading not required.)

Place	Date	Hour	Summary of Events and Information	Remarks and references to Appendices
	28/9/15	9am	Left by 36 omnibuses for MONT BERNENCHON where we arrived at 1.30pm. Transport arrived 5.7pm.	
	29/9/15	Noon	Joined brigade at GONNEHEM and arrived via CABOCQUES, VAUDRICOURT, ROUX LES MINES to LABOURSE (wet day) secured rail halts arrived at 7pm all men in billets.	
	30/9/15	4pm	Left LABOURSE for the trenches at LOOS. Considerable delays owing much rain & heavy traffic. Bn then reported present in support Trenches shambles after BURBURE road/5pm.	
	1/10/15			

35th Inf.Bde.
12th Div.

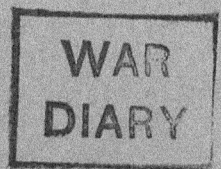

5th BATTN. THE ROYAL BERKSHIRE REGIMENT.

O C T O B E R

1 9 1 5

INTELLIGENCE SUMMARY.

(Erase heading not required.)

Place	Date	Hour	Summary of Events and Information	Remarks and references to Appendices
	1/10/15		Batalion finished relieving Guards shortly after midnight. Men employed strengthening parapets by night and by day erecting shelters in the Chalk for protection from Shell fire. Snipers and Machine guns about 1200 yards North of LOOS. Held 70 to 2760 yards S.E. of HULLOCH about 2000 yards N.E. As have Trenches cut in full view of the Germans no work can be done by day above the parapet.	
	2/10/15			1 killed and 6 wounded
			A few moments of shelling by the Germans caused casualties. Two parties of 110 men were sent up by night to dig and finish off from refuges and to connect up with the armed Division on Right.	
	3/10/15		Enemy shrapnel burst over and over our support trenches causing 3 killed and 4 wounded in afternoon.	
		7.30pm	Relief of Battalion by 1st East Lancashire Regt. Trenches to gain and complete by about 10 pm. Work continued on new trench over Ridge.	
	4/10/15		Work on Parapet by night. Shelled by Enemy most of the day.	1 killed & 15 wounded

INTELLIGENCE SUMMARY.

(Erase heading not required.)

Instructions regarding War Diaries and Intelligence Summaries are contained in F. S. Regs., Part II. and the Staff Manual respectively. Title pages will be prepared in manuscript.

Place	Date	Hour	Summary of Events and Information	Remarks and references to Appendices
	5/10/15		Heavily shelled by enemy all morning and part of the afternoon. 1 killed 21 wounded	
	6/10/15	9 p.m.	Relieved by Gloucesters & Leicester Lincolns 2nd Brigade	
		3 a.m.	Battalion reported present at NO 5555 billets at 3 a.m. Standing by. 3 wounded	
↓	7/10/15		In billets. Quiet day. nil	
	8/10/15		Billets shelled from Noon to 5 p.m. Men took shelter in cellars and communication trenches. 5 wounded	
		6 p.m.	Battn ordered to "Stand To" & to be ready to move at once.	
		9 p.m.	Battn stood down & went to bed.	
	9/10/15	5 a.m.	Battn "Stood To" till 8 a.m. Ready to move. Quiet day. nil	
	10/10/15		Quiet day. 2 wounded	
	11/10/15		Quiet morning. Germans shelled us from 2 p.m. to 4 p.m. 5 wounded.	
	12/10/15		Left billets at 11 a.m. and relieved Welchroom Guards in support Trenches. 9 wounded	

INTELLIGENCE SUMMARY.

(Erase heading not required.)

Instructions regarding War Diaries and Intelligence Summaries are contained in F. S. Regs., Part II. and the Staff Manual respectively. Title pages will be prepared in manuscript.

Place	Date	Hour	Summary of Events and Information	Remarks and references to Appendices
	13/8/15	10 a.m.	Steel coats ~~bodies~~ and caps were started in Deep Gully. Re men put on their Sun-Helmets	
		12.30 p.m.	Head Quarters moved up to the firing line and on arrival there about 2.30 pm with one Company on the line H.Q. so far as I can ascertain No 8. I went out 1st Norfolks who were one that the majority of his 3 Coys. had been sent forward to the ahead had become casualties but that on had reached their objective, the heard in front of the Queries and were urgently in need of reinforcements. I at once despatched "P" Coy 5th Royal Scots under Major Bay-Ly to reinforce. This Company met with a very severe machine Gun fire from the trenches that the 8th Norfolks was under the impression that his own side, hardly any Gerking half way. It was reported Serious that the 1st Norfolks was mistaken & that the trench was held strongly by the Germans As the Brigadier gave out a free hand in the matter I did not deem it advisable to continue the attack. Re reinforcements needed, approximately a line drawn through from (G 12 of map 5) pivotted with 20nd running from Point 46 & 82. We now have 2 Divisions and news) from (F 12 a) 54, k (G 11 d) 9.3.	

1577 Wt.W10791/1773 500,000 1/15 D. D. & L. A.D.S.S./Forms/C. 2118.

INTELLIGENCE SUMMARY

Place	Date	Hour	Summary of Events and Information	Remarks and references to Appendices
	13/9/15		Bombing attack made by 6th Royal Scots. The attack was made by four parties of 2 & 1 men drawn from each Coy. of B.N.R.S.S. 1 Sergt & 1 Corp. under 2/Lt. R.Shand. "B" & "C" Party to be followed by the parties from D., A., & C. Coys. 2/Lt. R.Shand had arranged to station himself in the centre of the detachment of bombers. That the way that the German Trench had been arranged: Run along by the French, whose fire he took charge of, to leading parts. Our barricade was built. B. Coy to be to right of about 2 ft. to bayonet men of the B. Coy. party went over first followed by 2/Lt R.Shand carrying bombs. A machine gun opened fire from the right. 2/Lt R.Shand was hit in the jaw whilst on the barricade & two other men were also wounded. On the further side of the barricade were some French with showering bombs and revolver. No enemy came from his own trench about 10 metres off – so that it was necessary to crawl through the wire on the stomach – two men were raised themselves on their hands & knees being immediately hit. No men returned who escaped unwounded, towards the British trench which was supported ahead. 2/Lt R.Shand &c. As signed by Staff card. Followed by B & D Coy parties	

INTELLIGENCE SUMMARY.

(Erase heading not required.)

Place	Date	Hour	Summary of Events and Information	Remarks and references to Appendices
	13/2/		Scrambled over & bombed the several traverses. The R & C C.M. parties passed up their bombs & were following over the German barricade when the Rsgt of C.M. showing that no one was following and having urgent call for more bombs returned with 3 men taking him and shouted for bombs which they passed along as they came over the barricade. By this time the advance had been checked owing to shortage of bombs. Pte Randall Kitchener Bayonet man had been wounded but carried on firing steadily. Rendered 2 coy German Stores himself wounded but remained at this point. Unsupported on our front and either extremities. Wm. Rillingston a gun wounded but continued to throw bombs and direct operations. Four feet high so that the party were exposed to rifle and machine gun fire from various trenches. They rose to throw or reserve some of the Germans did so by an officer & attempts to reach the party from the trench on the 25th but were broken up by bombs and rifle fire. The heavy bombing of B Coy had done some serious damage; they fell back but continued to pass up bombs. Their places been taken by R. B Branch By noon of the day also, although 3 bombers continued to throw until it was but a second time when Pte Randall also wounded cannys ??? wounded	

1577 Wt. W10791/1773 500,000 1/15 D. D. & L. A.D.S.S./Forms/C. 2118.

INTELLIGENCE SUMMARY.

(Erase heading not required.)

Place	Date	Hour	Summary of Events and Information	Remarks and references to Appendices
	13.6.15		again experienced difficulty to the end. Lyttelton continued throwing bombs until unable to stand, he supported himself against the parapet still directing operations; in this position he was killed. The supply of bombs was unsatisfactory owing to the lemon bombs were unreliable owing to the fuzing being bad, during their passage over the two services – being thrown from hand to hand, either singly or in sandbags. At one point no bombs could be obtained & the counter attack pursued up could be used as the man bombarding had no bombs. Lyttelton endeavoured in vain to secure relief but some twenty during this period the parts were defending themselves with rifles only. In response to urgent calls for reinforcements four men of the Buffs came up under Lothian had a stretcher sustains the counter attack came. The party continued to hold their ground until the order to retire was given. They then retired in good order. Lyc Goddard carrying Lieutenant Wankerfield at P.M. 36 wrist. 16th 5.15 party Pte Hanson reported to be killed. L/c Berg died of wounds L/c Smith Pte Harrison and Ransell wounded. 5.9th. 5.15 party Pte Alloway Brown and Davies are reported to be killed.	bad message

INTELLIGENCE SUMMARY.

(Erase heading not required.)

Place	Date	Hour	Summary of Events and Information	Remarks and references to Appendices

and Pte Lambell & Smith wounded.
All the survivors agree in their praise of the gallantry shown by Lt Collins and of Captain [...] escaping by No 10311 Pte Lambell B.D.M. and by No 11106 L/c Day & 10299 Pte Duncan of "B" Coy — all of whom carried on in the forefront of the fight after they had been wounded.

INTELLIGENCE SUMMARY.

(Erase heading not required.)

Instructions regarding War Diaries and Intelligence Summaries are contained in F. S. Regs., Part II. and the Staff Manual respectively. Title pages will be prepared in manuscript.

Place	Date	Hour	Summary of Events and Information	Remarks and references to Appendices
			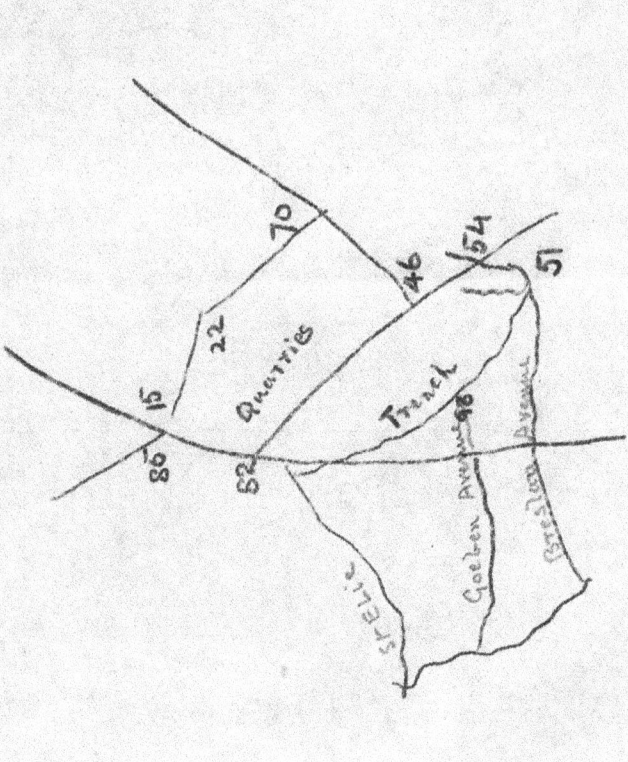	

1577 Wt. W10791/1773 500,000 1/15 D. D. & L. A.D.S.S./Forms/C. 2118.

INTELLIGENCE SUMMARY.

(Erase heading not required.)

Place	Date	Hour	Summary of Events and Information	Remarks and references to Appendices
	13/5		Our Casualties amongst Officers has been: Killed: Capt Spencer Machine Gun Officer Lieut R. Pepland in charge of Bombers Missing: Major W.H. Bay Sy } comdg 'A' Coy Capt D.G. Mount Lieut L Rees Lieut Freworth-Jones } 'B' Coy Capt & Adjt P.H. Good Wounded: Capt P.H. Hereford 'C' Coy Shock: Lt H.C. Hereford Capt E.C. Stacey R.A.M.C. last badly crushed by dug out 2nd Lieut J Leccent Station falling on him ? Killed Sgs Major Turner and 36 N.C.O.'s and men Wounded 91. Total 149 Missing 22.	

Instructions regarding War Diaries and Intelligence Summaries are contained in F. S. Regs., Part II. and the Staff Manual respectively. Title pages will be prepared in manuscript.

INTELLIGENCE SUMMARY.

(Erase heading not required.)

Place	Date	Hour	Summary of Events and Information	Remarks and references to Appendices
	13/15		Most of the night was spent clearing the Trenches of dead and collecting the wounded and also repairing the parapets	
	14		Quiet day	
	15		Quiet morning but about 4pm we were shelled for an hour	
	16		Quiet	
	17th		Germans on our left began a bombing attack at 5am our guns also fired for several hours. The Germans retaliated after our and shelled our Trenches heavily till 5pm. Suffering from shock 1 killed 19 wounded	
	18th		Quiet till 5pm. When Essex Regt on our left began a bombing attack & captured about 100 yards of trench. Germans shelled us heavily from 5.30pm to 6pm 2 killed 8 wounded, 3 shock	
	19th	5am	Relieved by 9th Royal Fusiliers & marched to billets at VERMELLES	
		5pm	Ordered to "Stand To" and eventually marched at 6.30pm to Trenches Old British front line. Returned to billets at 11.30pm 2 killed 5 wounded	
	20th	6.45am	Battalion left for BETHUNE which we reached about 11am	
	21st 25		Battalion marched in Orphanage, Refitting.	

1577 Wt.W10791/1773 500,000 1/15 D. D. & L. A.D.S.S./Forms/C. 2118.

INTELLIGENCE SUMMARY.

(Erase heading not required.)

Instructions regarding War Diaries and Intelligence Summaries are contained in F. S. Regs., Part II. and the Staff Manual respectively. Title pages will be prepared in manuscript.

Place	Date	Hour	Summary of Events and Information	Remarks and references to Appendices
	26/12/15	9.30 a.m.	Battalion left Bethune for Trenches and L.o.s. trenches at Noyelles	
		1.40 p.m.	Entered Communication Trench Gordon Alley.	
	27		Relieved by Norfolk Reg't. during afternoon	1 killed 3 wounded
	28		A&B Coys to Support line	
	29		Battalion relieved Norfolks in morning	2 killed 2 wounded
	30		Quiet day	1 killed wounded
	31st		Quiet day Relieved by Norfolks midday	

INTELLIGENCE SUMMARY.

(Erase heading not required.)

Place	Date	Hour	Summary of Events and Information	Remarks and references to Appendices
			14/10/15 Copies telegrams. The Brigadier has been informed that the Corps Commander was particularly pleased with the conduct of the Troops throughout yesterday's operations. The Brigadier desires to congratulate the 33rd-15th on having gained such excellent positions which he himself fully concurs.	M
			15/10/15 The Corps Commander has expressed his admiration for the performance of the Division and his satisfaction that we have achieved what has already been twice attempted. The Major General hopes that as far as possible no kits or equipments belonging to the 12th Division will be left lying about in front of or near the trenches when we are relieved and the Brigadier is sure Battalions will make it a matter of pride that every effort is made to get in all that is in our charge. 18/10/15. The following message received from Guards Division. "Well done neighbours. Stick to it. Sincere thanks for help and cooperation yesterday and to-day."	

INTELLIGENCE SUMMARY.

(Erase heading not required.)

Place	Date	Hour	Summary of Events and Information	Remarks and references to Appendices
			The following received from the Corps Commander. 15/10/15. "Please convey to the Officers, N.C.O's and men of 12th Division my appreciation of their successful attack against Gun Trench on 13th inst, and also of their efforts to gain possession of the Quarries where they have made an important and successful advance. This attack was carried out by troops who had been for some days in the trenches and reflects great credit on all." (sgd) R. Haking, Lieut-General, Commanding 11th Corps 14/10/15. The following message from Division received. 19/9/15. The Major-General is especially pleased with the behaviour of your Brigade not only against the attack of the Germans to-day but with its gallant conduct in the trenches during the recent operations. The 9th Essex Regt; are to be especially commended on their gallantry in capturing the Quarry Trench and on the manner in which they have withstood the determined attacks by the Germans this afternoon which reflects the greatest credit on their Officers and on all ranks.	

35th Inf.Bde.
12th Div.

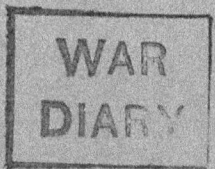

5th BATTN. THE ROYAL BERKSHIRE REGIMENT.

N O V E M B E R

1 9 1 5

Attached:

3 Maps.

INTELLIGENCE SUMMARY

(Erase heading not required.)

Place	Date	Hour	Summary of Events and Information	Remarks and references to Appendices
In billets at Vermelles	Nov 1/15			
	2nd			2 wounded
	3rd		Relieved Norfolk Reg't in Trenches during the afternoon. Communication trenches knee deep in liquid mud in many places. Men employed in clearing trenches & reverting parapets & parados once repaired.	1 wounded
	4th	10.30 am	Trenches slightly better. Work begun again on them at & continued all day.	1 wounded
	5th		Relieved by Norfolk Reg't during the morning. 2 Companies sent to support trenches. C Coy to support Trench in rear of Rupert Bastion (Sussex Regt) and one platoon of D & Hulloch Keep. Remainder of Batt'n in Bn HQ & 3 Platoon of B Coy & Head Quarters & billets in Vermelles. 8 wounded.	
	6th		2 Platoons of D/1st sent in support trenches to man trenches near Keeps	1 wounded

INTELLIGENCE SUMMARY.

(Erase heading not required.)

Instructions regarding War Diaries and Intelligence Summaries are contained in F. S. Regs., Part II. and the Staff Manual respectively. Title pages will be prepared in manuscript.

Place	Date	Hour	Summary of Events and Information	Remarks and references to Appendices
	Nov 7th		D Coy remained in Support and KEEPS. Bn HQ relieved by Royal West Kent Regt. Bn HQ marched to new billets at SAILLY LABOURSE	Reminder seen after 8 p.m. (relief) 5 Lorenges
	8th		Cleaning up and drying clothes	
	9th	Noon	Tour Hot baths at disposal of battalion at Annequin 18 suits clothes returned	
	10th	2 h	Bombing + Bayonet fighting + Physical Drill C Coy returned by 5 p.m. Roll Call + Bath + Shaving. Working parties improving CT Bathing parades turning day D Coy to Baths	
	11th		Musketry in Morning. Speech practice in afternoon	
	12th		Wet morning. Musketry Gallery not on. Working party in afternoon	
	13th		Marched to FOUQUEREUIL (8 miles) at 9 a.m.	

INTELLIGENCE SUMMARY.
(Erase heading not required.)

Instructions regarding War Diaries and Intelligence Summaries are contained in F. S. Regs., Part II. and the Staff Manual respectively. Title pages will be prepared in manuscript.

Place	Date	Hour	Summary of Events and Information	Remarks and references to Appendices
	14/15		Church Parade 10 a.m. Marching order inspection by O.C. at 11.30 a.m.	
	15th	9	Marching order inspection 9 a.m. Company drill	
		12.30	& Musketrie & Bombing till 12.30 pm	
		2pm		
		4pm	Route march.	
	16th	5.10am	Marched to ANNEQUIN arrived 11.10am.	
	17th	5.15am	Leading Platoon left for Trenches to relieve R. Welsh Fus⁰ & Kent Reg⁹. Relief completed by noon. A Coy on the Right "B" in Centre and "C" on left. D⁰ "A" The Suffolks were on our Right and the 5th Kings (L⁴) Liverpool Reg⁹ 6th Brigade on our left. (670 Scots mise) (killed 1 wounded)	
	18th		Artillery amount of French Mortars fired by the Germans, we replied with Stocker & Rifle Grenades 6 wounded.	
	19th		Relieved by Norfolk Reg⁹ & broken Vermelles by 2/pm. Batt⁰ all in cellars in village.	
	20th		Most of battalion away on carrying old equipment from Trenches	

INTELLIGENCE SUMMARY

(Erase heading not required.)

Place	Date	Hour	Summary of Events and Information	Remarks and references to Appendices
	21st		General fatigues	
	22nd	11.15	Leading Platoon marched off to trenches to relieve R. Norfolks. Relief completed by 2 pm. "D" on Right "B" in Center "A" on Left "C" in Support. Capt Elliot "D" Coy wounded whilst taking over from R. Norfolks. Capt Lace "A" Coy took his place for the two days. ("A" Coy hit a powder flare going up, report wounded Capt Elliot & 2 men & 2 men killed	
	23rd		German trench mortars busy. We replied with our own. The New divisional artillery not having registered were unable to retaliate properly. 2nd Lieut T.D.W. Buchel was wounded & wiring atom[?] 21 also 4 men and 2 more men killed	
	24th		Relieved by 4th Battn (T) Seaforth Highlanders & Kashis 13th Division arrived in billets at Sailly Labourne at 4 pm.	
	25th		Marched at 7.20 am for Bethune. Bath for the men & clean clothes	
	26th		Marched X & entrained at Fouquereuil Station at 8.30 am.	

INTELLIGENCE SUMMARY.

(Erase heading not required.)

Instructions regarding War Diaries and Intelligence Summaries are contained in F. S. Regs., Part II. and the Staff Manual respectively. Title pages will be prepared in manuscript.

Place	Date	Hour	Summary of Events and Information	Remarks and references to Appendices
	26		Detrained at Priemer Station & 20am. Billets in village 1/2 mile distance. Companies somewhat scattered	
	27		Inspection of clothing & kit. Quiet evening morning	
	28		Church Parade 10.45am	
	29	8.30 F	Companies at drill, saluting, Bayonet 2/S.Being, Platoon & Coy	
		12.30	Drill. Physical training. Special sunlight glass under 2/Lt Seymour Bsmt.	
		2.45pm	Short Route March. Recture for class under 2/Lt Morgan.	
	30		Drill as on 29	

[signature]

3 MAPS.

Army Form C. 2118.

Maps to illustrate
Various places where
battalion **WAR DIARY** has been billeted
5th R. Berks Regt

INTELLIGENCE SUMMARY.

(Erase heading not required.)

Summary of Events and Information

Date	Hour	Summary of Events and Information	Remarks and references to Appendices

...ructions regarding War Diaries and Intelligence
Summaries are contained in F. S. Regs., Part II.
and the Staff Manual respectively. Title pages
will be prepared in manuscript.

1577 Wt. W.10791/1773 500,000 1/15 D. D. & L. A.D.S.S./Forms/C. 2118.

Map to show Communication Trenches to Boulders
Squares 500 yards

WAR DIARY
or
INTELLIGENCE SUMMARY.

Army Form C.-2118.

5th R¹ Berkshire Reg¹

(Erase heading not required.)
Summary of Events and Information

Place	Date	Hour	Summary of Events and Information	Remarks and references to Appendices

Instructions regarding War Diaries and Intelligence Summaries are contained in F. S. Regs., Part II. and the Staff Manual respectively. Title pages will be prepared in manuscript.

Trenches shown:
FOSSE ALLEY, THE DUMP, DUMP TRENCH, NORTH FACE, SOUTH FACE, CROSS TRENCH, BIG WILLIE, LITTLE WILLIE, HOHENZOLLERN REDOUBT, FOSSE TRENCH, THE WINDOW, BRESLAU AVENUE, WHITE MOUND, BRESLAU TRENCH, HULLUCH ROAD, THE HARE, BOIS C, QUARRIES, RAILWAY, WATER TOWER, FOUNTAIN KEEP, QUARRY ALLEY, LEFT BOYAU, RIGHT BOYAU, V.1, JERMYN STREET, GORDON ALLEY, BART'S ALLEY (OUT), GORDON ALLEY (IN), HULLUCH ALLEY

1577 Wt. W10791/1773 500,000 1/15 D. D. & L. A.D.S.S./Forms/C.2118.

Map to illustrate Trenches 5th R. Berkshire Regt

X represent Right & Left of Battln in front line vis a vis Hanover Trench & East End of Bigger Willie

WAR DIARY
INTELLIGENCE SUMMARY
Army Form C. 2118.
(Erase heading not required.)

35th Inf.Bde.
12th Div.

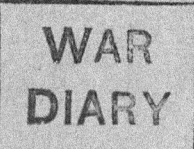

5th BATTN. THE ROYAL BERKSHIRE REGIMENT.

D E C E M B E R

1 9 1 5

Attached:

2 Maps.

WAR DIARY 5 Royal Berkshire Reg: Army Form C. 2118.

INTELLIGENCE SUMMARY.

December 1915

Place	Date	Hour	Summary of Events and Information	Remarks and references to Appendices
THIENNES	1st Dec.	10.20	Reorganisation, Battalion Route march	
		12.45	2nd Batt 2nd P.W.L.I. team came over to play us and even teams 6 goals to 0. About 100 men came over	
		2.30 pm	2nd Batt on VIII Division encamped in tents about 3 & 1/2 miles north of us.	
	2nd Dec		Companies at drill	
	3rd Dec		Wet all day, Companies went for short Route march.	
	4th		Another holiday. 35th Brigade 2nd Football competition	
			1st Round 5th Royal Berkshire beat 7th Suffolks 3 goals to 0	
			7th Norfolks beat 5th Essex Regt. 3 goals to 0	
	5th		2nd Round 7th Norfolks beat 5th Royal Berkshire Regt 2 goals to 0.	
	6th		Route march.	
	7th		Zieuveture Range 30 yards at disposal of Companies all day. One hour for each Company enemy firing onwards	

WAR DIARY
or
INTELLIGENCE SUMMARY.

Army Form C. 2118.

(Erase heading not required.)

Instructions regarding War Diaries and Intelligence Summaries are contained in F. S. Regs., Part II. and the Staff Manual respectively. Title pages will be prepared in manuscript.

Place	Date	Hour	Summary of Events and Information	Remarks and references to Appendices
	7th		Team competitions in afternoon.	
	8th		Journey of men from each Platoon, knock'out competition at Brigade targets winners as follows	
			A Coy No 1. Platoon	
			B Coy 5 also ains Battalion Prize	
			C Coy 11	
			D Coy 13	
	9th		Artillery Practice morning. Football in afternoon.	
			Brigade Rifle meeting. No 4 match viz. Lewis Helmet Competition won by 3rd Rl Berks Regt, 2nd & 3rd places referenced O. 2nd 9.3 Essex 3rd 7th Norfolks 4th 1st Suffolks	
	10th		Battalion left THIENNES at 7.65am for BELLERIVE (4 miles) after passing L'ECLEME/Morfield Bilady) Very wet day. We met the Corps Commander – General Gough. warned. at BELLERIVE just after 2pm & were also held up 2612	
	11th		Very wet night & morning. rain stopped 10.30am. Bn HQ marched at 10.15am for ESSARS 15 miles N.N.E. of Bethune. arrived Noon.	

1577 Wt.W10791/1773 500,000 1/15 D. D. & L. A.D.S.S./Forms/C. 2118.

WAR DIARY or INTELLIGENCE SUMMARY.

Army Form C. 2118.

(Erase heading not required.)

Instructions regarding War Diaries and Intelligence Summaries are contained in F.S. Regs., Part II and the Staff Manual respectively. Title pages will be prepared in manuscript.

Place	Date	Hour	Summary of Events and Information	Remarks and references to Appendices
	12th		Scheme for Officers all morning. 80 men arrived from 3rd Bn Rifles	
	13		Continuation of scheme near de Wamel	
	14th		Troops taken out to practise Brinsleys scheme near Hinges	Signal
	15		Battalion marched to LE QUESNOY at 9am in Brigade Reserve. Suffolks and Norfolks in front line & Essex in support.	
	16		Quiet day	
	17th		Tuesday. Bn Hd relieved Norfolk Bn in firing line and coys at 2pm to supports & Scottish Trench and ran out 1pm to Grove Butts, & 60 Risheled deer & Princes Street. B Coy 2 Platoons and HQ at LE PLANTIN. A Coy 2 Plats and HQ at LE PLANTIN. C & D Royal Sceistuin (36/134) men on Left. Crews on man dry at Battalion Head Quarters at WINDY CORNER near GIVENCHY. Nothing very important except several Whizz Bangs fell near GIVENCHY KEEP one unfortunately killing Lieutenant E.C. Morgan.	2 wounded
	18th		2/4th Norfolks buried in Cemetery near Windy Corner. 60thR.S. relieved 11am Battalion in support at Windy Corner village & Wild Keep. Whiz Keep, MOAT HOUSE FARM and HERTS KEEP.	
	19th		B Coys to Village. A Coys in GIVENCHY KEEP. B Coy to Village line & D C & C remained in LE PLANTIN	

Army Form C. 2118.

WAR DIARY
or
INTELLIGENCE SUMMARY.
(Erase heading not required.)

Instructions regarding War Diaries and Intelligence Summaries are contained in F. S. Regs., Part II and the Staff Manual respectively. Title pages will be prepared in manuscript.

Place	Date	Hour	Summary of Events and Information	Remarks and references to Appendices
	19		Givenchy Keep was heavily shelled from Noon to 4 pm but no one hit owing to the excellent cellars in the Keep (in Bacon Farm)	
	20		Last day. Spy reported to about 10 teams out to be Staff Officer belonging to the Corps. Inspected defences of Reg: at aid Posts.	
	21st		Lt Col Shaw Comdg 3rd (S.R.) R.M. Surrey Regt arrived 11 am for instruction in Givenchy with reference to a bombing attack (Lieut Wenrich suffering from swollen feet). Conference in Givenchy and between 2 & 3 Coys. just before Sunset. Col Day & Col Shaw left for billets 2nd trenches.	
	22nd	1am	On their return journey severe artillery barrage came over & burst close to them near junction of upper cut & Scottish Trench. Lieut J.S.L. Salk who was with them was killed. Col Day had his right paw broken & Col Shaw was thrown from his car & hurt. Later Col Day walked back to dressing station & then on to hosp. Ambulance.	
			Moved Village Line inspected by Brig Commander Lieut Genl Scott.	
		12.30pm	Conference of CO's Brig Genl re Gas Operation in evening. During the evening a rifle Grenade fell on a Gas cylinder cracking it & causing the gas to leak. 8 men were poisoned. 3 men Shock & Shrouded.	
			Special Instructions were issued with reference to Gas operation at 8pm. Bombers in 2nd Cos had to wear their smoke helmets. The Gas was discharged	

1577 Wt. W10791/1773 500,000 1/15 D. D. & L. A.D.S.S./Forms/C. 2118.

WAR DIARY or INTELLIGENCE SUMMARY

Army Form C. 2118.

(Erase heading not required.)

Place	Date	Hour	Summary of Events and Information	Remarks and references to Appendices
	22nd	at 9 pm	Re Sermans at once fired Red Rockets for artillery fire & also enemy's bonfires on their bombline trenches. Then artillery opened fire at 9.30 pm. Our artillery was ordered to begin firing till 9.20 pm. 2 Howitzers fired 4 rounds & 3 rounds Gun opened fire. Re wires to coys too weak. Screen out & also 4 coys & reinforced.	
		10.30 pm	Enemy's artillery ceased. Runners at once instructed to Companies and the Telephone Linesmen worked & repaired lines. Communication was soon reestablished. Re went to K.O.L. men were very good & ready for about 30 minutes.	
		midnight	Enemy's artillery began again & fired for about 20 minutes	
	23rd	4.30 am	Enemy's artillery again fired heavily. This time for an hour.	
		5.30 am	Telephone line again cut & mended at once and communication restored	
		10 am	Enemy shelled Guinchy & also Windy Corner & village. Our artillery retaliated at once. Also the Howitzers 5 killed. 23 November. 3 Guns, 1 shock.	
			Casualties during operations	

WAR DIARY
or
INTELLIGENCE SUMMARY.
(Erase heading not required.)

Army Form C. 2118.

Place	Date	Hour	Summary of Events and Information	Remarks and references to Appendices
	23	2pm	11th Middlesex relieved Batt. 2 D.C.L.I.'s in 2 pm. Out	
		4pm	Coys at 4 pm. Motor Buses conveyed Companies from RORE & the Tobacco Factory, BETHUNE. Officers Billets in the Rue de Lille. Head Quarters at 121 Rue de Lille.	
	24th		Battalion given the Baths at Brasserie Factory 8 A.M. 2.30 p.m and 2 & 4.30 pm.	
	25th		No Parade Service. Each man got pehen pudding for his dinner also Cigars Cigarettes. There were 300 Hommades sent out and a few parcels from villages in Berkshire i.e. from Abingdon for Abingdon men	
	26	9am	Church Parade. 12 men from Base rejoined.	
	27		Marched at 9.25 for Rue d'Epinette. 2 Companies & Head Quarters Viz: One Coy "C" at Zeshebert + One Coy "D" at Estaminet Corner Battalion in Support "B" Coy on Germans attacking reinforced	AMB

1577 Wt. W10791/1773 500,000 1/15 D. D. & L. A.D.S.S./Forms/C. 2118.

Army Form C. 2118.

WAR DIARY
or
INTELLIGENCE SUMMARY.
(Erase heading not required.)

Place	Date	Hour	Summary of Events and Information	Remarks and references to Appendices
	27		HQ British divn between Rue du Cailloux & Le Quinque Rue filling up the gap in support line between Right & Left Battalions of Left Brigade. Essex on Right, Norfolks on Left. Suffolks in Reserve at Le Tonnet	
	28		Quiet day. Kilt about 4 bn when Germans shelled "D.1.C." 1 wounded (accident) no damage done	
	29		Working parties on cleaning houses & repairing troops	
	30		Some German shelling about 7 am & again c. 2.30 pm at Les Rulout	
	31		Germans "Crumps" in Epinette at noon & again 2.30 pm B. C? 2am shelled men removed in time Relief began at 4.30 pm half hour late. Relief completed by 7.30pm. Norfolks returned to Le Tonnet. Essex relief ours in Epinette - Suffolks relieved Essex & became Right Batt? D on Right Coy C Left Coy A in Support in Richmond Trench 1 wounded with Battn Head Quarters	

Army Form C. 2118.

WAR DIARY
or
INTELLIGENCE SUMMARY.
(Erase heading not required.)

Instructions regarding War Diaries and Intelligence Summaries are contained in F. S. Regs., Part II. and the Staff Manual respectively. Title pages will be prepared in manuscript.

Place	Date	Hour	Summary of Events and Information	Remarks and references to Appendices
			Owing to the scarcity of water about and the drainage condition from present front line it is divided up into "Islands" posts. The right Battalion has 16 Islands. The Right Coy of left Battn has Nos 17 to 25 and the left Coy Nos 26 to 36. No men are relieved every night as a rest but some like to stay & leave. All men in the 3 front Companies are served with Long Sea boots owing to the scarcity of water about. Relief could only take place at night. No one could move out during the day in the two front Companies. There were two Machine Guns with the Left Company and two on the right of the Battalion. Rations for the front line Companies are carried up from Regimental area Roads to the Cart by the Company in Reserve from old Brick & lime	J.A.Mⁿ

1577 Wt W10791/1773 500,000 1/15 D. D. & L. A.D.S.S./Forms/C. 2118.

2 M A P S .

Army Form C. 2118.

WAR DIARY
or
INTELLIGENCE SUMMARY.
(Erase heading not required.)

FESTUBERT. Map k illustrate Trenches.

Place	Date	Hour	Summary of Events and Information	Remarks and references to Appendices

Labels on map: Princes St, Rose St, Deadmans French, Piccadilly, The Mall, Oxford St, Scottish Trench, Lyons Cut, New Cut, Moat House Keep, Guardsman Road, GIVENCHY KEEP, HILDA, George St, Grouse Butts, Suez Canal, HERTS, Fife Road, Le Plantin Road, Willow Road, Yellow Road, WINDY CORNER

WAR DIARY or INTELLIGENCE SUMMARY.

Map to illustrate Trenches

Army Form C. 2118.

(Erase heading not required.)

Instructions regarding War Diaries and Intelligence Summaries are contained in F. S. Regs., Part II. and the Staff Manual respectively. Title pages will be prepared in manuscript.

Place	Date	Hour	Summary of Events and Information	Remarks and references to Appendices

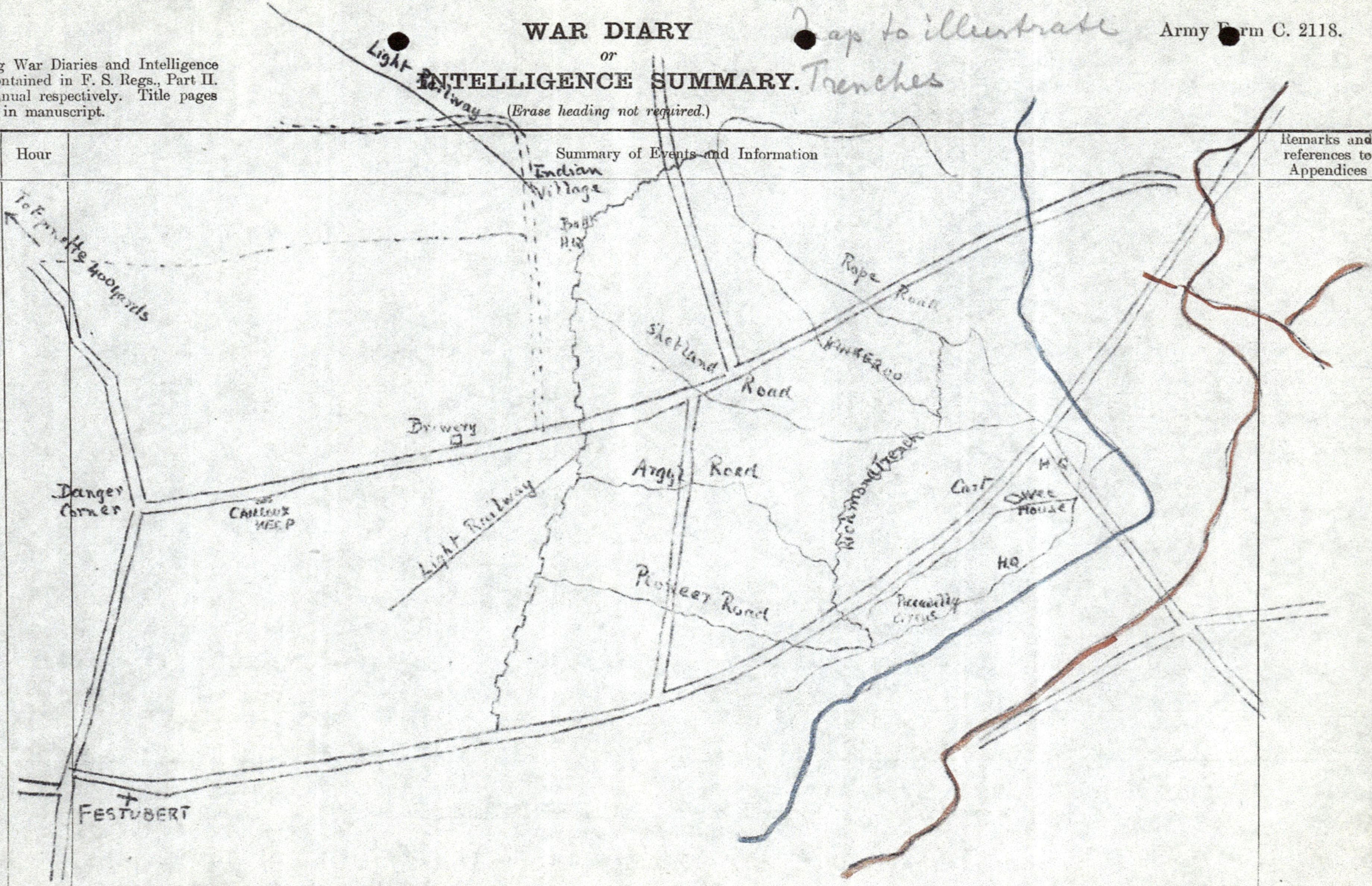

Map features (handwritten labels):
- Light Railway
- Indian Village
- Rope Road
- Shetland Road
- Argyll Road
- Rugby Road
- Cart Shed House
- H.Q.
- Piccadilly Circus
- Brewery
- Cailloux Kpe. P.
- Danger Corner
- To Epinette 400 yards
- To Festubert

5th R. Folio:
fol: 6

WAR DIARY
or
INTELLIGENCE SUMMARY

5th Royal Berkshire Regt.

Army Form C. 2118.

Place	Date	Hour	Summary of Events and Information	Remarks and references to Appendices
	January 1916			
	1st		Quiet day. "B" Coy at work on Trench and parapet in Old British line all the morning. By night "B" had to fetch Rations from Rickebush Cross Roads to the "Cuts" where they handed them over to "C" & "D" Coys also to "A" Coy. Later also had to be carried from water cart at Barrier to the Companies	
	2nd		"B" at work on Old British line south of the Piastoens Road on our left, at night Lieut Warner & 2 men made an excellent reconnaissance of the German Barrier across Caillou Road opposite the left of our line. The ground was very muddy and mostly covered with water which our men were unable to cross. Lieut Sucha Pumps sent to D Coy to enable them to pump out water from trench on to ground in front	
	3rd		About Noon Enemy began to Shell road from Dame Camp to our Old British line; they stopped as soon as our Artillery retaliated. "B" Coy at work at Old British Line under O.C.	JW

Place	Date	Hour	Summary of Events and Information	Remarks and references to Appendices
	4/5		The Enemy sent over shells at intervals during the day but did no damage. Relief by 11th Middlesex began at 6 pm and finished at 10 pm. Motor lorries provided to take Tonnet (2½ miles from Berthen) only 3 turned up (they made a gentle journey) 7 more were about 2 midnight so 3 coys A, C & D got a lift. B Coy marched, got to Billets at LES CHOQUAUX at 11:30 pm. Battalion all in by 1:30 am 5th	
	5/5	10 am 12:30	Cleaning up & drill during morning. A Coy on short range (30 yds) near Railway siding. 1 mile south of billets along the Canal. 2/Lieut Brown to Hospital with C.D.S.	
	6/5		B Coy on Range during morning. Remainder at drill & musketry during morning and Bombing during afternoon	
	7/5	9:30 am 10:45 12:30	Parade Service (C of E) R. C's at 8:30 am Parades drill & Bayonet exercise. C Coy on Range afternoon 2nd Lieut Waggoner joined from 9th Battn	

WAR DIARY
or
INTELLIGENCE SUMMARY

(Erase heading not required.)

Army Form C. 2118

Instructions regarding War Diaries and Intelligence Summaries are contained in F.S. Regs., Part II. and the Staff Manual respectively. Title Pages will be prepared in manuscript.

Place	Date	Hour	Summary of Events and Information	Remarks and references to Appendices
	8th	9.30	B Coy on Range all morning. Remaining Coys.	Route March
		12 no	under Company arrangements	
		2 pm	Kit Inspections	
	9th		Battalion marched by Companies at 1 km intervals to WINDY CORNER	
			D at 10.30 C at 11.30 am B at 1 pm H.Qrs. party 1.30 & A at 2 pm	B & C Villages
			A Coy went to the Plantion "B" in the Givenchy Keeps "D" in the Support Battalion	
			Relieved 8th Surreys & Support & sentries & trenches from the Quay	
	10th		Enemy shelled Keeps at intervals during morning & also village line	
			3 Shells hit Head Quarters of dept Battn	
			Shells burst amongst working party of Suffolk Regt & a carrying	
			party of our Regiment 6 killed 6 wounded	
		8 pm	more shells into Head Qrs of dept Battn New house	
	11th		Relieved about 300 yards further J.B. We began our Relief	
			of Norfolk Regt in Front line at 8.30 pm. finished at 11 pm	
			C Coys in Scottish Trench, New Rose D in Caledonian Trench	
			B in Grouse Butts A in Potsdam Princes St and H.Qrs	
			with 2 Platoons in J. Battn	

G.   H.Q.   4
      35th Bgde.

Herewith - War Diary rendered monthly in accordance with G.R.O. 1598. dated 30. 5. 16.

F W Hartley Dennett
           Lt Col.
31.10.17   Commdg 5th Royal Berks Regt.

WAR DIARY or INTELLIGENCE SUMMARY

Army Form C. 2118

Place	Date	Hour	Summary of Events and Information	Remarks and references to Appendices
	11		During Night several shells fell in La Plantin looking for one gun we had placed there, which fired 100 rounds during night. No transferred our H.Q. to the New House which the R.E. had been at work on during day. All furniture from old Quarters removed to New Quarters. Draft arrived 3 N.C.O.'s 31 N.C.O.'s men.	
	12	9am	Enemy shells began as usual.	
		10.40	Trench bombarded at Windy Corner & approaches to Kemmel.	
		Noon	Many shells fell on roads near La Plantin. Arrangements being made for replenishing shell Bomb Stores. Two put into R Sap & one near H.Q. I sap in Scottish Trench.	
	13		Quiet day. R.E. join hurg on H.Q.'s. On relief by Norfolks began at 6.30 pm, finished at 11.45 pm. It was a long slow move. Essex Reg't relieved Suffolk on Right of Brigade. Suffolk relieved Norfolk Reg't in Village Line and Norfolks relieved us on left of line. Last company arrived at de Queeroy 12.30 am 14th Battalion in Reserve. 2 killed 7 wounded.	

WAR DIARY
or
INTELLIGENCE SUMMARY

Army Form C. 2118

Place	Date	Hour	Summary of Events and Information	Remarks and references to Appendices
	14/5		Baths at disposal of Batt. Cleaning up no job press. Capt Rickman & Lieut Carey to Hospital. 2nd Lieut Stewart rejoined. Account of bombing attack made at 2 p.m. on 12th inst. he has to own 3 detachments in the Norfolk claim four casualties [13]. "Three West Spring Guns has been built into positions about A9a Central as shown on attached plan which also shows their line of fire and targets which were A9a 85 and 10 9 & 09. A telephone wire was also laid with emplacements hence No 1 & 2 guns for observation purposes. Each gun has a team of 1 NCO & 5 men and has provided with a box periscope and 60 Mills Grenades. During the previous days registration has taken place on the targets selected. Shortly before the operation were to commence a trench mortar bomb burst just in front of No 1 gun covering the parapet so as to expose the aim of the gun such time it was discharged. Accordingly, it was decided not to use this gun and	

Instructions regarding War Diaries and Intelligence Summaries are contained in F. S. Regs., Part II. and the Staff Manual respectively. Title Pages will be prepared in manuscript.

WAR DIARY
or
~~INTELLIGENCE SUMMARY~~
(Erase heading not required.)

Army Form C. 2118

Place	Date	Hour	Summary of Events and Information	Remarks and references to Appendices
			its team was withdrawn into PARKLANE as a Reserve.	
			At 2 pm both the remaining guns commenced firing and in 15 minutes	

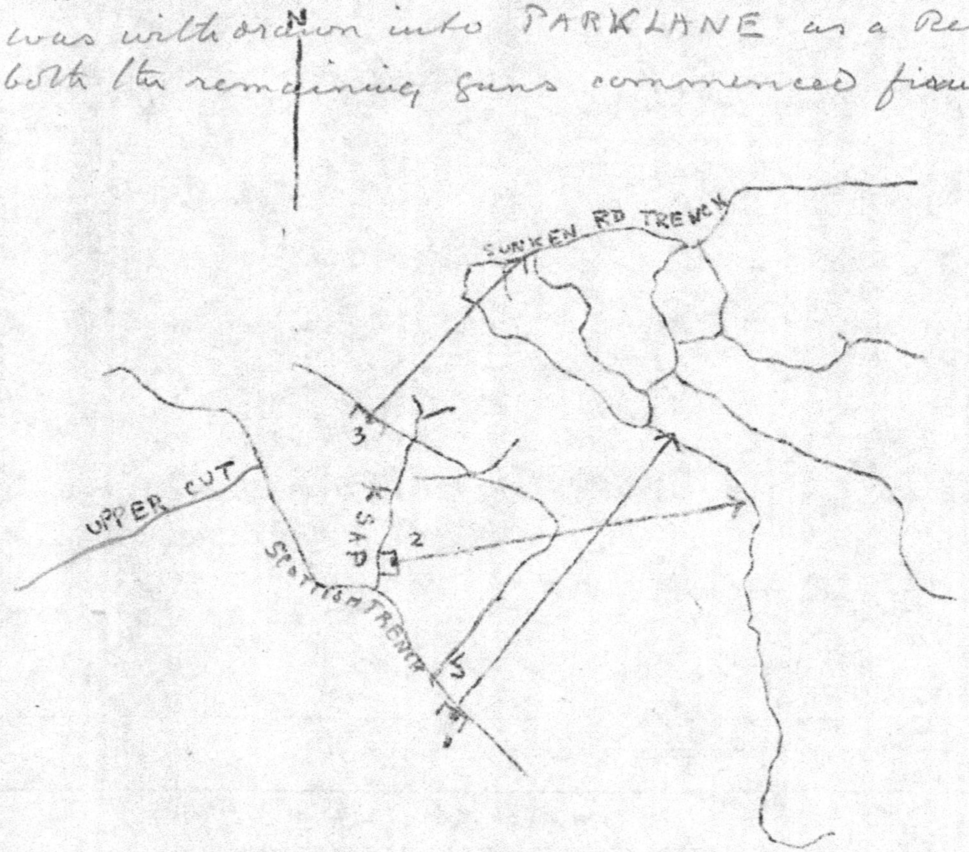

N
SUNKEN RD TRENCH
UPPER CUT
SCOTTISH TRENCH
SAP
1
2
3
5

1875 Wt. W593/826 1,000,000 4/15 J.B.C. & A. A.D.S.S./Forms/C. 2118.

fired No 2 Gun 18 Grenades & No 3 12 Grenades
The Grenades from No 2 landed and burst very well. The first
ones from No 3 burst high in the air but this was remedied at
the expense of a few minutes and the remainder burst right in
the Trench. At 2.15pm fire ceased and the Gun teams
hurried to cover which had been previously selected.
At 2.45pm fire started again & in the next 15 minutes No 3 Gun
fired 17 Grenades which burst well. During this second period
No 2 Gun was out of action as the team was unable to return to
it as a trench Mortar Bomb fell during the half hour interval,
at the junction of K Sap and SCOTTISH TRENCH completely
blowing in the latter and making it impassable.
The enemy retaliated only by fruitless shelling well to the Rear
and also by means of Trench Mortars which did some damage.
A sentry was posted to watch for them and there were no
casualties in the Gun teams. We rejoined the Bn H.Q. that Evening

WAR DIARY or INTELLIGENCE SUMMARY

Place	Date	Hour	Summary of Events and Information	Remarks and references to Appendices
	15th		Returned to Trenches at GIVENCHY and LE PLANTIN. Regts in same position as before. Relief completed by 3 p.m. Communication with Regts still much better and also with Princess Street. Seem to be not required to walk up in. Good work being done in recovering dead & wounded in Walker Street close to Princes Street. 1 wounded.	
	16th		Quiet morning till about noon, when the Germans shelled Le Plantin & also the Givenchy Keeps. Officers of the 2nd South Staffordshire Regt came to talk to our before taking over on 17th. 4 wounded.	
	17th		At 2 a.m. received orders to arrange Rifle Grenade attack for 2.30 p.m. 12 parties of 3 men each under 2nd Lt Steward and 2nd Lieut A. ?? tops off. Reg has to go into the Suffolks and a to fire. Reg fired for 20 minutes with some success. 2nd Lt Seymour Brown was wounded in the eye & Sergt Skinner suffering from Parapet being blown into his face. Enemy replied in support their but was soon silenced by our Artillery. Relief by 2nd South Staffords 6th Brigade 2nd Div began at 6.30 p.m. & finished at 8.10 p.m.	

Date	Hour	Summary of Events and Information	Remarks and references to Appendices
18th		Battalion had to march to BETHUNE (5 miles) carrying their Fur Coats and Steel Helmets. Men very tired. Battalion all in billets by 11.30 pm over the Railway Station. Fur coats and Steel Helmets given into Store soon	1 Officer 4 men wounded
	10.30	Battalion left by train at 10.30 am for LILLERS. marched	
	11.30	from Lillers at 11.30 and arrived at FONTES at 1 pm. The Regimental Transport left at 6.30 am and arrived at 3.15 pm. Good billets both for men and officers.	
19		Drills and firing on small Range in old Quarry 600 yards away. Practices preventing arms & cleaning up the same time for General Joffre.	
20th	12.30	Brigade had to be in position 50 yards between Companies by 12.30 pm. General Joffre due at 1.15 but he did not come till 2.30 pm. We had a hailstorm & rain from 1.30 to about 2 pm.	

WAR DIARY or INTELLIGENCE SUMMARY

Army Form C. 2118

Place	Date	Hour	Summary of Events and Information	Remarks and references to Appendices
	21		Battalion at drill morning & afternoon. Capt Rickman returned from Hospital.	
	22		Battalion seen by Major Genl. Scott Dick & Comdr at drill & during morning. Two football matches during afternoon in Corps competition.	
	23rd		Brigade Scheme for C.O. & 2nd in C. be Scheme continued on ground under supervision of the Div. E. Comdr. The Brigadier commanding it. 2nd Lieut E.C. Brown from 7th Battn arrived	
	24		Battalion at work on High Ground. Platoons & Companys in attack. 2nd Lieut Lloyd arrived. He has received his commission on 16th & was formerly a sergeant in "D" Coy.	
	25/12		Brigade Route March. Battalions in en routed at 2 different villages about 6½ miles away & then marched back by one Road along 3 miles. Capt Chadwyck Healey to Hospital and Lieut Avery from Hospital	

WAR DIARY
or
INTELLIGENCE SUMMARY
(Erase heading not required.)

Army Form C. 2118

Instructions regarding War Diaries and Intelligence Summaries are contained in F. S. Regs., Part II. and the Staff Manual respectively. Title Pages will be prepared in manuscript.

Place	Date	Hour	Summary of Events and Information	Remarks and references to Appendices
	26/6		Brigade practised the attack Two Battalions at a time. Norfolks & Essex first. Suffolks & ourselves afterwards. Did not get back till 6 p.m.	
	27/6		Battalion parade in morning. In afternoon C.O.'s meets refereed 6 miles off at 12.30 & took over. Screens in the Corps Staff Ride. Each by 5 p.m. (Conference afterwards)	
	28/6		Enemy parades during morning.	
		Noon	C.O.'s at Noon had competition over by the Bn.	
		2 pm	Brigade Tournament. Lieut Horner an incident with scouts available.	
	29/6		Parades during morning. Half holiday	
	30/6		Battn marched at 7.30 am as a Rt. Flank Guard to the Brigade which was marching as an I.G. to the Divn. There was a test on the sending of orders & messages & keeping communication by means of Cyclists DP 12 & two Cyclists carried at CHARQUES at Noon Locked till 1.15 pm	

1875 Wt. W593/826 1,000,000 4/15 J.B.C. & A. A.D.S.S./Forms/C. 2118.

WAR DIARY
or
INTELLIGENCE SUMMARY

Army Form C. 2118

Place	Date	Hour	Summary of Events and Information	Remarks and references to Appendices
	31st		and then put out outposts, in conjunction with Essex Regt on our left. At 3. 15pm position of billets & outposts changed. We moved to the left. At 5. 30pm Coys withdrew Outposts & no more work for the night. Very misty day. Good billets at CLARQUES near THEROUANNE. Bn marched on one road back to billets. He reached 9.30am. Formed starting point in THEROUANNE 10.12am, Brigade split up on arrival went B COTTES & remainder to Billets. We got back at 3pm. No one fell out	

Army Form C. 2118

WAR DIARY
or
INTELLIGENCE SUMMARY

(Erase heading not required.)

Confidential

War Diary

of

5th Royal Berkshire Regt

from 1st February 1916 to 29 February 1916

WAR DIARY or INTELLIGENCE SUMMARY

5TH ROYAL BERKSHIRE

Army Form C. 2118

Place	Date	Hour	Summary of Events and Information	Remarks and references to Appendices
	February 1916			
	1st		Inspection of Coys in marching order. Physical Training Squad & Platoon drill. Organisation of Squads for Instruction of Enemy working parties. Drill during morning. Baths at Bonnes for 1&2 Coys from 1pm to 6pm. Lewis Gun Classes began.	
	2nd		Ordinary drill near Billets.	
	3rd		Morning menace received. The G.O.C. 1st Army has expressed his appreciation of the good work performed by the 1st Army in minor Enterprises against the Enemy during past month. This is to be notified to all Ranks.	
	4th		Range at our disposal all day. Practice for Div. Rifle meeting.	
	5th	8:30 to 1pm	Practice for Rifle meeting on Range on Toogy Hill 2 miles away. Remainder Drill & Attack Practice	

WAR DIARY
or
INTELLIGENCE SUMMARY
(Erase heading not required.)

Army Form C. 2118

Instructions regarding War Diaries and Intelligence Summaries are contained in F.S. Regs., Part II. and the Staff Manual respectively. Title Pages will be prepared in manuscript.

Place	Date	Hour	Summary of Events and Information	Remarks and references to Appendices
	6th		Parade Services C.B. E.G. am. R.C.s 10.30 am. Nonconformists & Presbyterians 11am	
	7th	8.15	Battalion Rifle Meeting all day	
			Brigade Rifle Meeting } None not employed were on Battn parades	
	8th		Brigade Rifle meeting	
			Battⁿ won No 1 Event Sniperscope Competition	
			1st L/Corp Ash 5 R Berks	
			2nd Pte Pyke	
			Pte Musterman	
			No 2 Event Bullring Plate Knock Out 1st 5/R Berks	
			No 3. 1st Post "A" Essex	
			2nd Sgt Major Yardley 5' R/Berks	
			3rd L/Corp Hawes to	
			No 5. Field Firing 1st 7th Suffolks 2nd 5th Royal Berks	
			2nd 7th Norfolks	
			No 4 Rapid Competition 1st Norfolks 2nd 5th R. Berks	
			3rd Suffolks	

WAR DIARY
or
INTELLIGENCE SUMMARY
(Erase heading not required.)

Army Form C. 2118

Place	Date	Hour	Summary of Events and Information	Remarks and references to Appendices
	8		Brigade Rifle Meeting (continued)	
			No.6. Telescopic Rifles 1st, 2nd, 3rd Suffolk Regt	
			No.7. Gas Attack 1st 5th Royal Berkshire	
			No.8. Lewis Rifle Competition 1st 7th Suffolks 2nd 5th Royal Berkshire Regt	
			No.9 Machine gun ?	
	9th		Instruction in wiring by R.E. Making roads to rear. All C.OS met HQ in Brigade to visit trenches	
	10th		Inspection by Divisional Commander & presentation of Ribbon to L/Cpl Powell & Cas to 7th Perris.	
			Battn Parades. All C.OS in Brigade to visit trenches	

Army Form C. 2118

WAR DIARY
or
INTELLIGENCE SUMMARY
(Erase heading not required.)

Instructions regarding War Diaries and Intelligence Summaries are contained in F.S. Regs., Part II. and the Staff Manual respectively. Title Pages will be prepared in manuscript.

Place	Date	Hour	Summary of Events and Information	Remarks and references to Appendices
	11th		Bn HQ Paraded at 6.30 am and marched to La Perriere. Lt Col. 2nd S Miller D.S.O. K.R.R. took over command on arrival of Battn	6 miles
	12th		Battn reviewed at La Perriere. 2nd Lt. Cooper joined	
	13th		Battn marched at 5 am & arrived at Cte Orpheon	
	14th		Bethune at 12 noon.	
	15th		Breakfast at Neuve. for Noyelles & arrived at 4 pm 2nd Lieut J. Ashley Cooper joined	
	16th		Corpl G.J. Power	
at NOYELLES	17th		The Battalion relieved the 7th Suffolks in the trenches in the Loophost system - Casualties - 1 man killed -	

WAR DIARY
or
INTELLIGENCE SUMMARY
(Erase heading not required.)

Army Form C. 2118

Place	Date	Hour	Summary of Events and Information	Remarks and references to Appendices
	18th		Remained in Support - Very Quiet time - No Casualties -	
	19th		In VERMELLES in Support - The Battalion was chiefly employed furnishing fatigue parties - Things were very Quiet. Casualties - 1 man wounded, on the 21st -	
	20th 21st 22nd			
	23rd	11-20 p.m.	The Battalion relieved the 7th Suffolks in the front system of trenches in "C" Sector. About 11-20 p.m. the parties a mine opposite ERNEST CRESCENT, with the object of destroying a hostile gallery - The enemy's retaliation was slight -	
	24th		A quiet day on the whole, as nothing unusual occurred - A few casualties were caused by rifle grenades and trench mortars - Casualties - 9 men wounded - Nothing to report - Trench rifle, the first 3 days has been very cold, but with Thermitraw - Casualties - 1 man wounded -	
	25th			
	26th		The Bn. relieved by the 9th Essex, and the Battalion went back to billets at NOYELLES - Casualties - 5 men wounded -	
	27th 28th 29th		At NOYELLES - Nothing to report -	

D. Wilson Lt Colonel
Comdg. 5th Battn R. Berkshire Regt
29-2-16

Army Form C. 2118

WAR DIARY
~~Border Redoubt~~ or
INTELLIGENCE SUMMARY
Hulluch — Pagechendaele
(Erase heading not required.)

Instructions regarding War Diaries and Intelligence Summaries are contained in F. S. Regs., Part II. and the Staff Manual respectively. Title Pages will be prepared in manuscript.

Place	Date	Hour	Summary of Events and Information	Remarks and references to Appendices

[Hand-drawn trench map with labels including: Crown Trench, Rabbit Hole, Lancer Lane, St Elie Avenue, Stansfield Road, Old G.2, Old G.1, Fosse Way, Goeben Alley, Stafford Lane, Breslau Avenue, Chapel Alley, Devon Lane, Left Leg, Right Leg, Hairpin, Foxmer's Hole, Brookwood Street, Lancet Sap, Swinburn, Tom wise way, Lookout Crater, Dugdale Road, Lookout, Pilgrims Progress, Drummond Trench, Chapel Alley, Devon Lane, Crescent, German (5-2-16), QUARRIES, T, 12, 11]

1875 Wt. W593/826 1,000,000 4/15 J.B.C. & A. A.D.S.S./Forms/C. 2118.

Army Form C. 2118.

WAR DIARY
or
INTELLIGENCE SUMMARY

(Erase heading not required.)

Instructions regarding War Diaries and Intelligence Summaries are contained in F. S. Regs., Part II. and the Staff Manual respectively. Title Pages will be prepared in manuscript.

Place	Date	Hour	Summary of Events and Information	Remarks and references to Appendices

Map labels: Hulluch Alley, Gordon Alley, Stansfield Road, Fosse Way, Stafford Lane, Chapel Alley, Devon Lane, O.B.L.1, O.B.L.2, O.B.L.3, O.B.L.4, O.B.L.5, Bois Carrie Keep, Chapel Alley, Gordon Pump, Gordon Alley, Hulluch Alley, Stansfield Road, CURLEY CRESENT

Army Form C. 2118

WAR DIARY
or
INTELLIGENCE SUMMARY
(Erase heading not required.)

S R Berks
Vol 10

Confidential

War Diary
of
5th Royal Berkshire Regiment

from 1st March to 31st March 1916.

WAR DIARY or INTELLIGENCE SUMMARY

(Erase heading not required.)

Army Form C. 2118

Place	Date	Hour	Summary of Events and Information	Remarks and references to Appendices
	29.2.16	9 P.m.	The Battalion left NOYELLES and relieved the 7th Bn. Suffolk Regt in Sector C II. C and D Coys in front line A and B Coys in support trenches. Draft of 43 N.C.O's and Men arrived from Etaples. The 7th Bn. Norfolk Regt occupied the line on our right. " 11 " Middlesex " " " " " left.	
	1.3.16		Dispositions as for 29.2.16. 1 other rank killed.	
	2.3.16		Dispositions as for 29.2.16. Mine exploded in front of D Coy. and Crater occupied by Coy. Bombers. Casualties O.R. 3 killed 7 wounded. 2 Compenies 4th Bn. R.J. Fusiliers attached for instruction.	
	3.3.16		Casualties O.R. 2 killed 3 wounded. The Battalion was relieved by the 7th Bn. Suffolk Regt and moved into VERMELLES	
	4.3.16		Billets at VERMELLES	

Army Form C. 2118

WAR DIARY
or
INTELLIGENCE SUMMARY

(Erase heading not required.)

Instructions regarding War Diaries and Intelligence Summaries are contained in F.S. Regs., Part II. and the Staff Manual respectively. Title Pages will be prepared in manuscript.

Place	Date	Hour	Summary of Events and Information	Remarks and references to Appendices
	5.3.16		Battalion in Billets in VERMELLES. A and B Coys to the Support trenches. Casualties O.R. 1 Killed 1 Wounded.	
	6.3.16		Headquarters, C.D and 2 Coys. R.I. Fusiliers moved into the front line in relief of the 7' Bn. Suffolk Regt. Casualties O.R. 1 Killed 2 Wounded. 2/Lt. Transeer to Hospital Sick.	
	7.3.16		Disposition as for 6.3.16 Casualties 1 O.R. wounded.	
	8.3.16		Disposition as for 6.3.16 Casualties O.R. 5 wounded. One slight remained at duty	
	9.3.16		The Battalion was relieved by the 7' Bn. Suffolk Regt. and moved into billets at NOYELLES.	
	10.3.16		Battalion moved into Billets in BETHUNE being relieved in NOYELLES by the 11' Bn. Middlesex Regt. Draft of 41 O.R. joined from Etaples	

Army Form C. 2118

WAR DIARY
or
INTELLIGENCE SUMMARY
(Erase heading not required.)

Instructions regarding War Diaries and Intelligence Summaries are contained in F. S. Regs., Part II. and the Staff Manual respectively. Title Pages will be prepared in manuscript.

Place	Date	Hour	Summary of Events and Information	Remarks and references to Appendices
	11-14. 3.16		Battalion in Billets in BETHUNE. Drum & Fife band played in the Grande Place.	
	15.3.16		Battalion moved into Billets in SAILLY LABOURSE relieving 7th Bn Suffolk Regt. Capt C Nugent joined from Ebaplin.	
	16.3.16		Billets. The Battalion Snipers won the Brigade Competition for Sniping with telescopic Sight. Working parties found for trenches. Casualties O.R. 1 killed 1 wounded.	
	17.3.16		Billets. 2/Lt C A Mallam joined from Ebaplin. Drum and fife band played at Divisional Headquarters.	
	18.3.16		Inspection of C and D Companies by General Sir Charles Monro. Comdg 2nd Army and presentation of Ribbons. Military Cross to 1st Lt L.D. Cotterell and D.C.M. to Corporal Gee and Pte Holford. Brigade Boxing Tournament at Bethune. One entry in each weight. Drum and Fife band played at the Tournament.	

WAR DIARY
INTELLIGENCE SUMMARY

Army Form C. 2118.

(Erase heading not required.)

Instructions regarding War Diaries and Intelligence Summaries are contained in F. S. Regs., Part II. and the Staff Manual respectively. Title pages will be prepared in manuscript.

Place	Date	Hour	Summary of Events and Information	Remarks and references to Appendices
	18.3.16	5.4 pm	The enemy attacked and captured the Craters in Sector D 2 held by the 7 East Surrey Regt. The Battalion stood to Arms all night. Bombing Counter-attack stopped owing to the above attack.	
	19.3.16	3.30 pm	Battalion moved into Front line Trenches from SAILLY LABOURSE, relieving 7 Bn. E. Surrey Regt. in SECTOR D II. Disposition :- A Company in Crater Area. C Company to the left in Shickby and Mud Trenches. 2 Platoons B Company in support of A Company in Northampton Trench 2 " " " " " " " in the Quarry D Company in the Reserve Trenches. Units on Flanks. Left 2 Worcestershire Regt. Right 7 Norfolk Regt. Casualties. 5. O.Ranks wounded 1. O.R. shell shock	
	20.3.16		A change in dispositions was made. The Battalion taking over more line from the 7 Norfolk Regt. D Company was moved up from the reserve trench and took over the line from the right of A Company to SAVILLE ROW. Casualties. O. Ranks. 1 Killed 5 wounded 3 Shell Shock.	
	21.3.16		Dispositions as per 20.3.16. Considerable amount of shelling by the enemy between 2.45 pm and 5 pm Casualties Captain C Nugent to Hospital (Sick) O. Ranks 1 Killed 6 wounded 1 Shell Shock.	

Army Form C. 2118.

WAR DIARY
INTELLIGENCE SUMMARY.

(Erase heading not required.)

Instructions regarding War Diaries and Intelligence Summaries are contained in F.S. Regs., Part II and the Staff Manual respectively. Title pages will be prepared in manuscript.

Place	Date	Hour	Summary of Events and Information	Remarks and references to Appendices
	22.3.16		Dispositions as for 21.3.16 Casualties Officers 2/Lieut G.H. BLACK wounded. O. Ranks 1 Killed 4 wounded.	
		2 P.M.	The Battalion was relieved by the 7" Suffolk Regt. in the Reserve Trenches. A and C Companies in Lancashire Trenches. B Company in Reserve Trench D " " in Railway Reserve Trench.	
	23.& 24. 3-16.		The Battalion were in the Reserve Trenches finding working parties every night in the front line. A draft of 40 N.C.O.s and men joined the Battalion on the 23.3.16. Casualties Nil.	
	25.3.16.	12 Noon	The Battalion relieved the 7' Suffolk Regt in the front line Trenches. Disposition. D Company on the right C " Centre (or Crater Area) A " on the left B " 2 Platoons supporting C Company, 2 Platoons in the Quarry, Units on the Flanks. Right 7" Norfolk Regt, left Scottish Fusiliers? Casualties O. Ranks. 1 Killed 6 wounded 2 Shell Shock Officers Lt. J.E. WARNER joined from Hospital	

Army Form C. 2118.

WAR DIARY
INTELLIGENCE SUMMARY.
(Erase heading not required.)

Instructions regarding War Diaries and Intelligence Summaries are contained in F. S. Regs., Part II. and the Staff Manual respectively. Title pages will be prepared in manuscript.

Place	Date	Hour	Summary of Events and Information	Remarks and references to Appendices
	26.3.16		Dispositions as for 25.3.16.	
			Casualties O. Ranks. 5 wounded 1 Shell Shock.	
			2 Lieut. A. G. Pennett joined for duty from England.	
	27.3.16		Dispositions as for 2 Sh. Coys. A Company changed positions with C Company	
			B " " " D "	
			Casualties Lt. J. E Warner admitted to Hospital (Sick)	
	28.3.16		Dispositions as for 27.3.16.	
			Casualties Officers 2 Lt. J. Astley Cooper to Hospital Sick	
			2/Lt R Haywood — " —	
			O. Ranks 1 Killed 2 wounded.	
		12 noon	The Battalion was relieved in the front line trenches by the 7th Suffolk Regt. and our Companies took up positions in Reserve Trenches. A Company Reserve Trench	
			C " Railway Reserve Trench	
			B + D Lancashire Trenches.	

Army Form C. 2118.

WAR DIARY
or
INTELLIGENCE SUMMARY.
(Erase heading not required.)

Instructions regarding War Diaries and Intelligence Summaries are contained in F. S. Regs., Part II. and the Staff Manual respectively. Title pages will be prepared in manuscript.

Place	Date	Hour	Summary of Events and Information	Remarks and references to Appendices
	29.3.16		Battalion in Reserve. Draft of 24 O.R. joined. Casualties 2/Lt. A. G. Pennett to Hospital (sick)	
	30.3.16		Battalion in Reserve. Bn. Headquarters in Cannon Street shelled for 2 hours no damage. Casualties nil.	
	31.3.16	12 noon	7th Battalion relieved the 7th Suffolk Regt. in the front line trenches. Dispositions D Company on the Right. A " " Centre C " " on the Left B " " 2 Platoons in support of A Company and 2 Platoons in the Quarry. Units on the flanks. Right 7 Norfolk Regt. Left 2/6 Royal Fusiliers.	
		9.30 pm	The Germans sprang a mine about 40 yards E of Craters 3 & 4. doing no damage to the latter Craters. Casualties through the explosion 2 killed and 20 wounded or shaken by falling debris. John Casualties 6.Ranks 5 killed 20 wounded. Captain C. Nugent joined from Hospital. There was a great deal of Bombing and Trench Mortar Grenades for about 2 hours.	

D. Wilmot Colonel
Comdg. 5 Bn. Royal Berkshire Regt.

Army Form C. 2118.

WAR DIARY
or
INTELLIGENCE SUMMARY.
(Erase heading not required.)

5th Berks
Vol II

Confidential

War Diary
of
5th Royal Berks Regiment

from 1st April 1916 to 30th April 1916

Volume II

Army Form C. 2118.

WAR DIARY
or
INTELLIGENCE SUMMARY.
(Erase heading not required.)

Instructions regarding War Diaries and Intelligence
Summaries are contained in F. S. Regs., Part II.
and the Staff Manual respectively. Title pages
will be prepared in manuscript.

Place	Date	Hour	Summary of Events and Information	Remarks and references to Appendices
	1.4.16.		The dispositions were as on 31.3.16.	
		6 am to 6.10 am	At 6 am 6.10 am. 6.40-6.47 and 7.80-7.55 am an offensive operation against the German lines opposite the Brigade Front by the Heavy, Field Artillery, Trench Mortars, Stokes Guns and Rifle Grenades. The enemy retaliated during the Afternoon.	
			Casualties. O. Ranks. 4 Killed 12 Wounded H.M.	
			2/Lt. L.G. Cook and E.V. Biles Joined the Battalion from the 9th Bn. The 16th Bn. NOTTS and DERBY. REGT. relieved the unit on our left.	
	2.4.16	7 am	The enemy sprang a mine opposite Sap 8 (Unit on our Right) and opened up with Artillery and Trench Mortar Batteries on our trenches, without doing much damage.	
		9 am	The dispositions of Companies was changed. C with A and B with D Company.	
		7.30 pm	The enemy opened up an intense bombardment with artillery of all calibres, Trench Mortars and aerial Torpedoes and continued until 9 pm. There were no casualties at all from this bombardment. Our Artillery and Trench Mortars retaliated and the remainder of the night passed quietly.	
			Casualties 2 Killed 8 Wounded - O. Ranks.	
			2/Lt. R.D.H. Norman reported from Hospital	

Army Form C. 2118.

WAR DIARY
INTELLIGENCE SUMMARY.
(Erase heading not required.)

Instructions regarding War Diaries and Intelligence Summaries are contained in F. S. Regs., Part II. and the Staff Manual respectively. Title pages will be prepared in manuscript.

Place	Date	Hour	Summary of Events and Information	Remarks and references to Appendices
	3.4.16		The dispositions of Companies were as for the 2.3.16.	
Bethune		9.3 a.m.	The Battalion was relieved in the front line trenches by the Royal Fusiliers 36' Brigade, and the Battalion moved into Billets in the Tobacco Factory, Bethune, the relief being complete by 1.45 p.m. Casualties	
	4.5+6 4.16		The Battalion in Billets as for the 3.4.16. Drill and individual training exercises	
SAILLY LABOURSE	7.8.9 4.16		On the 7th the Battalion moved into billets at Sailly Labourse and training Continued, relieving the 7' Bn. Norfolk Regt.	
	10" 4.16		The Brigade relieved the 37' Brigade in the trenches and this Battalion relieved the 7 Bn. Norfolk Regt in the Support line of trenches the disposition of Companies. A Company Au Bombers Au Gunners Bn. H. Qrs. Curley Crescent D & C " in O.B.1. ⎫ N.B. O.B. means Old British Trench B " in O.B. 4+5. ⎭ in front of the left Quarry Section.	
	11+12 4.16		Dispositions as for 10"	

WAR DIARY
INTELLIGENCE SUMMARY
(Erase heading not required.)

Army Form C. 2118.

Instructions regarding War Diaries and Intelligence Summaries are contained in F. S. Regs., Part II. and the Staff Manual respectively. Title pages will be prepared in manuscript.

Place	Date	Hour	Summary of Events and Information	Remarks and references to Appendices
	13 April		The Battalion relieved the 7th Bn. Suffolk Regt in the Front line at 12 noon being relieved in the Support line by the 9th Essex Regt. Dispositions in left Sub of Quarry Sector. C Company Regt Front. D " " Hairpin Crater A " " left Sub B " " Reserve in O.B.1. Units on the flanks 7th Norfolks on the right 11th Middlesex on left. Casualties 2nd Lt H.M. Cook wounded.	
	14 April		Dispositions as for 13 April Casualties 2nd Lt Mallam wounded. O. Ranks 1 killed 5 wounded.	
	15 April		Dispositions as for 13th Casualties O. Ranks 4 wounded.	
	16 "		12 noon Relieved by the 7th Suffolk Regt. when the Battalion moved back into Reserve. 2 Comps. reliev A & C at Vermelles. H.Q. B & D Comps. Rue des Bordeurs. Lewis Gunners & Snipers to Noyelles. Casualties O. Ranks 1 killed 1 wounded.	

Army Form C. 2118.

WAR DIARY
or
INTELLIGENCE SUMMARY.
(Erase heading not required.)

Place	Date	Hour	Summary of Events and Information	Remarks and references to Appendices
In Reserve	17th 18th		Draft of 35 N.C.O.s & men joined Battalion on 17th	
	19th		Relieved 7th Bn Suffolk Regt in front line at 10 a.m. Disposition: On the right C Coy - Hairpin Craters. B Coy & Left A Coy - D Coy in reserve in O.G.I. which joins It. Nuffels MR 6th Green on left. There was some trench mortar activity but not serious. Casualties. 1 O.R. killed 1 O.R. wounded	
	20th		Enemy shelling us on our right. There was a quiet day. Casualties. 2nd Lt Burkby wounded early in the morning and died same day in No 33 C.C.S. 1 O.R. killed 5 O.R. wounded	
	21st		Fairly quiet till nightfall when mining officer exploded that German here mining under cubic leg of Hairpin - Sap was cleared but nothing happened. Rained all night. Trenches in very bad state. Casualties 1 O.R. killed 6 O.R. wounded & 2 mis[sing]	

WAR DIARY or INTELLIGENCE SUMMARY

Army Form C. 2118

(Erase heading not required.)

Place	Date	Hour	Summary of Events and Information	Remarks and references to Appendices
	22nd		Relieved in front line by 8th Royal Scots - and proceeded to Auregnin in reserve. Heavy rain, very wet and in places knee deep in water.	
	23rd		2/Lt Malcolm evacuated to club from hospital. Draft of 37 N.C.O.s & men from the base.	
	24th		In reserve. Had to find some working parties.	
	25th		Moved into "C" Sect area. Took over billets from 9th K.O.S.B. at Rainhut. A mining village. Billets not good - men to scatter and in small houses. Battn HQ & Coys B & D scattered and billeted at Kilun. Settling down in the billets - making up training programme.	
	26th		Company individual training carried out.	
	27th		Orders to be attack by enemy at Pub 14 - held in readiness to be prepared to move at 1 hour notice. Later this was cancelled and work was resumed.	
	28th		2/Lieut Partridge & Bradley joined Battn from Base and reported for duty.	

Army Form C. 2118

WAR DIARY
or
INTELLIGENCE SUMMARY
(Erase heading not required.)

Place	Date	Hour	Summary of Events and Information	Remarks and references to Appendices
	29th		Training continued	
	30th		Draft 16. N.Cos & men joined the battalion	

5th R. Berks
Vol: 9

Army Form C. 2118

5 Berks
Vol 12

XII

WAR DIARY
or
INTELLIGENCE SUMMARY
(Erase heading not required.)

Confidential

War Diary
of
5th Royal Berkshire Regiment

from 1st May 1916 to 31st May 1916.

Army Form C. 2118

WAR DIARY
or
INTELLIGENCE SUMMARY
(Erase heading not required.)

Instructions regarding War Diaries and Intelligence Summaries are contained in F. S. Regs., Part II. and the Staff Manual respectively. Title Pages will be prepared in manuscript.

Place	Date	Hour	Summary of Events and Information	Remarks and references to Appendices
	May 1st		Training continued.	
	2nd		do.	
	3rd		Lieut P. May. joined for duty.	
	4th		Practised BB Scheme. i.e. to mount up by train to be in free to be.	
	5th		Training continued. Lieuts Lorenathan - Holloway joined for duty.	
	7th		Training continued	
	8th		Marched to 1st Army Manœuvre Area. Batt" billets #8.	
	9th		2 coys in SERNY - 2 coys in FLECHINELLE.	
	10th		Company training - or manœuvre found.	
	13th			

1875 Wt. W593/826 1,000,000 4/15 J.B.C. & A. A.D.S.S./Forms/C. 2118.

WAR DIARY
or
INTELLIGENCE SUMMARY

Army Form C. 2118

(Erase heading not required.)

Place	Date	Hour	Summary of Events and Information	Remarks and references to Appendices
	14th		Sunday.	
	15th		Battalion Training.	
	16th		Draft of 13 N.Co's men joined battalion from 12 I.B.D.	
	17th		Bazaar field day	
	18th		Battalion field day	
	19th		Batt. marched back to Rainbert. Capt. James	
	20th		joined the batt. for duty	
	21st			
	22nd		Batt. marched to Rabuguoy and took over billets from 7 Royal Sussex Regt.	
	23rd		Individual training —	

WAR DIARY
or
INTELLIGENCE SUMMARY

Place	Date	Hour	Summary of Events and Information	Remarks and references to Appendices
	24th		Training carried on -	
	25th		do -	
	26th		Battalion received orders that they were temporarily attached to 49th Infantry Brigade relieving 8th Royal Inniskilling Fusiliers 49th Infantry Brigade consists of 7th Royal Inniskilling Fusiliers & 7th & 8th Royal Irish Fusiliers. Moved accordingly into billets in PHILOSOPHE EAST, being Reserve Battalion to Brigade in left subsection LOOS- 1 Platoon of D Coy sent to LENS ROAD REDOUBT - 2 Lt F.G. Thorne & 110 O.R. joined for duty -	
	27		In billets in PHILOSOPHE - Kept our Lewis gun teams sent up into the line 1 Platoon of C Coy dispatched as reinforcements to LENS ROAD REDOUBT 2nd Lt Crowther joined for duty 1 O.R. killed -	

WAR DIARY
or
INTELLIGENCE SUMMARY

Army Form C. 2118

Place	Date	Hour	Summary of Events and Information	Remarks and references to Appendices
	28th		Two Platoons in LENS ROAD REDOUBT relieved by 2 Platoons of B Coy - whole of "C" Coy moved to VILLAGE LINE.	
	29th		Battalion relieved 7th R. Inniskilling Fusiliers in LOOS sector. On our right 8th Royal Irish Fusiliers - on left 6th Connaughts. 7th R. Innis killings moved back to PHILOSOPHE. 7th R Irish Fusiliers in support in LOOS. Our dispositions were B Coy less 2 Platoons in centre, D Coy on right - C Coy & 2 Platoons of B in cellars in A Coy on left - in support.	
	30th		A quiet day. D Coy front Coy knocked flat had to be repaired all night - 2nd Lt H.K. May wounded at duty - 6.O.R. wounded.	
	31st		A quiet day. D Coy front line again knocked down 2nd Lt F.G. Young killed - 7 O.R. wounded 2nd Lt H.M. Thurota joined for duty -	

E.J. William Lt. Colonel
Commdg. 5th Royal Berks Regt.

Army Form C. 2118

WAR DIARY
or
INTELLIGENCE SUMMARY
(Erase heading not required.)

XV. S.L Berks
Vol 13

Confidential

War Diary
of
5th Royal Berkshire Regiment

from 1st June 1916 to 30th June 1916

Volume 13.

Army Form C. 2118

WAR DIARY
or
INTELLIGENCE SUMMARY
(Erase heading not required.)

Place	Date	Hour	Summary of Events and Information	Remarks and references to Appendices
	1		A quiet day. Casualties 1 other rank killed, 4 " " wounded, 2 " R.E. badly wounded	
	2		Batt: was relieved by 7th Royal Irish Rifles and marched back into billets at Manynegarbe. Casualties Killed 3 O. ranks, Wounded 10 O. ranks	
	3		In billets. Casualties wounded 1 O. rank (shell shock)	
	4		In billets. 2 Lieut J. + L. Edwards admitted to hospital. 2 Lieut F.H. Lloyd struck off strength (to England)	
	5		In billets. 2 Lieut A.D. Beech joined for duty.	

Army Form C. 2118

WAR DIARY
or
INTELLIGENCE SUMMARY
(Erase heading not required.)

Instructions regarding War Diaries and Intelligence Summaries are contained in F.S. Regs., Part II. and the Staff Manual respectively. Title Pages will be prepared in manuscript.

Place	Date	Hour	Summary of Events and Information	Remarks and references to Appendices
	6		Batt relieved in 49th Brigade by 7th Suffolks and then came under orders of C.R.E. 16th Division - Billets not changed -	
	7		In billets - many working parties found by battn. Casualty wounded - 1 O. rank	
	8		Relieved at Maurepas by 11th Middlesex of 36th I.B. & marched back to Lapugnoy, taking over billets from 9th Royal Sussex Regt. Casualties wounded - 1 O. rank Lieut Adams transferred to 2nd Battn.	
	9		Company & individual training commenced.	
	10		Company Training	
	11		(Sunday) 2 Lieut A. Wilkinson Taylor & W.A. Frew joined for duty.	

WAR DIARY
or
INTELLIGENCE SUMMARY

Army Form C. 2118

Place	Date	Hour	Summary of Events and Information	Remarks and references to Appendices
	12		"C" Company went to 1 Cnfs Head quarters to furnish guards etc - relieving a company of 1st Norfolks. Company Training	
	13.		Company Training. Weather has been good also	
	14.		Company Training. 2 Lieut A.G.W. Butler joined for duty. Lieut R H Causton employed as "Galloper" to Brigadier	
	15		Company Training	
	16.		Battalion entrained at Lillers at 9 pm and travelled to Longeau. Kune marched to Vignacourt. arriving about 6 am - on 17/6/16	
	17.			
	18		C.O. + Company Commanders went to see trenches about Albert.	

WAR DIARY
or
INTELLIGENCE SUMMARY

(Erase heading not required.)

Army Form C. 2118

Place	Date	Hour	Summary of Events and Information	Remarks and references to Appendices
	19		Company Training -	
	20		Brigade field day at Montmirchen. -	
	21.		Company Training - Battalion Training	
	22		Battalion Training	
	23		Brigade field day at Montauville	
	24		Battalion Training	
	25		(Sunday)	
	26		Battalion Training - Capt Rickman admitted to Hospital	
	27		Battalion moves to Molliens. Major Lotier admitted to Hospital	

Army Form C. 2118

WAR DIARY
or
INTELLIGENCE SUMMARY
(Erase heading not required.)

Instructions regarding War Diaries and Intelligence Summaries are contained in F.S. Regs., Part II. and the Staff Manual respectively. Title Pages will be prepared in manuscript.

Place	Date	Hour	Summary of Events and Information	Remarks and references to Appendices
	28th		Remained at Rollins du Bois - Training orders to move being cancelled -	
	29th		Remained at Rollins du Bois. Coy training -	
	30th		Battalion moved to Franvillers -	

E. Mellan
Lt Colonel
Comdg. 5th R. Berks Regt

5th Bn. Royal Berkshire Regt.

— July 1916 —

THE GALLIPOLI CAMPAIGN.

~~CHAPTER XIII.~~

Corrections to Chapter XII (formerly XI).

CONFIDENTIAL

12/5

5 Berks
Vol 14

WAR DIARY –

5th Battalion Royal Berkshire Regiment

29-7-16

2262
SB
A. Niven
Lt Colonel
Comdg. 5th Royal Berks Regt.

WAR DIARY or INTELLIGENCE SUMMARY

Army Form C. 2118

Place	Date	Hour	Summary of Events and Information	Remarks and references to Appendices
	July 1st	9 a.m.	The Battalion left FRANVILLERS and marched to HENENCOURT WOOD, arriving there about 11 a.m. - All packs were collected and stored in a hut. - Two extra bandoliers and two bombs per man issued to all ranks, and 200 entrenching tools were issued. - Received a sudden order to take to ALBERT to relieve the 8th Division.	
		5 p.m.	The relief was not complete until daybreak on 2nd, the Battalion occupying the front system of trenches from RYCROFT Street to ARGYLL Street. B. and C. Companies occupied the front system of trenches - A. and D. Battalion H.Q. in support.	* See map attached
	2nd	3 a.m.	Continued here in support to RYCROFT Street - Battalion H.Q. to VINCENT Street. The 37th Infantry Brigade were holding the trenches on our left the 19th Division on our Right. to men in a very filthy state, with many dead Germans lying about - In the evening men were issued hot dinner the following day the Battalion was to capture the village of OVILLERS LA BOISELLE -	

WAR DIARY or INTELLIGENCE SUMMARY

Army Form C. 2118

Place	Date	Hour	Summary of Events and Information	Remarks and references to Appendices
	2nd	10 p.m.	Operation Orders by Lieutenant Colonel WILLAN. J.L.O.	

1. At daybreak on the morning 3rd July the 12th Division will capture and consolidate the village of OVILLERS LA BOISSELLE.

2. The order of battle will be :— 36th Infy. Bde :— Right Brigade
                     37th   Do   Left   Do
                     36th   Do   Divisional Reserve.

3. The frontage allotted to the Brigade is from ARGYLL Street to X.7.d.3.8. — The frontage allotted to the Battalion is from ARGYLL Street to VINCENT Street inclusive. — The 7th Suffolks will attack on the left of the Battalion, and will direct. — The portion of front line trench from which the actual assault will be issued to the frontage VINCENT Street inclusive, to a point where the track cuts our front line at X.7.d.2.0. That is about 120 yards frontage.

WAR DIARY or INTELLIGENCE SUMMARY

Army Form C. 2118

4/ The attack will be carried out the B Battn, in a two Company front - Each Company will attack on a two Platoon front, about 30 yards distance between the two Platoons will assault on a frontage of 60 yards - Suitable gaps in the wire must be cut -

5/ The order of battle will be "C" Company, supported by "D" Company, on the left - "B" Company supported by "A" on the right - The left of "C" Company will direct, and keep touch with the 7th Suffolks -

6/ The two supporting Companies will be accumulated in the rear O.B.1. and take leading up to it, between X.7.d.2.0. and ARGYLE Street - They must be prepared to take into position vacated by the two assaulting Companies, as quickly as possible, and to follow in close support of the front troops. The actual distance will depend on circumstances -

7/ The first objective will be the enemy's support trenches, from X.8.c.5.4. to the east - trenches at the Western Extremity of the village, near X.8.c.7.4½

Army Form C. 2118

WAR DIARY or INTELLIGENCE SUMMARY
(Erase heading not required.)

Place	Date	Hour	Summary of Events and Information	Remarks and references to Appendices

and including the trenches, farms, etc.: in these tracks:— The first two tracks will be directed on their objectives, the Trench known as Shrapnel Trench, the fourth taken in the Trench, the Trench known as the Enemy's front line Trench. Each tank will be responsible for clearing all dugouts, cellars, C.T.'s etc: and consolidating their own objective. A Vickers flank hurt to form on the right, and special bombing parties told off to secure that flank from a terrible hostile attack — No troops will be assaulting in our immediate light —

Plus to Zero there will be a 10 minutes intense bombardment of the Enemy's trenches, with the object of driving him into his dugouts — During this period the first two or three tanks will crawl forward to their easy assaulting distance, and will assault as he man at Zero. At Zero the Artillery will lift for 30 minutes, and barrage a line through the Church — Half an hour after Zero, the artillery will lift again, and the two Supporting Companies which will take tanks up

WAR DIARY or INTELLIGENCE SUMMARY

Army Form C. 2118

Place	Date	Hour	Summary of Events and Information	Remarks and references to Appendices

to a position of readiness will await the next line of trenches, from B.M. 126.5 to a point about 200 yds. S.E., and consolidate them. There will be no further advance for a period of 45 minutes when the 9th Cheshire Regt. may be called upon to carry out a further attack.

9. The hour of Zero will be notified later.

10. The direction of the attack will be a line drawn through X.7.d.3.7. to the Chapel in OVILLERS, this line will mark the left of the Suffolks who will direct the attack throughout all its phases.

11. Battalion H.Q. to be established in VINCENT Street at 1 a.m. — Attacking Brigade H.Q. will be in FURNESS Street.

12. The last two lines will carry entrenching tools, all other orders as regards dress, sandbags, bombs, S.A.A. etc. will hold good — Flares will be issued to all Companies to fix to denote the position of our most advanced troops —

Issued about midnight 2/3 July.

Sgd: C.A. Gold.
Maj.

WAR DIARY or INTELLIGENCE SUMMARY

Army Form C. 2118

Summary of Events and Information

Narrative of Operations:-

The Artillery arrangements here allotted at the last moment, and the towed Inhabitants actually took their place prior to Zero, which was at 3-15 a.m.

The Bay Inhabitants had the effect of drawing considerable hostile fire on our front system of trenches. The result was that companies suffered casualties whilst waiting for the moment to assault, and also in crossing 'No Man's Land' from the little humps of trenches and H.E.

The assaulting Companies proceeded to crawling forward through the M.G.s cut in our wire, and advancing in quick time about up to the German front line trenches, before our Artillery lifted, and buttressed being hindered by the companies of the trenches.

The line in front of the enemy's front line has been completely destroyed, but there were many long held tales, which form considerable obstacles. There were in front of Shrapnel Terrace, but casualties:-

WAR DIARY or INTELLIGENCE SUMMARY

Army Form C. 2118

All four Companies appear to have kept good direction with the exception of the Right Assaulting Company which advanced too far to the right, this Coy was verified before entering the German Front Line Trench. - The leading waves appear to have suffered little or no casualties from rifle or machine gun fire until they had broken the German Front Line. - There appear to have been none of the enemy actually in the Front Trench. - After carrying the Front Line the leading waves pushed on after the second Trench and into what is known as "Thorofare Terrace" - Here some of the enemy were encountered and had to be had fighting tactics - Many dugouts were taken, and it became obvious that unless the ones between were taken a plentiful supply of bombs, it would be impossible to carry on to what proved to the Boa Grenel. - It proved to be a very back thing, and in the darkness it was entirely different to recognise

WAR DIARY
or
INTELLIGENCE SUMMARY.
(Erase heading not required.)

Army Form C. 2118.

Place	Date	Hour	Summary of Events and Information	Remarks and references to Appendices

Fired four shots, & even the Howitzer which had been carefully damaged by our Hell fire, assisted which, the noise of the bombardment which had startled to the Northern outskirts of the village, and the fire of innumerable Machine Guns, was deafening, and made it quite impossible to see over ridges —

There is no doubt that some men penetrated as far as the village, and were eventually killed or cut off —

The German dugouts appear to have been quite undamaged by the heavy bombardment, and as soon as the commenced to throw trench mortars down into them, the enemy streamed out of entrances further along fully armed with bombs, to that they were observed by our heard advancing coun —

There is no doubt that the heavy witnesses of evidence today by whole violates thinking parties, and which were all defeated by the supply of bombs becoming exhausted. —

WAR DIARY or INTELLIGENCE SUMMARY

Army Form C. 2118.

The Commanding Officer and Adjutant went forward shortly after the last wave had left. It was still quite dark, and impossible to discern friend from foe. On reaching the German Front line trenches about 100 men were found, between these and the rear line - considerable bombing was heard on the right and in front, and the enemy could be seen advancing from the left. There were much confusion in the darkness, & men from the 7th Suffolks and 9th Essex were seen to be heaped up with our own - The twice that Serjeaning, and it was impossible to make oneself heard - The bulk of the men fell back to the German Front line trench, where declined to go further, their stay on the top and exposed, not to know what to do - My re Officer and he found the Casualty - [Captain WACE] and he was endeavouring to rally the men, and to get them to go forward - After a brief reconnaissance the Commanding Officer decided that it would be quite impossible to retain

Army Form C. 2118.

WAR DIARY or INTELLIGENCE SUMMARY

(Erase heading not required.)

Place	Date	Hour	Summary of Events and Information	Remarks and references to Appendices
			we told us the German front line trench which was almost entirely obliterated, was extremely deep, expressed as to have to an attack from both flanks, as well as from the front - It would have been impossible to have carried it sufficiently in the time available, also to the fact that we would probably take too to leave there throughout the entire day. Quite unoccupied, and certainly cut off, with no chance of touch of S.A.A. By this time the enemy had started a heavy Arc fire with Machine Guns across "No Man's Land" from the direction of X.14.a.3.5 and X.7.d.9½.9½. To the commanding officer therefore went then to the line) collect and take them dig in on a the ALBERT — OVILLERS — number Road facing front - This was effected complete protection from the north, and was deployed from the start - About 80 to 100 men were dug in here, They were entrenched All remained there throughout the day. Quite undisturbed - They were withdrawn by order of the G.O.C. as soon as it was dark - Lieutenant and Adjutant GOLD was killed in this Road, just below the C.O.	

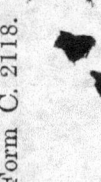

WAR DIARY or INTELLIGENCE SUMMARY

Army Form C. 2118.

(Erase heading not required.)

Instructions regarding War Diaries and Intelligence Summaries are contained in F. S. Regs., Part II and the Staff Manual respectively. Title Pages will be prepared in manuscript.

Place	Date	Hour	Summary of Events and Information	Remarks and references to Appendices

The failure to maintain our hold on the captured trenches may be put down to the following facts:-

(a) The extreme darkness, which had not been anticipated.

(b) The length of our bombardment, which resulted in the enemy putting up a heavy barrage at Thiepval & P.7.E.

(c) Excessive casualties caused to Officers, Non Com. Offrs., bombing Parties and Lewis gun teams (the men first out of action) at an early stage in the operations.

(d) Little or no damage was done to the enemy's dugouts by our bombardment.

(e) Our men undoubtedly lost direction, and therefore (i) not real the objective, thereby causing loss of cohesion, and (ii) operation and (iii) Vast losses of heavy casualties incurred in crossing "No Man's Land".

Army Form C. 2118.

WAR DIARY
or
INTELLIGENCE SUMMARY

(Erase heading not required.)

Instructions regarding War Diaries and Intelligence Summaries are contained in F. S. Regs., Part II. and the Staff Manual respectively. Title Pages will be prepared in manuscript.

Place	Date	Hour	Summary of Events and Information	Remarks and references to Appendices
	3rd	4pm	The Battalion total consisted of about 70 men, and the C.O. (as above) to go to the ALBERT Refugees for the night. Here the men made extreme shelter, and the officers & men's kit had been left at the transport lines behind, & indeed there brought up — the evening 2nd Lieutenant BREACH and MAY, and about 60 men who had been sent on in advance (can's Land) rejoined — The there all very glad to see them —	
	4th 5th		Going to the extreme left the Battalion has taken into the vacant trenches in ALBERT, and three two days have spent in resting and refitting — Casualties for the operations against OVILLERS, are:- Officers — Killed 2. Ptn. Ranks Killed 2. Wounded 212. Missing 104. 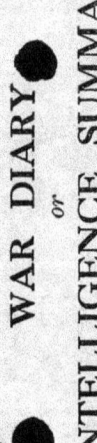 Killed 2. 2nd Lieuts 2. Wounded 3. Missing 7. The Medical Officer and the later Reverend Emanuel Selow in the Aid Post in STANDISH Street when the Battalion was withdrawn from the trenches, they (Singdine) excellent work in bringing in many wounded —	

2449 Wt. W14957/M90 750,000 1/16 J.B.C. & A. Forms/C.2118/12.

WAR DIARY or INTELLIGENCE SUMMARY

Army Form C. 2118.

Place	Date	Hour	Summary of Events and Information	Remarks and references to Appendices
	6th	11 am	Lieutenant and Adjutant GOLD was buried in AVELUY Cemetery —	
		2 pm	The Battalion strength 340 all ranks, the Brigade Commander arranging for us (2 officers & other ranks from the Transport Lines) to relieve the 7th Suffolks — leaving behind A and B. Companies who accompanied the Front Line Battalion. ※ DORSET West and DUNFERMLINE West ※ C and D companies and Battn. H.Q. to the USNA Redoubt. The relief was completed without incident, and the trenches then stood to be very hot — Casualties. Nil.	※ See map attached
	7th		A hot night and morning making trenches very dusty — The attack by the 7th Infantry Brigade and the 58th Infantry Brigade from LA BOISELLE on the morning — against OVILLERS has been reported — They show a certain amount of retaliation against our trenches, fortunately the shy led to 3 men wounded —	

WAR DIARY or INTELLIGENCE SUMMARY

Army Form C. 2118.

Place	Date	Hour	Summary of Events and Information	Remarks and references to Appendices
			The Battalion was to assist the attack of the 8th Regulars by enveloping our Lewis Guns a to the head of the MASH Valley. An Officers' patrol that went out during the night found many wounded, there were brought in. — Casualties - Other Ranks - Wounded 3.	
	8th	1 a.m.	The O.C. and Lieutenant EDWARDS were asked to guide 2 Battalions of the 75th Inf. Brigade into the new-assembly trenches that had been dug astride the MASH Valley — This was successfully carried out, and left Battalions ready their objective, i.e. the enemy's front line trench at the head of the MASH Valley before day light, without any opposition.	
		5 p.m.	About 5 p.m. the Battalion was ordered to withdraw and proceed to billet at BOUZINCOURT, the rest of the Brigade were at ALBERT. Billets were reached about 11 p.m. Casualties. Other Ranks - Killed 1. Wounded 2.	

Army Form C. 2118

WAR DIARY
or
INTELLIGENCE SUMMARY

(Erase heading not required.)

Instructions regarding War Diaries and Intelligence Summaries are contained in F. S. Regs., Part II. and the Staff Manual respectively. Title Pages will be prepared in manuscript.

Place	Date	Hour	Summary of Events and Information	Remarks and references to Appendices
	9th	11 a.m.	The Battalion moved to VARENNES where the remainder of the Brigade joined us.	
	10th		The whole Brigade marched to, and have accomodated in huts and tents, in the BOIS du WARNIMONT.	
	11th		Commenced training.	
	12th		Training continued – 3 Officers and 150 other Ranks proceeded to BERTRANCOURT and came under orders of the 4th Division, for took a transfer in their tests.	
	13th		Training continued.	
	14th		Do. Do. The party lent to the 4th Division returned about 5 p.m.	
	15th		Do. Do. Reinforcement, consisting of 46 men of the Warwick Regt. arrived.	
	16th		Training continued.	

WAR DIARY or INTELLIGENCE SUMMARY

Army Form C. 2118.

(Erase heading not required.)

Place	Date	Hour	Summary of Events and Information	Remarks and references to Appendices
	17th		Training Continued – 30 Reinforcements arrived, all men of the Royal Berkshire Regiment.	
	18th		The Battalion carried out exercises in the attack over a piece of training area.	
	19th		Training Continued – Throughout the past week, the 1st (1st) innumerable football matches, and some presented sports for the Transport. In the afternoon the Brigade took to BERTRANCOURT, and were killed in huts – C.O. Brigadier the AUCHENVILLERS Sector.	
	20th			
	21st		The Battalion Relieved the 1st K.O.R.L. Regt in the AUCHENVILLERS Sector and occupied the trenches from FOX Street to JACOB'S LADDER – The 7th Suffolks were on our right, and the 9th Royal Fusiliers on our left. The trenches were good, and on the whole fairly peaceful. Casualties Other Ranks 3 wounded –	

WAR DIARY
or
INTELLIGENCE SUMMARY

Army Form C. 2118.

Place	Date	Hour	Summary of Events and Information	Remarks and references to Appendices
	22nd		A quiet day – Battalion was employed at night in digging a new O.B.L., about 200 yards in advance of the present line – The Transport had a lively time coming up with the rations at night, and sustained some casualties. Casualties – Nil	
	23rd		A similar day to the 22nd – A draft of 30 other ranks of the Ox & Bucks L.I. arrived in the trenches – Casualties – Nil	
	24th		About 1 Run the enemy Lombarded our sector with H.E. am) throughout causing oly slight casualties, but doing some damage to the trenches – Works continued at night on the O.B.L. Casualties – Other Ranks – Wounded 16.	

Army Form C. 2118.

WAR DIARY
or
INTELLIGENCE SUMMARY
(Erase heading not required.)

Instructions regarding War Diaries and Intelligence Summaries are contained in F. S. Regs., Part II. and the Staff Manual respectively. Title Pages will be prepared in manuscript.

Place	Date	Hour	Summary of Events and Information	Remarks and references to Appendices
	25th		In the afternoon the Battalion was relieved by the and marched to billets at BUS-les-ARTOIS. Reinforcement consisting of 33 men of the Regiment arrived. Casualties - Nil.	
	26th		The Brigade marched at 9am to VARENNES. Training was carried out in the afternoon.	
	27th 28th		Training continued. Reinforcement consisting of 30 other ranks of the Royal Berks. Regt. arrived and were posted to Companies.	
		7pm	In the evening a Brigade Concert was held.	
	29th	9am	The Brigade marched to billets at BOUZINCOURT.	

D. Millar Welch
Cmdg. 5th Battn. R. Berks. Regt.

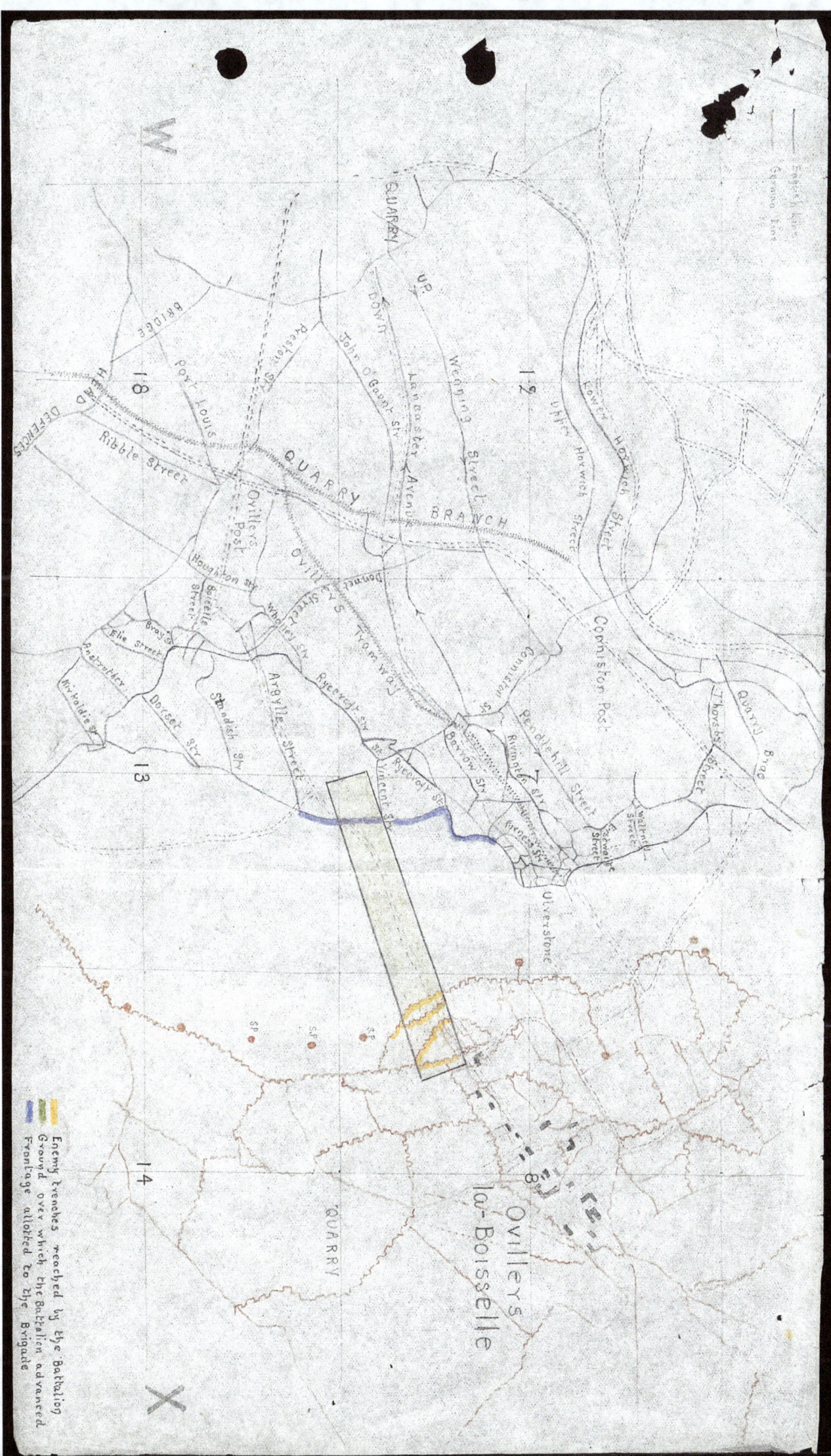

35th Brigade.
12th Division.

1/5th BATTALION

ROYAL BERKSHIRE REGIMENT

AUGUST 1916

1/5 Bn
12th

5 Books
Vol 15

2282
sb

WAR DIARY

5th Royal Berkshire Regiment

from

July 30th/1916 — August 30th/1916

Army Form C. 2118.

WAR DIARY
or
INTELLIGENCE SUMMARY
(Erase heading not required.)

Instructions regarding War Diaries and Intelligence Summaries are contained in F.S. Regs., Part II and the Staff Manual respectively. Title Pages will be prepared in manuscript.

Place	Date	Hour	Summary of Events and Information	Remarks and references to Appendices
	July 30		At BOUZINCOURT - Training commenced.	
	31		do do continued	
	Aug. 1		do 2Lt. E. DAVIS invalided sick to England.	
	2		do 2Lt. G.P. DEBONO and 2Lt. A.J. SHIPTON joined the Battalion	
	3		do do	
	4		do do	
	5		do do	
	6		do do - Draft of 10 O.R. joined from 12/13.D.	
	7		Left Bouzincourt at 4 p.m. and marched up to relieve the 36th Brigade in the trenches N.N. of POZIERES. The Battalion occupied 5th Avenue, 4th Avenue and 3rd Avenue.	

Army Form C. 2118.

WAR DIARY
or
INTELLIGENCE SUMMARY
(Erase heading not required.)

Place	Date	Hour	Summary of Events and Information	Remarks and references to Appendices
	Aug 8th		On the morning of August 8th the Germans made 4 counter attacks on our position in 5th Avenue. (1) On our left flank at 3 a.m. They made a bombing attack and were cut into our trenches but were immediately driven out. (2) At the same place they attempted a second attack at 4.30 a.m. which was easily repulsed. (3) Simultaneously with (2) the enemy made a determined attack on the barricade which formed the right flank of our position in 5th AVENUE. The enemy employed flammenwerfer which were cut of the smoke got into the trenches. After three hours of fighting they were driven out and beyond the barricade. (4) At 5.30 a.m. They repeated the attack and this time succeeded in getting into the trench and bombing our men to within down the trench. A fresh barricade was erected about 30 yards from the old one and the enemy was checked there, whilst supervising the construction of this barricade the company commander, Lt. E. A. L. EDWARDS who had conducted the defence with great gallantry was wounded. Subsequent to his wound a days later Sgt. G. M. HUGHES who was sent out to be relieved and the first G. attack was found to be missing and Lt. H. CROWHURST who was wounded by enemy bombs. The situation was preceded by an intense bombardment. Lts. H.M. THURSTON, 2 Lt. A. BUDMEAD and 2Lt. A. J. SHIPTON were wounded.	2302

WAR DIARY or INTELLIGENCE SUMMARY

Place	Date	Hour	Summary of Events and Information	Remarks and references to Appendices
	Aug. 8 Contd.		The net result of the 4 attacks was that the enemy gained about 50 yards of trench with great loss of life. Casualties 6 officers and 128 other ranks. Major P.W. NORTH (of 2nd Bn. Royal Berkshire Regt.) and 2.Lt H.H. COOK (from 9th Bn.) joined the Battalion.	23/C
	Aug. 9		During the attacks of ANZACS and 7th SUFFOLK Regt. on our right the Bn. attention was heavily shelled and this was far more often casualties, all from shell fire in RATION TRENCH (5TH AVENUE) Lt. R. A. BANCE was killed; Lt. C. du V. HINDE, Lt. A.G. C. RICE & Lt. H.C. TOOGOOD were wounded. Casualties 4 officers & 39 other ranks.	
	Aug. 10		Battalion was relieved by 9th ESSEX Regt. and returned to trenches near OVILLERS – 2 Companies in old German Front line and 2 Companies on USNA Hill. Battalion employed in working and carrying parties. Casualties 4 other ranks.	

Army Form C. 2118.

WAR DIARY
or
INTELLIGENCE SUMMARY

(Erase heading not required.)

Place	Date	Hour	Summary of Events and Information	Remarks and references to Appendices
	Aug 11th		Near OVILLERS — employed on working and carrying parties. Casualties:- 3 OR wounded.	
	Aug 12th		Near OVILLERS — Battalion organized as two Companies and held in reserve to support 9th ESSEX & 1st NORFOLK Regiments in attack on trenches in front of 5th AVENUE. The attack being successful, Battalion was not called up. Casualties: 3 OR wounded.	
	Aug 13th		The Brigade was relieved and marched to bivouacs about ½ mile W. of BOUZINCOURT.	
	Aug 14th		Brigade marched to ACHEUX & was billeted there.	
	Aug 15th		Brigade marched to BOIS du WARNIMONT. Battalion accommodated in huts occupied in July.	
	Aug 16th		Battalion marched to LUCHEUX & billeted there — a very beautiful and comfortable village with a fine old castle.	
	Aug 17th		Battalion moved to NANQUIETIN & went into billets. At midday we came under the orders of VI th Corps IIIrd Army	

Army Form C. 2118.

WAR DIARY
or
INTELLIGENCE SUMMARY
(Erase heading not required.)

233℅

Place	Date	Hour	Summary of Events and Information	Remarks and references to Appendices
WANQUETIN	Aug 18th		Training commenced. 2/Lt A.D. BREACH invalided sick to England.	
WANQUETIN	19th		Training continued. Major P.W. NORTH left Bn. to take command of our 1st Bn.	
WANQUETIN	20th		G.O.C. 12th Division presented decorations given to Officers and men for operations on July 3rd/1916. Honours awards (only those marked with asterisk were able to be present for decoration by G.O.C.)	

Military Cross
  2/Lt. H.M. BROWN (since died of wounds)
  2/Lt. A.D. BREACH (since sick to England).

Distinguished Conduct Medal
  8000 Cpl. Howard. C.*
  10375 Sgt. Nicholls. H.

Military Medal

10291 Sergt. Woodley.E.*	11129 Pte. Smith.A.L.*	
9499 " Bruce.J.*	9284 " Gardiner.J.	
7493 Corpl. Hammond.W.*	10254 " Purchell.A.J.	
11876 " Rearman.W.*	12016 " Macfarlane.J.	
11117 " Pte Alston.P.*	15996 " Robins.E.J.	

2449 Wt. W14957/M90 750,000 1/16 J.B.C. & A. Forms/C.2118/12.

Army Form C. 2118.

WAR DIARY
or
INTELLIGENCE SUMMARY

(Erase heading not required.)

Instructions regarding War Diaries and Intelligence Summaries are contained in F. S. Regs., Part II. and the Staff Manual respectively. Title Pages will be prepared in manuscript.

Place	Date	Hour	Summary of Events and Information	Remarks and references to Appendices
	Aug. 21st		The Battalion left NANQUETIN at 11 a.m., marched to WATHUS and bivouacked there till 8.30 p.m. Leaving transport and Q.M. Stores at BERNEVILLE the battalion then marched up through ARRAS and relieved the 6th LINCOLNSHIRE Regt (33rd Brigade) in H2 sector in front of ARRAS. Very good and quiet twelve. Battalion Headquarters in RONVILLE.	D34C
	22nd		H2 sector - Casualties nil.	
	23rd		do. do.	
	24th		Captain E.P.C. AMPHLETT (4th T.B. WORCESTERSHIRE Regt.) joined for duty.	
	25th		H2 sector - Casualties nil.	
	26th		do. do.	
	27th		do. Our left company front bombarded with aerial torpedoes from 10.10 - 10.40 p.m. Enemy attempted a small raid, which was entirely unsuccessful. Casualties 5 other ranks.	

Army Form C. 2118.

WAR DIARY
or
INTELLIGENCE SUMMARY
(Erase heading not required.)

Instructions regarding War Diaries and Intelligence Summaries are contained in F.S. Regs., Part II. and the Staff Manual respectively. Title Pages will be prepared in manuscript.

Place	Date	Hour	Summary of Events and Information	Remarks and references to Appendices
	May 28th		Hz Sector - Our left Company again att bombarded with aerial torpedoes from 10.10 - 11 p.m. Enemy attempted a raid with 20-30 men but succeeded in cutting two passages through our wire. None of the enemy however succeeded in entering our trenches and they must have suffered casualties from our Artillery Barrage and Lewis gun fire. Casualties 7 OR ranks wounded.	
	29		Hz Sector - The Battalion was relieved in the afternoon by the 9th Essex Regt. and moved into Billets in ARRAS.	
	30.		ARRAS - Battalion in Divisional Reserve provided working and carrying parties for Division. Major P.W. NORTH rejoined the Battalion.	

War Diary

of

5th Royal Berkshire Regt.

from

September 1st 1916 - September 30th

Army Form C. 2118.

WAR DIARY
INTELLIGENCE SUMMARY
(Erase heading not required.)

Place	Date	Hour	Summary of Events and Information	Remarks and references to Appendices
ARRAS	Aug. 31st		Battalion in divisional reserve.	
	Sep. 1st		do. - Draft of 8 other ranks arrive.	
	2nd		do. - Casualty - 1 Other Rank wounded.	
	3rd		do.	
	4th		do. - Following officers attached to this Battalion for duty 2/Lt. M.R. READ, 6th Queens, 2/Lt. J.E. BURKE, 6th Buffs and 2/Lt. C.W. LEGGETT, 7th E. Surreys.	
	5th		do.	
	6th		Battalion relieved 9th Essex Regiment in H.2 sector in front of ARRAS. 2/Lt. L.D KONENSTAM admitted hospital sick. Draft of 10 O.R. arrives. Casualties - nil	
	7th		H.2 sector - Casualties 1 O.R. wounded.	
	8th		do - Casualties nil. Captain & P.C. AMPHLETT admitted hospital sick.	

Army Form C. 2118

WAR DIARY
or
INTELLIGENCE SUMMARY
(Erase heading not required.)

Place	Date	Hour	Summary of Events and Information	Remarks and references to Appendices
	Sep 9th		Hg Sector - Casualties nil.	
	10th		do.	
			Corps Commander F.M. Cof.s granted Military Medals to the following for gallant conduct during the fighting of Aug 7th, 8th & 9th	
			10506 Cpl H.T. Matthews 1966 Cpl. W.H. Heath	
			10861 Pte T.J. Baker 10363 L/Cpl J. Auer	
			9309 L/Cpl B. Ensley 9872 L/Cpl. E. Horwood	
			10441 Pte. E. Garlick (Bar) 10660 L/Cpl J. Bennett	
			6101 Sgt W. James 8730 Pte A. Bothill	
			10283 Pte J.J. Allen 11763 Pte J. Pike	
			10635 Pte W.R. Parris 11020 Pte A. Clarke	
	11th		Hg Sector - Casualties nil. Draft of 12 O.R. arrived.	
	12th		do. do.	
	13th		do. do.	
	14th		do. Relieved in evening by 9th Essex Regt and took over down billets in ARRAS, coming 18th Divisional Reserve.	
	15th		ARRAS — Lt. H.C. HORSFORD rejoined the Battalion. Draft of 7 O.R. arrived.	

WAR DIARY / INTELLIGENCE SUMMARY

Army Form C. 2118

Place	Date	Hour	Summary of Events and Information	Remarks and references to Appendices
	Sept. 16th		ARRAS - Following distinctions granted by the Army Commander for gallantry during fighting of July 3rd - 6th & 7th - 9th. Military Cross Captain J.J. Barthalomew (R.A.M.C. attached) Lt. J.A. Burton (Transport officer) Lt. J.M. Wykes. 2/Lt. H.A.L. Edwards (died of wounds 10/8/16) C.S.M. T. Perkins Distinguished Conduct Medal 10673 C.S.M. A. Waite 12810 Pte. E.T.B. Ware 10743 C.S.M. J. Faulkner 17231 Pte. S. Beatewick.	
	17th		ARRAS - Following granted Military Medals by H.M. the King :- 10459 Pte. W. Cousins 10286 Pte. W. Lewis. 10411 Pte. J. Garlick 10861 Sergt. J. Redford 10822 L/C. C. Gorland 16239 Cpl. P. Reynolds 10763 L/C. A. Histed	
	18th		ARRAS - Draft of 15 O.R. arrived.	

WAR DIARY or INTELLIGENCE SUMMARY

Army Form C. 2118

Place	Date	Hour	Summary of Events and Information	Remarks and references to Appendices
ARRAS	Sept 19th 20th 21st 22nd 23rd		Relieved 9th ESSEX Regt. in H2 Sector. H2 Sector - Draft of 128 arrived all of Royal Berkshire Regt. On night 23rd-24th a raid was attempted on the enemy trenches. The party consisted of two officers and 36 other ranks under Lt. A.W. TAYLOR. The scheme was to cut through the enemy wire with a 36 ft. torpedo and then let the raiding party through. The torpedo was successfully fired but on the wire not being cut and not been successful, the party was withdrawn. Casualties 1 o.r. wounded.	Appendix A Sketch
	24th 25th		H2 Sector - On night 25th-26th a second attempt was made to raid the enemy trenches. The 1st attempt in enemy wire had been kept open and a second tape was successfully got into position & front distant this remains of the wire within cover of which the Bangalore Gun fire, the Raiding Party hung through the Gap but found the wire in a condition with the enemy's parapet in front enabled on top of it. They found no sign of enemy, so lay up keeping a watch on enemy's parapet. They partly returned unmolested fired on and 2nd Lt. A.W. TAYLOR was killed. The party returned to the trenches from the enemy line. Casualties in the process. Herewith sketch showing position.	

A

Sketch showing enemy's parapet and wire at
the point where Torpedoes were exploded.

PARAPET

CRATER

2nd Torpedo
Exploded
XXXXX

1st Torpedo Exploded
XXXXX

|—12ft—|—5yds—|—10ft—|—10yds—|—12yds—|

barb wire
cut through
1 ft wide
XXXXX

ACTUAL GROUND.

It was supposed after the first attempt that the
crater was the enemy's trench & the second the
parapet.

Army Form C. 2118

WAR DIARY or INTELLIGENCE SUMMARY

(Erase heading not required.)

Place	Date	Hour	Summary of Events and Information	Remarks and references to Appendices
	25th		Cont'd.	

Lt. A.N. TAYLOR conducted both patrols with great skill & gallantry, until he was killed and Lt. R. COBB took his machine & returned volunteer assistance made a brave attempt to rescue his body.

No. 9376 L/Cpl A. COX was responsible on both occasions to disentangle and firing the torpedo, and showed the greatest courage & resource in twice getting it into exactly the required position and detects and in recovering it. He was defended and after firing the torpedo —

Casualties:- Killed Lt. A. N. TAYLOR. - Wounded - 4 O.R's ranks
Missing - 4 O.R's ranks

26th — Hd. Qrs. Casualties — 2 O.R. wounded.

27th — The Batn — Battalion returned by night by the 10th D.L.I. 14th Div.- moved from ARRAS and proceeded to IVERGNY.
Lts. H.S. BARRATT & Lt. B. H. A. FELLOWES joined the Battalion

28th
29th — IVERGNY — in billets
do — Transport which in advance of Battalion to VILLERS-BOCAGE

30th — Bun Coume in command of
XVth Corps IVth Army

P.W. Beak
Lieut Colonel
Commanding
5th R. Berkshire Regt.

1875 Wt W593/826 1,000,000 4/15 J.B.C. & A. A.D.S.S./Forms/C. 2118.

Vol 17 35/12

5th Royal Berkshire Regt.
Octr 1916

Army Form C. 2118.

WAR DIARY
INTELLIGENCE SUMMARY
(Erase heading not required.)

Place	Date	Hour	Summary of Events and Information	Remarks and references to Appendices
	Sep. 30th		The Battalion was conveyed by buses from IVERGNY to RIBEMONT. After detraining Battalion marched into camp near BECORDEL.	
	Oct. 1st		Transport rejoined unit. In camp near BECORDEL.	
	2nd		Battn. marched via FRICOURT, MAMETZ & MONTAUBAN to BERNAFAY WOOD, where we settled in bivouacs. 35th Brigade in Divisional Reserve.	
	3rd		Major P.W. NORTH left Battn. to take command of 20th Bn. D.L.I. BERNAFAY Wood. Bn. finding working and carrying parties for Bde. in the line. 2Lt. H.S. BARRATT admitted to hospital sick.	
	4th		do:- 2Lt. G.E. COLLINS joined for duty. Casualty:- 1 O.R. killed in action.	
	5th		do:- Casualties - nil.	
	6th		do:- Casualties:- 1 O.R. wounded.	
	7th		do:- 36th and 37th attacked with the object of capturing BAYONET SCABBARD and BARLEY trenches. The attack was carried out in conjunction with 124th Bde. on left and 61st Bde. on right. The 35th Infy. Bde. was in support Divisional Reserve. The attack was unsuccessful. 2Lt. T.M. READY and 2Lt. A.C.B. STOREY joined the Bn.	

WAR DIARY
INTELLIGENCE SUMMARY
(Erase heading not required.)

Army Form C. 2118.

Instructions regarding War Diaries and Intelligence Summaries are contained in F. S. Regs., Part II. and the Staff Manual respectively. Title Pages will be prepared in manuscript.

Place	Date	Hour	Summary of Events and Information	Remarks and references to Appendices
	Sept. 8th		Bn. Received orders at 6 p.m. that we were to be temporarily attached to 36th Bde. Bn. march up via LONGUEVAL and took over FLERS Trench from 8th and 9th Bn. Royal Fusiliers. Casualties :- Nil	
	9th		FLERS Trench - Casualties:- 1 or. Killed, 1 or. wounded	
	10th		do:- Remainder of 36th and 37th Bdes relieved by 35th Bde. 7th Norfolk and 7th Suffolk Regts in front line. Bn. in next area of 35th Bde. again. Casualties :- 6 or. wounded	
	11th		do:- Casualties:- 1 or. wounded	
	12th		do:- At 1.50 p.m. the 7th Suffolk and 7th Norfolk Regts. attacked with the object of capturing BAYONET and SCABBARD Trenches. Though successful in places some parts of the line were held up. By about 5 p.m. nearly all the line was back in its front line trenches. By 7 p.m. both Bns. were back in the 9th ESSEX Regt. took on the front line also the remaining Bns. went to this assault and at 8.30 p.m. we received orders to take on the position in SMOKE support to Butt's Road. Bn. Headquarters transferred to Butt's Road. Casualties:- 2 or. killed, 6 or. wounded	

WAR DIARY
or
INTELLIGENCE SUMMARY
(Erase heading not required.)

Army Form C. 2118

Place	Date	Hour	Summary of Events and Information	Remarks and references to Appendices
	Oct. 13th		SMOKE TRENCH - Bn. in support to 9th ESSEX Regt. Lt. R. COBB and C.S.M. T. PERKINS killed by shell near Bn. Headqrs. Casualties:- 1 officer and 1 or. killed, 6 or. wounded.	
	14th		-do- Casualties:- 4 or. killed, 8 or. wounded.	
	15th		8348 Sergt. J. HACKETT and 9376 L/Cpl A.C. COX granted Military Medal for gallant conduct on Sep. 25th. Relieved 9th ESSEX Regt. in front line from N.19.b.4.3 - N.26.a.8.8. (ref. 57.c.S.W. 2000) - 2 Companies in front line, 2 Companies in support. Casualties:- 4 or. wounded. Draft of 86 other ranks arrived - all of 2/4th Bn. of the S. Regiment.	
	16th		Front line - Casualties:- 2 or. killed, 13 or. wounded.	
	17th		-do- Orders received to take over front line from GRAVENNEY K.N.20.d.1.0. by 2.40 am. 7th ESSEX Regt. who were ordered to attack BAYONET Trench at 3.40 am. This Bn. was in support and was ordered to take over the front line as soon as the Enem. advance to the assault. At 3.40 am. the assault was launched and at 5 am. it was known that	

WAR DIARY

INTELLIGENCE SUMMARY

(Erase heading not required.)

Army Form C. 2118.

Place	Date	Hour	Summary of Events and Information	Remarks and references to Appendices
	Oct. 18th		The attack had not been successful. The Brigadier ordered Indian mtn. gun right and support there would be attempt to advance through the Bn. on our right and support the attempt to advance from the Right. Hd. and. so it was that in almost light the movement was executed and by 8 a.m. all the 9th Essex Regt. were back in the original trenches. Meanwhile the Brigade on our right had (from 88th Bde.) had taken their objective. Casualties:- 4 O.R. wounded. The situation being near that the 8th Bn. was established in GRENSE Trench and HLT Trench to form N.20.d.4.5. Orders were issued for the 35th Bn. to capture BAYONET Trench from N.20.d.4.5 to N.20. Central. The attack was to be carried out by a company of this Battalion attacking from the Right and a company of the 7th R. Sussex (attached to us for this operation) from the Left. The attack was timed for 3 a.m. - The company of 7 R. Sussex Regt. was seen to launch a bombing attack from N.20.c.5.6, mm Bn. was to launch two bombing attacks simultaneously from the Right. The success of the operation was made improbable by the enemy opening a steady barrage at 2.45 a.m. Barrage was rifle by patrols, the attack was launched,	
			Casualties:- 2/Lt. H.H.K. MAY wounded, 3 O.R. killed, 22 O.R. wounded, 3 O.R. missing	

Army Form C. 2118.

WAR DIARY
or
INTELLIGENCE SUMMARY
(Erase heading not required.)

Instructions regarding War Diaries and Intelligence Summaries are contained in F. S. Regs., Part II and the Staff Manual respectively. Title Pages will be prepared in manuscript.

Place	Date	Hour	Summary of Events and Information	Remarks and references to Appendices
	Sept 19th		The Bn. was relieved by 16th MIDDLESEX Regt. of 86th Bde., 29th Divn. The relief was very tedious and the march to Brick TREE the Bn. did not reach MAMETZ until 6.30 a.m. Casualties: 9 O.R. killed, 23 O.R. wounded, Bn. in Bivouacs just E. of MAMETZ wood. Casualties: 3 O.R. wounded, 18 stragglers rejoined (Not eventually rejoining).	
	20th			
	21st		Marched to DERNANCOURT into billets for one night. Following Officers ceased for duty from 5th Bn Stokes Trench Mortar. Lt. E.S. MOSS, Lt. E.A. SUTTON & Lt. H.R.S. KING	
	22nd		Marched to RIBEMONT - entrained there and proceeded to HAUTEVILLE coming under orders of III Corps again in the III rd Army Area. Transport went upon 23rd Inst.	
	23rd		HAUTEVILLE - Bn. in billets. Draft of 130 other ranks arrived all of other Regiments	
	24th		do	
	25th		do	
	26th		do - Embarked at KATTRE ST QUENTIN at 10.30 p.m. and were conveyed to HAPLAS, which we took over Army billets and were occupied in September as Divisional Reserve Battalion	

Army Form C. 2118.

WAR DIARY
or
INTELLIGENCE SUMMARY

(Erase heading not required.)

Place	Date	Hour	Summary of Events and Information	Remarks and references to Appendices
	Oct 27th		ARRAS - Training commenced -	
	28th		do.	
	29th		do.	
	30th		do. Relieved 9th ESSEX Regt in the trenches taking on some trenches do not occupied in September. Casualties :- Nil.	

D. Miller
Lt Col.
Commanding 5th R. Berkshire Regt

31/10/16

Vol 18.

Confidential

WAR DIARY
November 1916

5th Bn Royal Berkshire Regt

WAR DIARY
or
INTELLIGENCE SUMMARY
(Erase heading not required.)

Army Form C. 2118

Place	Date	Hour	Summary of Events and Information	Remarks and references to Appendices
H2 Sector	Oct. 31st		Casualties:- Nil	
	Nov. 1st		Casualties:- Nil	
	2nd		Casualties:- Nil	
	3rd		Relieved by 9th ESSEX Regt. Divisional Reserve Bn in Barracks in ARRAS. Casualties:- Nil	
ARRAS	4th		Lt. J.E. BURKE (attached from 6th BUFFS) rejoined his Bn.	
	5th		Following Officers joined this Bn for duty:- 2Lt. L.E. WHITE, 2Lt. M.B. BEATTIE, Lt. K.C. BICKERDIKE, Lt. K.C.B. STOREY	
	6th		do. (last named rejoined from hospital)	
	7th		Relieved 9th ESSEX Regt. in H2 Sector. Casualties:- Nil	
H2 Sector	8th		Casualties:- Nil	
	9th		Casualties:- Nil - Draft of 6 Other Ranks joined Bn.	
	10th		Casualties: Nil	

WAR DIARY
INTELLIGENCE SUMMARY
(Erase heading not required.)

Army Form C. 2118

Place	Date	Hour	Summary of Events and Information	Remarks and references to Appendices
H2 Sector	Nov. 11th		Relieved by 9th ESSEX Regt. and returned to billets in ARRAS as Div'l Reserve Battalion. Casualties:- Nil - Lieut. W.E. FRASER (R.A.M.C.) attached to Bn for duty.	
ARRAS	12th		Draft of 16 O.R.s joined the Battalion. 2nd Lt. S.H. MAYO joined the Battalion for duty.	
do	13th		Relieve 9th ESSEX Regt. in H2 Sector. Casualties: 1 O.R. wounded	
	14th		Casualties :- nil -	
H2 Sector	15th		" :- nil -	
	16th		" :- nil -	
	17th		Relieved by 9th ESSEX Regt. and returned to ARRAS as Battn. in Divisional Reserve. Casualties :- Nil.	
	18th		Lieut W.E. FRASER (R.A.M.C.) returned to C.C.S. Capt. D. WOOD (R.A.M.C.) attached to Bn. for duty.	
	19th			

WAR DIARY
INTELLIGENCE SUMMARY

(Erase heading not required.)

Army Form C. 2118

Place	Date	Hour	Summary of Events and Information	Remarks and references to Appendices
ARRAS	Nov. 20		Draft of 5 other ranks arrived.	
	21			
	22		do:- Relieved 9th ESSEX Regt. in H2 Sector	
	23		Casualties:- Nil.	
	24		H2 Sector:- Casualties:- 1 O.R. Killed, 1 O.R. wounded. Captain D. H. AVERY rejoined his Battalion.	
	25		do:- Casualties:- 2 O.Rs wounded. Lt. M.R. READ (attached for duty from 6th QUEENS)rejoined his Bn.	
	26		do:- Casualties:- 1 O.R. accidentally wounded.	
	27		do:- Relieved by 9th ESSEX Regt. and returned to billets in ARRAS as Battalion in Div. Reserve. Casualties:- 1 O.R. wounded.	
ARRAS	28			
	29			
	30			

D. M---
Lt-Col.
Commanding 5th R. Berks his Regt.
30/11/16

(6202) W 11186/M1151 350,000 12/16 McA. & W., Ltd. (Est. 731) Forms/W 3091/3.   Army Form W. 3091.

35/12

Cover for Documents.

Nature of Enclosures.

War Diary
of
5th Royal Berks.
~~Jerny to~~ Decbr 1916.

Notes, or Letters written.

169th Inf Bde.

May 1917

Volume No. _____

BRITISH SALONIKA FORCE

WAR DIARY.

27th DIVISION

PERIOD

Vol. No.	Unit	From	To
13	80th Trench Mortar Battery	1/3/18	31/3/18
17	81st do	do	do
19	82nd do	do	do

Vol 19

War Diary

5th Royal Berks Regt.

Hampshire

Army Form C. 2118

WAR DIARY
INTELLIGENCE SUMMARY
(Erase heading not required.)

Instructions regarding War Diaries and Intelligence Summaries are contained in F.S. Regs., Part II. and the Staff Manual respectively. Title Pages will be prepared in manuscript.

Place	Date	Hour	Summary of Events and Information	Remarks and references to Appendices
	Aug. 1st		ARRAS - Relieved 9th ESSEX Regt. in Hz Sector. Casualties :- N.e.	
	2nd		Hz Sector Casualties:- 4 other ranks killed 2 other ranks wounded 2/Lt. J.E. BURKE transferred to Batt'n from 6th E.KENT Regt.	
	3rd		do. Casualties:- 1 other rank died of wounds	
	4th		do. Casualties:- 2 other ranks wounded	
	5th		do. Relieved by 9th ESSEX Regt. Casualties.. 3 other ranks killed	
	6th		ARRAS	
	7th		do. 2/Lt. H.H. KING (attached from 5th N. Staffs Regt.) to Hospital sick	
	8th		do.	
	9th		do.	
	10th		do. Relieved 9th Essex Regt. in Hz sector	
	11th		Hz Sector - Casualties :- 1 other rank wounded	
	12th		do. " N.e.	
	13th		do. " N.e.	
	14th		do. " N.e.	

WAR DIARY / INTELLIGENCE SUMMARY

Army Form C. 2118

Place	Date	Hour	Summary of Events and Information	Remarks and references to Appendices
	Dec. 15th		Hr Sector - Relieved by 9th ESSEX Regt.	
ARRAS	16th			
	17th		do:- The Battalion moved from the Barracks in ARRAS at 4 p.m. and marched into billets for one night distributed as follows:- 1 Company GOUVES, 2 Companies AGNEZ les DUISANS, 1 Company and Headquarters MONTENESCOURT. Transport and Details moved direct to MONTENESCOURT.	
	18th		The Battalion moved off at 9 a.m. and marched into VI Corps reserve "C". BERNEVILLE to MONTENESCOURT. The Battalion was billeted as follows 3 Companies + Headqrs. DENIER 1 Company - SARS-les-BOIS.	
	19th			
	20th		Battalion in Billets. Rest Cure.	
	21st		Training Carried out	
	22nd			
	23rd		Lieut Q.M. F. Tuttle to Hospital sick	
	24th		2Lieut H.E. White to Hospital sick and transferred to 6th Bn. Royal Berkshire Regt. being found for duty from the
	25th		Lieut L. St. J. Mowbray rejoined the Battalion from the 6th Bn. Royal Berkshire Regt.	

Army Form C. 2118

WAR DIARY
INTELLIGENCE SUMMARY
(Erase heading not required.)

Instructions regarding War Diaries and Intelligence Summaries are contained in F. S. Regs., Part II. and the Staff Manual respectively. Title Pages will be prepared in manuscript.

Place	Date	Hour	Summary of Events and Information	Remarks and references to Appendices
	Dec 25th		Battalion in Billets in Rest Area Training Continues	
	26th			
	27th			
	28th			
	29th			
	30th			
	31st			

31/12/16

A. Miller
Lt. Col.
Commanding 5th Bn
Royal Berkshire Regt

1st 5th (S) Batt R. Berkshire Reg.
Vol 20

War Diary

January 1917

WAR DIARY
or
INTELLIGENCE SUMMARY
(Erase heading not required.)

Army Form C. 2118

Place	Date	Hour	Summary of Events and Information	Remarks and references to Appendices
	Jan 1st 1917		III rd Army Rest Area - Battalion in Billets - 3 Companies DENIER 1 Company SARS-les-BOIS.	
			Football:- Divisional Tournament - 1st Round :- R.Bucks. 5 - M.G. Coy. 0.	
	2nd		do:- 2Lt. L.P. BARTLETT joined Battn. for duty gazetted from 145th M.G. Coy.	
	3rd		do:- Capt. D. WOOD R.A.M.C. (attached) to Hospital sick	
	4th		do:- Football - Divisional Tournament - 2nd Round R.Bucks:- 2 - 9th ESSEX Regt:- 0	
	5th 6th 7th 8th		do:-	
			Football - Divisional Tournament - Final of Brigade Group R.Bucks:- 2 - 7th Suffolk Regt:- 0.	
	9th		do:- 10 a.m. Inspectra in Full Marching order by Brigade Commr.	
	10th		do:- 2Lt. C.H. COOKE (1/4th Battery) joined for duty Captn D. WOOD R.A.M.C. (attached) rejoins from Hospital	
	11th		do:- Football:- Divisional Cup - Semi final R.Bucks:- 3 - 6th Queens :- 2	
	12th		do:- Capt. T.V. BARTLEY DENNISS (1st B") joined for duty 2Lt. J. WOODWARD joined for duty gazetted from Inniskillin Dragoons 2Lt. S. H. MAYO admitted Hospital sick.	

WAR DIARY
or
INTELLIGENCE SUMMARY
(Erase heading not required.)

Army Form C. 2118

Place	Date	Hour	Summary of Events and Information	Remarks and references to Appendices
	Jan. 13	11 a.m.	DENIER and SARS-les-BOIS. Battalion Inspected by G.O.C. 12th Division - Decorations Presented to brave on the SOMME - Lt. Col. F.G. NIXON D.S.O. Proceed on one month's leave. Major D.H. AVORY takes command of the Battalion.	
	14th		do:- Battalion Cross Country Run held.	
	15th		do:- Football - Divisional Tournament Final - R.E. (Signals) 5 - R. Berks - 0.	
	16th		do:- Divisional Marathon Race held - 7th Battalion team won the First Regimental team home - Sergt. BURTON (B) being 3rd.	
	17th 18th 19th		do. Training continued.	
	20th		do:- 2/Lt. C.H.P. MAURICE posted to Bn. crushed by motor lorry and died of injuries, on way to join the Battalion.	
	21st		do:- 3rd Army Travelling Cinema gave performance in DENIER.	
	22nd		do:- 2/Lt. T. ROWELL joined for duty posted from 1st N or th ants. Regt.	
	23rd		do:- Draft of 89 O.R. Ranks joined the Battalion.	
		11 a.m.	do:- Battalion practiced the attack to illustrate cooperation with Contact Patrol Aeroplanes.	

Army Form C. 2118

WAR DIARY
or
INTELLIGENCE SUMMARY

(Erase heading not required.)

Instructions regarding War Diaries and Intelligence Summaries are contained in F. S. Regs., Part II. and the Staff Manual respectively. Title Pages will be prepared in manuscript.

Place	Date	Hour	Summary of Events and Information	Remarks and references to Appendices
	Jan 24th		DENIER and SARS les BOIS — Training Battalion	
	25th		do:- Lt. E. A. SUTTON left Bn for one month's probation with IX Div. Signals Brigade Wiring Competition R. Berks Regt. 3rd.	
	26th		do:- Lt. A. MAYBURY joined for duty Pugilist Comn 1st Bn R. Berks Regt	
	27th		do:- Transport Sports, 1st day — Cooker Turnout:- 3rd Pack Pony do:- 1st Limber do:- 2nd	
	28th		do:- Brigade Tug of War — R. Berks Regt. 1st — 7 Suffolk Regt. 2nd	
	29th		do:- Battalion Boxing Competition	
	30th		do:- Brigade Rifle Meeting — Following events were won by this unit :- Lewis Gun Competition Sniperscope Competition Rapid fire Competition Supervision of fire Competition	

D. H. Avery
Commandg 6th Bn
R. Berks Regt.

Vol 2¹

Sar Durup

of

5" Batl" R. Berks Regt.

Got mob Feby 1917

Army Form C. 2118.

WAR DIARY
or
INTELLIGENCE SUMMARY
(Erase heading not required.)

Place	Date	Hour	Summary of Events and Information	Remarks and references to Appendices
DENIER and SARS les BOIS.	Jan. 31st.	10.30 a.m.	Marched via LATTRE St. QUENTIN to AGNEZ les DUISANS. Billeted in Nissen Huts at BLENHEIM CAMP (2 Companies + Headers)	
BLENHEIM CAMP.	Feb. 1st.		Battalion finding working parties of 500 other ranks for work on construction of new railways	
BLENHEIM CAMP.	Feb. 2nd.		do.	
	3rd.		do. Capt. T.V. BARTLEY DENNISS rejoined from hospital and took command of "C" Company.	
	4th.		do.	
	5th.		do.	
	6th.		do.	
	7th.		do.	
	8th.		do.	
BLENHEIM CAMP.	9th.	9.30 a.m.	Battalion marched to Billets in LATTRE St. QUENTIN, for Battalion Training.	

Army Form C. 2118.

WAR DIARY
INTELLIGENCE SUMMARY
(Erase heading not required.)

Instructions regarding War Diaries and Intelligence Summaries are contained in F.S. Regs., Part II. and the Staff Manual respectively. Title Pages will be prepared in manuscript.

Place	Date	Hour	Summary of Events and Information	Remarks and references to Appendices
LATTRE St. QUENTIN	Feb. 10.		Battalion Training States. Reorganization of Companies on new lines.	
do.	11		Lt/Col. J.G. WILLAN D.S.O. returned from leave & resumed command of the Battalion. Companies practise the attack.	
do.	12		Battalion Training Continues. Major J.S. SHARP to Hospital.	
do.	13.		do.	
do.	14.		do.	
do.	15.		do.	
do.	16.		do.	
		10:30 a.m.	Battalion marched to MONTENESCOURT taking over from 6th Bn. The Buffs.	
MONTENESCOURT	17.		Marched to LATTRE to practise the Battalion in attack. Lt.Col. J.G. WILLAN D.S.O. takes command of 35th Infy. Bde. Major D.H. AVORY commando Bn. Lt.E.S. MOSS rejoined 1st/5th Bn North Staffs. Regt.	

Army Form C. 2118.

WAR DIARY
or
INTELLIGENCE SUMMARY

(Erase heading not required.)

Place	Date	Hour	Summary of Events and Information	Remarks and references to Appendices
MONTENESCOURT	Feb. 18.		Company Training.	
do	19.		2Lt. M.B. BEATTIE rejoined from Hospital. Draft of #3 O.R. from 46th I.B.D. joined the Battalion.	
MONTENESCOURT	20.		do	
	21.	4:30 p.m.	Moved to ARRAS - occupied billets in N.E. portion of town near the GRANDE PLACE. Very comfortable quarters Battalion find 550 all ranks for working parties on dugouts in I. Section under the R.E. 2Lt. H.S. BARRATT and 31 other ranks (Lewis Platoon) proceeded to GIVENCHY - le NOBLE to join Div'l Depôt Battalion.	
ARRAS	22		Lt. N.C. ADAMS & Lt. A.T. WESTON } joined the Battalion for duty.	
ARRAS	23			
ARRAS	24.		Major J.S. SHARP rejoined from Hospital.	

Place	Date	Hour	Summary of Events and Information	Remarks and references to Appendices
ARRAS	Feb 25		Following officers joined the Battalion for duty. Lt. C.R.B. WRENFORD, Lt. E. BEAKE, Lt. L.G. HOWARD.	
	26.	8.30 am	The 11th Middlesex Regt. of 36th Bde. carried out a raid from I sect. capturing 24 prisoners and inflicting 12 casualties. Following casualties caused among our working parties by enemy retaliation. Killed:- 1 O.R. Wounded:- 3 O.R.	
ARRAS	27.			

A. Savory
Major
Commanding 5th Bn
R. Berkshire Regt.

Vol 23

CONFIDENTIAL.

5ᵗʰ R. BERKS RGT.

War Diary
for
March 1917.

Army Form C. 2118.

Instructions regarding War Diaries and Intelligence Summaries are contained in F. S. Regs., Part II. and the Staff Manual respectively. Title pages will be prepared in manuscript.

WAR DIARY
INTELLIGENCE SUMMARY.
(Erase heading not required.)

Place	Date	Hour	Summary of Events and Information	Remarks and references to Appendices
ARRAS	Feb. 28		Attached to 36th Infantry Brigade for work.	
do.	March 1st		Capt H.C. HORSFORD admitted Hospital sick.	
do.	2nd		2Lt A.D BREACH joined the Battalion for duty.	
do.	3rd		35th Bde. Hdqrs moved to ARRAS, and Battalion came under the orders Lt-Col. F.G MILLAN D.S.O & received command of "B" echelon on ceasing to command the 35th Bde.	
	4th	10am	Battalion relieved the 11th Middlesex Regt. in I.2 subsector. Dispositions 2 companies front line, each with one platoon in support line - One company in Reserve - 3 platoons CAMBRAI Rd., one platoon in Rue Martin, Bn Company in Reserve. Bn Headqrs in RUE PASTEUR. Casualties - 2 other ranks wounded.	
	4th		I.2 Subsector - Casualties killed - 2Lt A.L.H. BUTCHER wounded - 4 other ranks	
	6th		I.2 Subsector - Relieved in Cemetery Subsector by 146th Infty Bde. - Company accommodated in cellars in Cemetery Road.	
	6th		I.2 Subsector. Inter Company relief.	
	7th		do. Casualties - 2 other ranks wounded	

WAR DIARY or INTELLIGENCE SUMMARY.

(Erase heading not required.)

Army Form C. 2118.

Place	Date	Hour	Summary of Events and Information	Remarks and references to Appendices
	March 8th		I.2 Intrsector - Casualties - 2 other ranks Killed 8 " " wounded.	
	9th	10am	Battalion relieved by the 7th Suffolk Regt in I.2 sector. Moved into billets in ECOLE des JEUNES FILLES, Battalion Hdqtrs in the RUE GAMBETTA. During daily working parties for Battalion. In view of hostile Raid, a wire party consisting of 10 officers and 220 other ranks under command of Major J S SHARP proceeded to THÉATRE St. QUENTIN for special training. 2/Lt A T WESTON rejoined from hospital. 2/Lt C H COOKE promoted Lt. (Apt 31st/1916) APRAS - Casualties - 3 other ranks wounded	
	10th		do " " " " 6 " " " Killed	
	11th		do " " " " 2 " " " wounded	
	12th		do " " " NIL	
	13		do Capt. H C HORSFORD rejoined from hospital	
	14th		do - 2Lt T C ORR joined the Battalion for duty	

Army Form C. 2118.

WAR DIARY
or
INTELLIGENCE SUMMARY.
(Erase heading not required.)

Place	Date	Hour	Summary of Events and Information	Remarks and references to Appendices
	March 15/16		ARRAS - Casualties - 1 or. wounded	
			do:- Casualties :- Nil.	
		11.15 p.m.	Special party returned in busses from LATTRE ST QUENTIN. A raid was carried out on the German trenches at 11 p.m. by a party of 10 officers and 200 other ranks. O.C. Raid Major J.S. SHARP 2nd in Command. Lt. W.C. ADAMS. Objective - Enemy front line from G.30.b. 3.65 to G.30.b.4.0. Support line from G.30.b. 45.70 to G.30.b. 65.30. The raiding party was divided into 6 parties, 3 for front and 3 for support line. Right Centre and Life Throw parties were commanded by Lt. A.P. DEBONO, Lt. J.H. READY, Lt. H.B. BEATTIE, Lt. T.E. COLLINS, Lt. L.P. BARRETT, Lt. B.H.A. FELLOWES, Lt. T. ROWELL, Lt. A. HANBURY. All parties reached their objectives. Three gaps had been successfully cut and Bangalore torpedoes only has to be used, and by the right party. The left party was held up for a short time by M.G. fire, but this M.G. was dealt with by the Centre party. Opposition in the trenches was not serious. All the Germans in the dugouts were killed or taken prisoner, and all dugouts were destroyed with stokes bombs. The parties returned at Zero +25 minutes.	

WAR DIARY
INTELLIGENCE SUMMARY.
(Erase heading not required.)

Army Form C. 2118.

Place	Date	Hour	Summary of Events and Information	Remarks and references to Appendices
Mont	18.		We find that casualties had been very slight, only wires 2Lt H.A. FELLOWES wounded going over, and one Or wounded when enemy front line returning. The party had to come back through heavy barrage which caused serious casualties. Major J.S. SHARP was killed by a shell when only 10 yards from our parapet. Total result of the operation was that 2 machine guns and 6 prisoners was captured, about 120 Germans were killed. Enemy front and Support line in front of 300 yards were thoroughly bombed. Total Casualties - Killed. Major J.S. SHARP and 6 other ranks. Wounded - 2Lt. B.H.A. FELLOWES and 28 " " Missing believed killed. 1 Or. Missing. Congratulations were sent to the Battalion by the Divisional Commander and the Corps Commander on the result of the raid.	
	19.		ARRAS. Casualty - Nil.	
	20.		do. Casualty.. 6 O.r. wounded. Lt. C.H. COOKE admitted to Hospital sick.	
	21		do. Lt. K.C.B. STOREY rejoined from Hospital. do. Casualties.. Wounded.. One other rank	

WAR DIARY
INTELLIGENCE SUMMARY

Army Form C. 2118.

Place	Date	Hour	Summary of Events and Information	Remarks and references to Appendices
	March 22		ARRAS - 2Lt B.H.A FELLOWES died of wounds & buried at AVESNES.	
	23		do - 9th ESSEX Regt carried out a raid from I.2 sector.	
	24		do - Following officers joined for duty. 2Lt A.H. HAMER SMITH, 2Lt G.E. LOUGHLIN. Divisional Concert party entertain the troops & bivouac to be worn as follows: Capt. T. BARTLEY-DENNISS - Major, Lt. N.C. ADAMS - Captain, 2Lt. A.D. BREACH - Lieutenant	
	25		ARRAS - Draft of 68 O.R.s ranks joined - all transferred from Oxford & Bucks Light Infantry 6th and 1/4th Bn.	
	26		ARRAS - At 5.40 am the Battalion marched out - breakfasted en route at HABARCQ and reached HANIN at 11.30 am. March of 13 miles carried out in pouring rain. Battalion billets very comfortably in HANIN.	
	27		HANIN - Reorganization of Companies in preparation for active operations.	

Army Form C. 2118.

WAR DIARY
or
INTELLIGENCE SUMMARY.
(Erase heading not required.)

Instructions regarding War Diaries and Intelligence Summaries are contained in F. S. Regs., Part II. and the Staff Manual respectively. Title pages will be prepared in manuscript.

Place	Date	Hour	Summary of Events and Information	Remarks and references to Appendices
MANIN	March 28th		Battalion Training	
do	29th		Battalion Training. Companies reorganized into 3 platoons, fourth platoon being broken up.	
MANIN	30th	2.30 p.m.	Battalion Training. Battalion practised the attack on trenches now existing. German trenches opposite I sector.	

J. Nelson
Lt. Col.
Commanding 5th Bn R. Berks Regt.

31/3/17

5. R Buch Rg.
Vol 23
April 1914.
35/12

Army Form C. 2118.

WAR DIARY
INTELLIGENCE SUMMARY.
(Erase heading not required.)

Instructions regarding War Diaries and Intelligence Summaries are contained in F. S. Regs., Part II. and the Staff Manual respectively. Title pages will be prepared in manuscript.

Place	Date	Hour	Summary of Events and Information	Remarks and references to Appendices
HANIN	March 31st		Battalion Training Continued	
	April 1st		Major T.V. BARTLEY-DENNISS proceeded to ENGLAND for course	
HANIN	2nd		do: - Lt. S.H. MAYO rejoined from Hospital. The Brigade was inspected by G.O.C. II Corps after practice attack.	
	3rd		"U" day. Draft of 65 O.R. arrived all of Royal Berkshire Regt. Lt. E.H. LLOYD rejoined the Battalion for duty.	
	4th		"V" day 13th Field day – attack on AGNEREUIL	
	5th	7 a.m.	"W" day. The Battalion marched from HANIN to AGNEZ les DUISANS and went into accommodation in Billets.	
	6th	8 p.m.	"X" day – Expected front attack on ARRAS. Marched from AGNEZ les DUISANS to ARRAS. Battalion were under the Threaven.	
	7th		"Q" day – ARRAS	
	8th		"Y" day – ARRAS	
	9th		"Z" day. 1st day of Battle of ARRAS (account of operations attached)	
	10th		13th Captured Dainvy Hill – marched to CHAPEL Redoubt. CHAPEL Redoubt. Capt. R.H. CHUSTON rejoined for duty.	
	11th		Battalion marched to ARRAS	
	12th	11 a.m. 5.35 p.m.	VIII Div moved back and relieved XXXVII Division near MONCHY – 35th Bde in Div Reserve – This Battalion held outpost line on FEUCHY-NANCOURT line	

A5834 Wt.W4973/M687 750,000 8/16 D.D.&L.Ltd. Forms/C.2118/13.

Army Form C. 2118.

WAR DIARY
INTELLIGENCE SUMMARY.
(Erase heading not required.)

Place	Date	Hour	Summary of Events and Information	Remarks and references to Appendices
	13th		Battalion was relieved by unit of XXIX Div" and went back to ARRAS. Into billets in Rue Chanzy.	
			Casualties during operations 9th – 13th April.	
			Officers. 3 killed. 3 wounded.	
			Other Ranks. 6 killed. 96 wounded.	
	14th	9 a.m.	Battalion marched from ARRAS to MANQUETTN.	
	15th	8 a.m.	" " " MANQUETTN to HALLOY.	
	16th		HALLOY.	
	17th		do	
	18th		do :- Capt. L. St J. de MAUBRAY to hospital sick.	
			Lt. M.E. DUNHAM, Lt. H.R. HAY and draft of 39 joined for duty.	
			Marched to FOSSEUX	
	19th	6 p.m.	Marched from FOSSEUX to GOUY EN ARTOIS	
	20th		GOUY:- Battalion Training commenced	
	21st		" " " continued	
	22nd		"	
			Lt. A.J. JONES and draft of 86 other ranks arrived.	
	23rd		GOUY.	
	24th		GOUY – Marched by bus from GOUY to ARRAS. Battalion accommodated in GRANDE PLACE.	

Army Form C. 2118.

WAR DIARY
INTELLIGENCE SUMMARY.
(Erase heading not required.)

Instructions regarding War Diaries and Intelligence Summaries are contained in F.S. Regs., Part II and the Staff Manual respectively. Title pages will be prepared in manuscript.

Place	Date	Hour	Summary of Events and Information	Remarks and references to Appendices
	25th	4 a.m.	Battalion left ARRAS and marched up the valley to the JEDBURGH of FEUCHY. Spent day there and at 8.30 p.m. went forward to relieve the 17th Division in front line twixt SCARPE to INFANTRY. The 35th Bde held a two Battalion front from MONCHY to INFANTRY covering East from MONCHY. Frontage of Bn (Ref Map FAMPOUX 10000) - H.36.b.5.4, H.36.b.4.9, H.36.d.3.2, H.30.d.3.8, H.30.a.4.3, T.25.a.1.9. with 7th Norfolk Regt on right. Dispositions. 3 Companies in Front line - one in Reserve. Battalion held this line and continuous heavy shell fire.	
	26th		Casualties not severe	
	27th			
	28th		35th Bde received orders to capture BAYONET TRENCH, that part of RIFLE Trench still occupied by enemy and eventually a line of outposts in advance of new line. Capture of BAYONET and RIFLE T. was allotted to 5th Suffolk Regt on left. 7th Norfolk Regt on right, Suffolk Regt being responsible for capturing 2nd objective, 9th Essex Regt being in Brigade Reserve. Division lines between the Bn and 7th Norfolks I.31.a.0.6, I.31.a.6.4, I.36.c.1.8. The Battalion attacked at 4.25 a.m. on a two Company front. "C" Coy on Right "D" Coy in Centre, "A" Coy on Left. "B" Coy in Reserve. Surmounting first obstacle, got clear up under barrage and took the objective in most difficult fighting. Consolidating BAYONET and RIFLE Trenches. The 7th NORFOLK Regt was not successful - and two companies Suffolk Regt. on going through up to and two coys who were not in Reserve after... M.G. fire and could not get in.	

Army Form C. 2118.

WAR DIARY
or
INTELLIGENCE SUMMARY.
(Erase heading not required.)

Instructions regarding War Diaries and Intelligence Summaries are contained in F.S. Regs., Part II. and the Staff Manual respectively. Title pages will be prepared in manuscript.

Place	Date	Hour	Summary of Events and Information	Remarks and references to Appendices
	29th		The left company of the 10th Australian Regiment lost one Machine Gun, 1 Officer and 16 other ranks prisoners.	
	30th	9 a.m.	The situation was that this Bn. held BAYONET Trench and RIFLE Trench as far as I.31.a.55.75. when a bomb attack was made. The enemy occupied RIFLE Trench as far as the HARNESS LANE. Por Jumend 4th NORFOLKS and 7th SUFFOLKS made charge. One company of 9th ESSEX Regt. was attached to this Bn. & came under the Commanding Officer's orders. Now his maintaining under heavy shell fire – owing to proximity of enemy in captured trenches, no attack could be made to oust the enemy out of Rifle Trench.	
	May 1st	3 a.m.	The 9th Essex Regt. were ordered to assault and capture 150 yards of Rifle Trench held by enemy by means of frontal attack by 2 Companies and a bombing attack by one Company from near flank. The attack was not successful. By night the 35th Bn. was relieved by 36th and 37th Bns. This Battalion afterwards relieved by 6th R. Fusiliers men of trek to the RAILWAY TRIANGLE. Casualties April 28th – May 1st (Inclusive) Officers: Killed: 2/Lt T.R. ORR. Wounded 143, Missing 22.	

Other Ranks: Killed 81, Wounded 143, Missing 22.

Noted:- Major D.H. HAVORY
 Lt A.J. JONES
 Lt E.A. SUTTON
 Lt E. BEALE

D. Millar
Comd. 4/5 R. Bat. R.F.

A 5834. Wt. W 4973/M 687 750,000 8/16 D.D. & L. Ltd. Forms/C.2118/13.

ACCOUNT OF OPERATIONS EAST OF ARRAS
April 9th – 12th/1917.

Ref. map TILLOY 1/10000

The objective of VIth Corps in the IIIrd Army Attack was MONCHY le PREUX

Objective of XIIth Division:- The BROWN LINE, as follows:-

Phase I. The 37th Infantry Brigade capture the BLACK LINE

Phase II. The 36th Infantry Brigade capture the BLUE LINE

During this period the 35th I. Bde. was in Divisional Reserve

Phase III. The 35th I. Bde. pass through the 36th and 37th Bdes and

① 5th R. Berks Regt. on left advance with left on HOUDAIN LANE into BATTERY VALLEY

7th Norfolk Regt. take MAISON ROUGE

② 7th Suffolk (Right) and 9th Essex (Left) Regts pass through 7th Norfolks and attack the BROWN LINE, the 5th R. Berkshire Regt cooperating by either supporting the 9th ESSEX Regt. or attacking the BROWN LINE at H.34 central

The XVth Division cooperate on the Left and the IIIrd Division on the Right of the XIIth Division

5/R Berks

Zero Hour 5.30 a.m.
On Zero -1 day the Battalion was billeted in the cellars of ARRAS museum.
The Battalion moved off from the cellars at 4.45 a.m. on April 9th and entered the sewer at the PORTE de FER entrance at 5.15 a.m., moved via St. SAUVEUR tunnel and emerged into BROAD WALK at 7.15 a.m.
Battalion in position at 8 a.m.

    2 leading Companies :- "A" (left) "B" (Right)
in Reserve and Duplicate Reserve lines
    2 support Companies :- "C" (left) "D" (Right)
in BROAD WALK
    Bn Head qrs in INK ST.

At 10.30 a.m. orders were received for the Battalion to advance to position in rear of BLUE LINE.
The advance from our line commenced in lines of platoons in single file disposed as follows :-

"A" Coy + 1 platoon "C" Coy   "B" Coy
"C" Coy (less 1 platoon) with 2 machine   "D" Coy
        guns attached
    Bn Head qrs

Advance was unopposed as far as HEILLY Trench. Right front Company there came under machine gun and rifle fire from HERON WORK, which was found to be occupied by the enemy.
The advance was delayed for ¾ hour while the situation on the right was cleared up, then the Battalion resumed the advance (11.45 a.m.) one platoon of "B" Coy. working round the rear of HERON WORK and capturing the garrison (1 machine gun and 35 Officers & men).
The advance was continued in same formation with left on HOUDAIN LANE.
Casualties very slight, and very little opposition

At 12.45 p.m. the two leading Companies extended and crossed the ridge into BATTERY VALLEY. Four enemy batteries were found to be in action & these guns fired point blank at about 200x range. By means of concentrated rifle fire and short rushes these batteries were rushed and the valley was cleared of the enemy. The following were captured:-

About 40 prisoners
One battery 4.2 Howitzers (4 guns)
18 77 m.m. guns (4 Batteries & 2 isolated guns)

By 2.30 p.m. Companies had reached their positions of assembly for the assault of the BROWN LINE being disposed as follows:-

"A" Coy in neighbourhood of B.4 ⑬
"B" Coy   "   "   "   "   ㉗
"C" Coy   "   "   "   "   ㊷
"D" Coy in HIRSON LANE

Bn Headqrs. established at about H.33.a.7.8. Owing to delay in HEININ Trench, the Battalion was too late to take advantage of barrage on BROWN LINE.

In attempting to advance on to line of road, heavy machine gun & rifle fire were opened and it was evident that a frontal attack was impracticable, especially as information shewed that the BROWN LINE had not been captured on left or right flanks.

These approximate positions were maintained till nightfall.

At 7.30 p.m. information was received that the XV th Division had captured the BROWN LINE and a Tank was seen moving along from the N. shortly in front of line.

An attack in cooperation with this Tank

was intended, but could not be carried out. At the same time 3 companies of 11th Middlesex Regt. came up as reinforcements, and at 8 p.m. 3 companies of 7th R. Sussex Regt., + came under the orders of O.C. 5th R. Bucks Regt.

Orders were then received (8.30 p.m.) that no further effort would be made to advance that night, but that O.C. 5th R. Bucks with 6 companies attached would move through the BROWN LINE where it had been captured by the XV" Div" and advance from the N onto ORANGE HILL. At the same time the 7th Suffolks with two companies attached would attack the BROWN LINE South of the CAMBRAI Rd, and the 9th ESSEX N. of the CAMBRAI Rd.

April 10th

The Barrage lifted off the BROWN LINE at 12 noon + the above operation was successfully carried out. By 12.45 p.m. the BROWN LINE on the whole Divisional front had been captured and this regiment had an outpost line on the extreme slopes of ORANGE HILL.

At 7 p.m. the 37th Division advanced through the XII" Division to attack MONCHY le PREUX, and our outpost line was withdrawn from ORANGE HILL.

Orders were received that the Battalion would reform in CHAPEL WORK + the night was spent in N.3.a.

April 11th

The Brigade had orders to march back and occupy dugouts in O.B.I. This was no sooner done than orders were issued for the XII" Div" to relieve the 37th Div".

The 27th Bde. on Left and 36th Bde on Right relieved the 37th Division in the advanced line in front of MONCHY the 35th Bde. being in Divisional Reserve in the neighbourhood of CHAPEL WORK.
The 5th R. Berks Regt was detailed to find 2 strong points on ORANGE HILL.

April 12th

The XIIth Division was relieved by the 29th Division. Relief complete at 3 a.m. on April 13th and Battalion marched back to billets in ARRAS.

NOTES

I Casualties - during the operations 9th -13th

Officers:- Killed:- Lt K.C.B. STOREY
            Lt L.P. BARTLETT

Wounded:- Capt. H.C. HORSFORD
          Capt. H. WYKES
          Lt. A.H. HAMEL SMITH
          Lt. L.G. HOWARD

Other Ranks:- Killed :- 5
              Wounded :- 92

II. SIGNALS

Throughout the operations on April 9th & 10th a single wire run from O.B.1 to BROWN LINE held intact and telephonic communication with Brigade was maintained throughout.

III Attached is list of Officers who took part in the operation.-

Lt. Col. F. G. WILLAN D.S.O.
        (Commdg)
Capt. H.C. HORSFORD (wounded)
Capt. L. St. J. de MOUBRAY
Capt. H. WYKES, M.C. (wounded)
Lt. J.M. READY
Lt. G.P. DEBONO
2Lt. K.C.B. STOREY (Killed)
2Lt. L.P. BARTLETT (Killed)
2Lt. A. MAYBURY
2Lt. G.E. COLLINS
Lt. A.D. BREACH
2Lt. J. WOODWARD
2Lt. L.G. HOWARD (wounded)
2Lt. A.H. HAMEL SMITH (wounded)
2Lt. J.C. ORR
2Lt. K.C. BICKERDIKE

2Lt. E.H. LLOYD (Liaison officer with
    XIIth H.L.I. on our left)

Capt. C.A. MALLAM (Adjt.)

Confidential

Vol 24

War Diary
of
5th. R. Berks Rgt.
for
May. 1917.

WAR DIARY
INTELLIGENCE SUMMARY
(Erase heading not required.)

Army Form C. 2118.

Place	Date	Hour	Summary of Events and Information	Remarks and references to Appendices
Railway Triangle	May 2.			
	3.	3.45 a.m.	Move off from Railway Triangle at 3.45 a.m. and forward up to BROWN LINE. The 35th Infy. Bde. in support of 36th & 137th Infantry Brigades who were ordered to attack in conjunction with Division on Right and Left N.E. of MONCHY. Battalion under orders to support the attack of 37th Bde. in rifle of columns to do so. No news in progress of their came through this Bn. received no orders to move from BROWN LINE. Casualties: 1 or wounded.	
	4.		BROWN LINE – Battalion found large working parties on Battalion front. Capt. R.H. CAUSTON to hospital sick, Lt G.E LAUGHLIN to England sick. Casualties: 8 or. s. wounded.	
	5.		BROWN LINE – Working Parties. Front trenches. Capt. L. S-f de MOUBRAY to England sick.	
	6.		BROWN LINE – Lt. C.R.B. WRENFORD to England sick. 35th Infy Bn. relieved 37th Infy. Bn. in Right sector N.E. of MONCHY, 7th Norfolk Rgt in front line. Casualties:- 2 or. wounded, 1 or. Killed.	
	7.	8.30 p.m.	Battalion left the BROWN LINE and relieved the 7th Norfolk Rgt. in right sector N.E. of MONCHY between HARNESS & BIT lanes. Dispositions 3 companies in front line, 1 company in MONCHY towers. Casualties – 5 Other Ranks wounded.	

Army Form C. 2118.

WAR DIARY
INTELLIGENCE SUMMARY.
(Erase heading not required.)

Instructions regarding War Diaries and Intelligence Summaries are contained in F.S. Regs., Part II. and the Staff Manual respectively. Title pages will be prepared in manuscript.

Place	Date	Hour	Summary of Events and Information	Remarks and references to Appendices
Railway Triangle	16.		announced to Battalion on April 9th. Following awards:- Military Cross :- Lt. J.M. READY. Lt. G.P. DEBONO. Military Medals :- 11099 Sjt. Stevens E. 7671S Cpl. Day F. 20058 L/Cpl. Munn W. 15448 L/Sjt. Jones H. 33749 Pte Gerwing D. 10375 Sgt. Blain A. 9760 L/Cpl. Fisher T. 12003 Pte. McAllister. 10580 Sjt. Burton J.	
	17.	2.30am	Left the Railway Triangle and marched to ARRAS. "D" accommodated in LEWIS Barracks.	
	18.		ARRAS - Lt. E.A. SUTTON seconded to R.E. Signals III Army.	
	19.	10.30am	Battalion marched out of ARRAS to SIMENCOURT, where billeted in huts.	
	20.		SIMENCOURT - Brigade Church Parade.	
	21.		do. } Training commenced.	
	22.		do. }	
	23.		do. - G.O.C. XII Divn inspected the Brigade and presented medals. Following decorations were presented to this Battalion: 1 D.C.M., 1 H.H. Bar, 9 Military Medals.	

Army Form C. 2118.

WAR DIARY
INTELLIGENCE SUMMARY.
(Erase heading not required.)

Instructions regarding War Diaries and Intelligence Summaries are contained in F. S. Regs., Part II. and the Staff Manual respectively. Title pages will be prepared in manuscript.

Place	Date	Hour	Summary of Events and Information	Remarks and references to Appendices
	May 24	10 a.m	Battalion marched from SIMENCOURT to SOMBRIN where it was very comfortably settled in billets. Army wide village without training area.	
	25		SOMBRIN – Company Training. Following Officers and NCOs and unposted in Sir Douglas Haigh's dispatches. Major J.S. Sharp, 10374 C/Sjt Elkin. P., 1137 Sjt L.P., 9380 A/Sjt Skinner. G. – Draft of 32 Ors joined "B" Coy	
	26.		Following officers joined for duty – Lt. H.W.P. Rawlin, Lt. C.J. Elsey, and Lt. J. Childe. Lt. A.D. Brench to hospital sick	
	27		do Church Parade in streets	
	28		do The XII Div. Concert Party Chimes gave two performances for "B"	
	29		do	
	30		do	
	31		do El-Coy Sjt J.G. Wilson DCM to England on leave & to be returned home and recommended for a Commission	

W. C. Adams Capt.
Commanding 5th "B" R. Berkshire Regt.

Confidential

War Diary

of

5th (Sr.) Bn. The Royal Berkshire
Regiment.

for

June, 1917.

Army Form C. 2118.

WAR DIARY
INTELLIGENCE SUMMARY.
(Erase heading not required.)

Instructions regarding War Diaries and Intelligence Summaries are contained in F. S. Regs., Part II. and the Staff Manual respectively. Title pages will be prepared in manuscript.

Place	Date	Hour	Summary of Events and Information	Remarks and references to Appendices
SOMBRIN	JUNE 1st		Battalion Training continued.	Battalion Sports held on ground near SOMBRIN
"	2nd		"	
"	3rd		"	
"	4th		Lt. B. LYONS joined the Battn. for duty	
"	5th		35th Brigade Sports held near SOMBRIN.	
"	6th		35th Brigade Boxing Comp. held at BARLY.	
"	7th		35th Brigade Horse Show held near SOMBRIN.	
"	8th		12th Divl. Sports held at GRAND RULLECOURT.	
"	9th		12th Divl. Boxing Comp. held at GRAND RULLECOURT.	
"	10th		Officers' Rifle Meeting held on Range. Lt. Col. H.G. Wilson D.S.O. returned from leave.	
SOMBRIN	11th		Battalion Training continued	
"	12th		Divl. Horse Show held at GRANDE RULLE COURT	
"	13th			

WAR DIARY
INTELLIGENCE SUMMARY.
(Erase heading not required.)

Army Form C. 2118.

Place	Date	Hour	Summary of Events and Information	Remarks and references to Appendices
SOMBRIN	June 14th		Battalion Training Continued	
"	15th		"	
"	16th		Lt. N.C. LIKEMAN joined for duty. Bayonet fighting Competition - Cross Country Run - Divⁿ presented medal ribbons to the following N.C.O.'s men before a representative Brigade parade. D.C.M. 10017 Sergt. E. Brookman. M.M. 7648 Cpl. J. Day 5874 L/Sgt. L. E. Minchin 10753 Pte. F. Allen 10747 Pte. E. Carroll 9313 Sergt. N. Vaughan	
	17th	4 p.m.	The Battalion left SOMBRIN and marched to ARRAS - Made broken by long halt 11 a.m. - 4 p.m. in BEAUMETZ wood. Arrived ARRAS 7.30 p.m. Battalion accommodated in SCHRAMM Barracks.	
	18th	8.30 p.m.	Battalion left ARRAS and relieved 1st Bⁿ Northumberland Fusiliers in BROWN LINE. Austrⁿ of the Railway. Lt. H.E. SMYTH left Bⁿ proceeded to England	
BROWN LINE	19th		Working parties found at work on front supervision at night. Casualties - 1 other rank wounded	
BROWN LINE	20th			

WAR DIARY
INTELLIGENCE SUMMARY
(Erase heading not required.)

Army Form C. 2118.

Place	Date	Hour	Summary of Events and Information	Remarks and references to Appendices
BROWN LINE	June 21st	9.45 p.m.	This Battalion left the BROWN LINE and relieved 9th ESSEX Regt. in the front line. Dispositions: "B" Coys in Front Line. "C" Coy. Bayonet Trench New Trench. "A" Coy Happy Valley. Lt. J. Childs left unit to rejoin East Kent Yeomanry.	
	22nd		Front Line — Casualties: 3 other ranks wounded.	
	23rd		do ": 3 other ranks killed, 4 other ranks wounded.	
	24th		do ": Nil.	
	25th		do ": Nil.	
	26th		do ": 2/Lt. A.R. JOSCELYNE Killed, 1 other rank killed, 9 O.R.s wounded. Lt. E.A.I. WYKES, & Lt. A.N. ADCOCK	
	27th		Following Officers joined for duty:-	
			do ": Nil	
	28th		" ": 1 O.R. Killed, 5 O.R.s wounded	
			" ": 1 O.R. Killed, 5 O.R.s wounded	
			Battalion was relieved by 2nd West Riding Regt. of 4th Div.n and marched back to ARRAS arriving about 4 a.m.	
ARRAS	29th		Battalion accommodated in LEWIS Barracks	
ARRAS	30th			

D. J. Allen
Commanding 5th "B" R. Berks Regt.
30/6/17.

Confidential.

War Diary

of

5th (Ter.) Bn. Royal Berkshire
Regt.

for

July, 1917.

Vol 24

WAR DIARY / INTELLIGENCE SUMMARY

Army Form C. 2118.

Place	Date	Hour	Summary of Events and Information	Remarks and references to Appendices
NEVIS Barracks ARRAS	July 1st		Draft of 18 other ranks joined.	
	2nd		ARRAS:- Battalion inspected in fighting order by G.O.C. 35th Bde. at RONVILLE. Major T.V. BARTLEY-DENNISS rejoined and assumed duties of Second in Command.	
	3rd		ARRAS - Battalion working under C.R.E. on ORANGE LINE by night.	
	4th		do.	
	5th	5.30 p.m.	Battalion two H.Q. proceeded to BROWN LINE and worked in forward area under C.R.E. - Battle for night in BROWN LINE. Casualties - 1 other rank wounded.	
	6th		BROWN LINE - On completion of work Battalion marched back to ARRAS arriving 2 a.m. (7th)	
	7th	9 p.m.	Battalion left ARRAS and marched to BROWN LINE relieving 8th Bn. Royal Fusiliers. Bn. H.Q. FEUCHY CHAPEL CORNER.	
	8th		BROWN LINE } Working parties found nightly in forward area. Regimental canteen established at FEUCHY CHAPEL Corner.	
	9th		do.	
	10th		do.	
	11th		do.	

Army Form C. 2118.

WAR DIARY
INTELLIGENCE SUMMARY
(Erase heading not required.)

Place	Date	Hour	Summary of Events and Information	Remarks and references to Appendices
	11/12th		The Battalion relieved the 9th ESSEX Regt. in front of approx. E. of MONCHY - with 7th NORFOLK Regt. on Left and 37th Infy. Bde. on Right. Dispositions :- 1 Company front line HOOK Trench. 1 Company support line HILL Trench. 1 Company Reserve line SHRAPNEL Trench. 1 Company in BROWN LINE. Casualties :- One other rank wounded.	
	12th		Trenches E of MONCHY - Casualties :- 1 Or. wounded.	
	13th		" Casualties :- 2nd Lt. C.F. ELSEY wounded. 2 OR. killed in action, 9 OR. wounded.	
	14th		" Casualties :- 2 OR. killed in action.	
	15th		" Casualties :- 1 OR. killed, 4 O.R. wounded.	
	16/17th		Relieved by 9th ESSEX Regt. and returned to BROWN LINE, taking our original billets.	
	17	4:45 a.m.	9th ESSEX Regt. in conjunction with 6th R.W. KENT Regt. (37th Bde) attacked LONG and SPOON Trenches; the attack was partially successful, and the Trenches were completed by a second attack at 9:45 p.m. Result of this operation was that SPOON and LONG Trenches remained in our hands.	

WAR DIARY or INTELLIGENCE SUMMARY

Army Form C. 2118.

Place	Date	Hour	Summary of Events and Information	Remarks and references to Appendices
	18th		The Battalion moved up to relieve 9th ESSEX Regt in left subsector of Right Sector of Brigade Front, dividing line between the subsectors being about the N. branch junction of HOOK mound Sap.	
	19th	3 pm	"D" Coy of the 13th carried out a small local attack with object of capturing culmination of LONG Trench opposite HOOK Trench and joining it up with MOUND SAP on right & HOOK Sap on left. Artillery Barrage was to come down in rear of objective at Zero + 10 seconds. The attack was carried out in two waves — the first wave consisting of 2 platoons in line & in Frontage of slightly equipped, & the second wave of our platoon carrying tools and prepared to consolidate. The plan of attack was founded on the assumption that the trench would be found very lightly held. At Zero the first wave closely followed by the second wave rushed across the enemy trench (120') entrenchment by a shower of christic bombs and by very stubborn resistance from a large number of enemy. Owing to the overwhelming opposition in the enemy trench for 15 minutes, but as this was considerably outnumbered, and their bombs were exhausted they had to withdraw and their conduct back to our own front line, to wait for reinforcements by 3.30 am were all	

2449 Wt. W14957/M90 750,000 1/16 J.B.C. & A. Forms/C.2118/12.

Army Form C. 2118.

WAR DIARY
or
INTELLIGENCE SUMMARY
(Erase heading not required.)

Instructions regarding War Diaries and Intelligence Summaries are contained in F.S. Regs., Part II. and the Staff Manual respectively. Title Pages will be prepared in manuscript.

Place	Date	Hour	Summary of Events and Information	Remarks and references to Appendices
	19th		Casualties: Lt. A. MAYBURY } Missing believed killed Lt. B. LYONS } 3 o.r.s. Killed, 24 o.r.s wounded, 14 o.r missing. In view of intelligence as to strength of enemy obtained during this operation, the Div. Commander now decided to adopt a defensive policy and orders are given for the Battalion to concentrate using HOOK and HILL Trenches.	
	20th		FRONT LINE Every night wiring parties worked in front of HOOK and HILL Trenches which were very good alterations. Battalion Commander was personally congratulated by the GOC 35th Bde. on their work Completed	CASUALTIES 2 o.r. Killed 6 o.r. wounded Lt. G. P. DEBONO M.C. to Hosp' sick 3 o.r. Killed 4 o.r. wounded 2/Capt. J.M. READY M.C. to Hosp' Sick 2 o.r. Killed 3 o.r. wounded 8 o.r. wounded 2Lt. H.E. DUNHAM wounded 3 o.r. Killed 6 o.r. wounded
	21st		do	
	22nd		do	
	23rd		do	
	24th		do	
	11th 21st Inst.		Lt. Col. F.G. WILLAN. D.S.O. was relieved to take command of 2nd Bn. K.R.R.C. after having commanded this Battalion for 18 months. Major T.V. BARTLEY DENNISS assumed command of the Battalion Capt. J.R.L. CARR joined for duty 24/7/17 & assumed duties of 2nd in command.	

WAR DIARY
or
INTELLIGENCE SUMMARY

Army Form C. 2118.

Place	Date	Hour	Summary of Events and Information	Remarks and references to Appendices
	24/25		The Battalion was relieved by 37th Infy Bde) and returned to very comfortable billets in ACHI COURT.	
	25.	3.7 a.m.	Enemy attacked and recaptured LONG and the greater part of SPOON Trenches	
ACHI COURT	26.		Working parties found by night to work further CRE in the forward area. Wire up and dump carried back by train from BONVILLE	
	27.		do.	
	28.		do.	
	29.		do.	
	30.		do. Working party found by night for work under CRE in forward area.	

M Whittingstall
Major
Commanding 3rd B"
R. Sussex Regt.

31/7/17

Vol 27

War Diaries
for
August, 1917.
5th Bn. R. Berks. Regt

Army Form C. 2118.

WAR DIARY
~~INTELLIGENCE~~ SUMMARY.
(Erase heading not required.)

Instructions regarding War Diaries and Intelligence Summaries are contained in F.S. Regs., Part II. and the Staff Manual respectively. Title pages will be prepared in manuscript.

Place	Date	Hour	Summary of Events and Information	Remarks and references to Appendices
ACHICOURT	July 31st	9 p.m.	The Battalion marched up to BROWN LINE and relieved 9th ESSEX Regt in position immediately North of CAMBRAI Rd. Battalion in Bde Reserve.	
BROWN LINE	Aug. 1st		Battalion employed working in the forward area. Casualties :- 4 o.r. wounded	
	2nd		do. 5 o.r. wounded	
	3rd		do.	
	4th		do.	
		9.30 p.m.	Battalion left the BROWN LINE and relieved the 9th ESSEX Regt in the Right sub-sector, immediately N. of CAMBRAI Rd. Dispositions :- A Coy - Left Front - TITES COPSE to POMMIER ALLEY. D Coy - Right Front - POMMIER ALLEY to GORDON AVENUE B Coy - Support - SPADE RESERVE C Coy - 1 Platoon "D" S.P., 1 Platoon "C" S.P., 1 platoon LES FOSSES Farm. Draft of 42 other ranks joined for duty.	
CAMBRAI Rd Sector	5th		Casualties :- N.E.	
	6th		do. :- 5 o.r. ranks wounded.	
	7th		do. :- Nil.	
	8th		do. :- Nil.	
			Lt.Col. E.H.J. NICOLLS (E. Surrey Regt.) joined for duty and assumed command of the Battalion.	

WAR DIARY or INTELLIGENCE SUMMARY

Army Form C. 2118.

Place	Date	Hour	Summary of Events and Information	Remarks and references to Appendices
CAMBRAI Rd Sector	Aug 9th	7.45 P.M.	Enemy trenches from BIT LANE to STIRRUP LANE subjected to 1½ hours bombardment. At times our front line, holding it with posts only. The enemy trenches were raided along whole front contributed by 35th Bde on right (2 Companies 300 Officers and men of 7th Suffolk Regt (-), 37th Infy Bde in Centre and 4th Division on left. The operation was very successful 89 prisoners being captured and a large number of the enemy being killed. The 12th Division are to be congratulated by the Commander in Chief on the success of the enterprise. Casualties :- 1 OR Killed 6 OR wounded.	
CAMBRAI Rd Sector	10th		do. Casualties:- 2 OR Killed, 3 OR wounded. Lt F.J. OKEY wounded 6 2 OR.	
	11th		do. - 3 OR wounded.	
	12th			
	13th		Relieved in front line trenches by the 9th ESSEX Regt and at night moved to Billets in ACHICOURT, reoccupying same and continued duties as before. Draft of 55 other ranks arrived 2nd of Royal Berks Regt. Decorations: H.H. The King of the Belgians awarded the following decorations to Lt M.B. BEATTIE - "CHEVALIER de l'ordre de la COURONNE". Following notification awarded for gallantry during operation in NOTK T, July 19-20. Bars to Military Medal. 537th WSgt MINCHIN. Military Medals 11799 L/Cpl WATLING. S. 8730 Cpl. DOBIE. 311545 Pte63 Cpl COULTON. G. 15374 Sgt STEWER. E. VARNEK. F.	

A 5841 Wt W4973/M687 750,000 8/16 D.D. & L. Ltd. Forms/C.2118/13.

Army Form C. 2118.

WAR DIARY
or
INTELLIGENCE SUMMARY.
(Erase heading not required.)

Instructions regarding War Diaries and Intelligence Summaries are contained in F. S. Regs., Part II. and the Staff Manual respectively. Title pages will be prepared in manuscript.

Place	Date	Hour	Summary of Events and Information	Remarks and references to Appendices
ACHI COURT	Aug 14		Following officers joined for duty:- Capt. D.E. WARD M.C. 2Lt H. SCHOFIELD 2Lt F.C.R. HILL 2Lt AT WINCHESTER.	
	15		2Lt H.T. NESTON wounded a musketry school while on leave and struck off strength.	
	16		Battalion Route March to NALLI and DAINVILLE. 30 O.Rs joined for duty, all of Royal Berkshire Regt.	
	17		Commanding Officer ionnoitred all Craters in full march order.	
	18		do.	
	19	6.30 p.m.	Left ACHI COURT and relieved 9th ESSEX Regt. in BROWN LINE North of CARNOY Rd.	
BROWN LINE	20		Battalion finding working parties in the front line area. Casualties :- Nil.	
	21		"	" Nil.
	22		"	" 3 O.R. wounded.
	23		"	" Nil.
			A message of Congratulation received from 35th Bn on work done by the Battalion during past period	

WAR DIARY
or
INTELLIGENCE SUMMARY.
(Erase heading not required.)

Army Form C. 2118.

Place	Date	Hour	Summary of Events and Information	Remarks and references to Appendices
BROWN LINE	Aug 24	8.30 pm	Left BROWN LINE to relieve 9th ESSEX Regt in Bn. sectors. Dispositions:- Left Front :- HOOK PURSE ALLEY - "C" Coy Right " :- CATS ALLEY to Sap 9 - "B" Coy Support Coy. and TWIN POSTS :- "D" Coy Reserve Coy :- SHRAPNEL Tr. - "A" Coy	
	25th		MONCHY PRETU :- Draft of 12 O.R. joined. Following officers joined Bn. 2/Lt H.S. NOBLE, 2/Lt A. WAITE, 2/Lt F.K. JUDD and 2/Lt H.K. de VRIES.	
	26th		do. ⎫	
	27th		do. ⎪ Exceptionally quiet period in Front Line -	
	28th		do. ⎬ Casualties :- One Other rank wounded.	
	29th		do. ⎪	
	30th		do. ⎭	
	31st		Relieved by 8th Bn. R. Fusiliers in MONCHY area and moved over to BROWN LINE taking over 7th R. Sussex Regt. trenches North of CAMBRAI Rd.	

E.H.Nicholls, Lt Col
Commanding 3rd Bn
R. Sussex Regt

War Diary
of
5th Bn. Royal Berks
for
September 1917.

Vol. 29

WAR DIARY
INTELLIGENCE SUMMARY

(Erase heading not required.)

Army Form C. 2118.

Instructions regarding War Diaries and Intelligence Summaries are contained in F. S. Regs., Part II. and the Staff Manual respectively. Title pages will be prepared in manuscript.

Place	Date	Hour	Summary of Events and Information	Remarks and references to Appendices
BROWN LINE	Sep 1st		Parts of CAMBRAI Rd - Battalion found working parties in forward area under C.R.E.	
	2nd		do - do - do - At A.T. WINCHESTER Hospital sick.	
	3rd		do - do - do	
	4th		do - do - do	
			DIVISIONAL GYMKHANA held on Race Course. West of AREAS Lt C.F. ELSEY up as 2nd in Bowrentli Mare and C.O's 2nd Charger won the INFANTRY CUP, and NH1ZZ BANG Cup. 200 men of Battalion went down by train from the BROWN LINE	
BROWN LINE	5th	5.30 p.m.	Relieved by 1st NORFOLK Regt and marched back to cause billets in ACHICOURT.	
	6th		Battalion Training	
	7th			
	8th			
ACHICOURT.	9th		Church Parade - Band of 7th E. SURREY Regt. played at service. Divine Service held by night - won by "C" Coy. Lt K.C. BICKERDIKE transferred to 2nd Bn Middlesex Regt.	
	10th		Companies Inspected by Commanding Officer in full marching Order	

WAR DIARY or INTELLIGENCE SUMMARY

Army Form C. 2118.

Place	Date	Hour	Summary of Events and Information	Remarks and references to Appendices
	Sep 11	4/10/50	Battalion came up by light Railway to FEUCHY CHAPEL, unloaded & front line and relieved 7th F. Lanc. Regt in left subsector of MONCHY sector. Dispositions:- A Coy. Front line Right. B " " " Left (and TWIN POSTS) } Dividing line OPSE ALLEY C " SHRAPNEL Trench D " BROWN LINE.	
	12		FRONT LINE MONCHY - 1 O.R. struck wounded.	
	13		MONCHY - 5:15 p.m. enemy opened a very heavy Barrage on front, support and Reserve lines (with intention of raiding), as was reported and obtained from prisoners. Our artillery opened very rapidly and though the Barrack was continued till 6.30 p.m. there was no infantry attack. "B" Coy were mixed up during the Bombardment in front near point DALE and part of EAST trench blown. Casualties:- 4 O.R. Killed, 13 O.R. wounded.	
	14		MONCHY - B Coy relieved "A" Coy } Casualties:- 1 O.R. Killed, 5 O.R. wounded. " " " " "C" " "D" Coy	
	15		MONCHY - Troop in our Right carried out 2 successful raids at CHERISY. Lieut and Q.M. T.R. OXLEY joined to duty from 8th SEAFORTH H.Y.	
	16		MONCHY - 1 O.R. wounded.	

Army Form C. 2118.

WAR DIARY
or
INTELLIGENCE SUMMARY.
(Erase heading not required.)

Instructions regarding War Diaries and Intelligence Summaries are contained in F. S. Regs., Part II. and the Staff Manual respectively. Title pages will be prepared in manuscript.

Place	Date	Hour	Summary of Events and Information	Remarks and references to Appendices
MOTCHY	17th		MOTCHY - 6 p.m. Relieved by 9th ESSEX Regt. and relieved them in the MOTCHY Defences.	
	18th		Disposition:- A Coy. "D" & "E" Strong Points B Coy. CIRCLE Trench C Coy. EAST Trench D Coy. ORCHARD RESERVE	
	19th		MOTCHY Defences - No 9779 Pte J. EDMANS wounded. Military Medal. - Enemy quiet - from 8.15 p.m. an intruder in road between trenches checked by our sentry.	
	20		do	
	21		do	
	22		do - 2.30 p.m. 9th Essex Regt. carried out small successful raid on enemy post opposite HOOK - Capturing prisoners & getting back without a casualty.	
	23		do - 8.30 p.m. Relieved by 7 R Sussex Regt. and moved into very comfortable billets bivouacs in BOIS du BOEUFS.	
BOIS du BOEUFS	24 25 26 27 28		BOIS du BOEUFS - Finding working parties under C.R.E.	

Army Form C. 2118.

WAR DIARY
or
INTELLIGENCE SUMMARY.

(Erase heading not required.)

Place	Date	Hour	Summary of Events and Information	Remarks and references to Appendices
Bois des Botleufs	Sept 29			
	30	5.30 p	Relieved by 7th NORFOLKS and went to ACH COURT. Lt Col. E.H.J. NICHOLAS was admitted hospital sick	
ACH COURT				

E.H.J. Nicholas
Lt. Col.
Commg. 8th Bn
30/9/17. R. Berkshire Regt.

WAR DIARY or INTELLIGENCE SUMMARY

Army Form C. 2118

5 R Berks B1 Vol 29

Place	Date	Hour	Summary of Events and Information	Remarks and references to Appendices
Achicourt	Oct 1st		The Battn were in billets at Achicourt. The morning was devoted to training.	
	Oct 2nd		Training at Achicourt. 2nd Lt. M. Schofield was sent to Hospital sick.	
	3rd		Training at Achicourt. In the afternoon an officers XI played the 7th Bn. East Surrey Regt at Cricket in Arras, and defeated them by 7 runs.	
	4th		The Battn held an inter company ambulance competition at Achicourt. The winners of the shield were "D" Company, with "B" Company Second.	
	5th		In the morning the Battn was inspected by the G.O.C. 12th Divn and mentioned were printed to 5 men of the Battn.	
	6.6	6.30 p.m.	The Battn marched to Monchy Defences and relieved the 8th Royal Fusiliers arriving about 10.0 pm. MONCHY DEFENCES.— Disposition: 1 Coy ORANGE TRENCH. 1 Coy STRONG POINTS 1 Coy EAST RESERVE 1 Coy CIRCLE TRENCH. HQ CIRCLE TRENCH.	
	7th		—	C.Q.M.S. Redford left for England on Commission.

1875. Wt. W593/826 1,000,000 4/15 J.B.C. & A. A.D.S.S./Forms/C. 2118.

Army Form C. 2118

WAR DIARY
or
INTELLIGENCE SUMMARY
(Erase heading not required.)

Instructions regarding War Diaries and Intelligence Summaries are contained in F.S. Regs, Part II and the Staff Manual respectively. Title Pages will be prepared in manuscript.

Place	Date	Hour	Summary of Events and Information	Remarks and references to Appendices
MONCHY	8th		DEFENSES. MAJOR T.V. BARTLEY-KENNIES to Hospital, sick. CAPTAIN J.L. CARR ASSUMED COMMAND of the Bn. Two other ranks wounded in ERCLE TRENCH.	
	9th		2Lt. A.H. PENN joined for duty. 2Lts. and Hon LT N.C.E. BUTCHER and attached to the Bn. 4 other ranks were wounded.	
	10th		The Bn. relieved 9th Bn. The ESSEX REGT. in the front line system E of MONCHY, with the 15th Divn on right. The 37th Div Bgde on left. Dispositions:- 1 Company front line HOOK TRENCH. 1 Company occupying left front company frontage. 1 Company occupying right company frontage - SHRAPNEL TRENCH, reserve line. 1 Company in BROWN LINE.	
MONCHY	10th		DEFENSES. MAJOR H.M.B. de SALES LA TERRIERE K.R.R.C. assumed temporary command of the Bn. and CAPT J.L. CARR 2nd-in-command.	

WAR DIARY or INTELLIGENCE SUMMARY

Army Form C. 2118

Place	Date	Hour	Summary of Events and Information	Remarks and references to Appendices
Front line system	12/5		3 Other Ranks wounded.	
— do —	13/5		Party to England for Commission.	
— do —	14/5		Hd-LEE to England for Commission. One signal from 54th Brigade to the Division made to said, "We had day acting in conjunction with our neighbour on the night of the 13/14 inst. The 7th NORFOLKS who represented the 35th Bgde took over the right front Company line, one Company relieved one Company relieved and stopped support to EAST RESERVE and SHRUBS SUPPORT. VINE AVENUE and SHRUBS SUPPORT. The bombardment opened at Zero - 8 hours. Zero hour was at 11—7 pm. The left Company front was cleared during the bombardment and by zero 18 wounded and by casualties had occurred including 3 Officers, and 1 Officer afterwards. The Company was heavily shelled and the left front Co. Hqrs. and the Company including TRENCH, the 7th NORFOLKS hqrs. the right front Company's line at 9.30 A.M. and 1 officer and several men were killed.	

WAR DIARY
or
INTELLIGENCE SUMMARY

(Erase heading not required.)

Army Form C. 2118

Place	Date	Hour	Summary of Events and Information	Remarks and references to Appendices
Front Line system	14/15			
	15/12		Major T.V. BARTLEY-DENNIS rejoined from hospital and resumed command. The following changes of rank were approved: Captain Crew-Major 2Lt G.E. Corbitt - Lieut. 1 other rank in Sgt. of S. other ranks joined 2Lt M.B. BEATTIE was wounded early this morning on patrol and died of his wounds later in the day in the Field Ambulance.	
	16/12	do		
	17/12	10 pm	The Bn. was relieved by the 8th Bn. Royal Fusiliers and marched back to ACHICOURT arriving in billets at 12 midnight. This day was spent in billeting and cleaning up	
ACHICOURT	18/12		The following changes of rank were effective this day: 2Lt J. Woodward Lt. 2Lt W.C. Linkeman Lt. 2Lt H.N. Cook Lt.	
	19/12		The Bn. spent the morning in training	
	20/12		This day was employed in bathing. A draft of 9 other ranks joined	

Army Form C. 2118

WAR DIARY or INTELLIGENCE SUMMARY

(Erase heading not required.)

Place	Date	Hour	Summary of Events and Information	Remarks and references to Appendices
ACHICOURT.	21st		In billets. The 13th attached Gunner fleurie et al.	
		10.0 a.m	Major H.M.B de SALES LA TERRIERE's Command.	
			to be attached to the Bⁿ. N⁻113-y Cpl SHARPE	
		11.45 a.m	to ENGLAND for Commission.	
	22nd	7.30 a.m	The Bn. left ACHICOURT and marched to HAUTEVILLE. Bn arrived at HAUTEVILLE. Operation order No. 2 5th Royal BERKSHIRE REGT dated OCTOBER 21st 1917, are attached. The Bn. was billeted in the village with H.Q. at the Chateau. Operation order No. 4 dated 22nd October 1917 is attached	
	23rd	8.45 a.m	The Bn. left HAUTEVILLE and marched to BERLENCOURT.	
		12 noon	The Bn. arrived and was billeted in the village.	
	24th 25th		This day was spent in cleaning up and informal billets. Operation orders No. 5 dated 24th October 1917 are attached	
		9.45 a.m	The Bn. left BERLENCOURT and marched to MANIN.	
		11.30 a.m	Bn. arrived at MANIN and were billeted in the village. Batt. H.Q. was at the Chateau.	
	26th		Billets at MANIN. The day was spent in cleaning up. A congratulatory message was received from the G.O.C. XVIIth Corps.	
	27th		Billets at MANIN. The morning was spent in training by the company. 1 company had baths	
	28th	6.40 a.m 12 noon	The 13th left MANIN and marched to REBREUVIETTE Bn arrived at REBREUVIETTE and was billeted in the village	

1875 Wt. W593/326 1,000,000 4/15 J.B.C. & A. A.D.S.S./Forms/C. 2118.

Place	Date	Hour	Summary of Events and Information	Remarks and references to Appendices
	29/10	9.15 a.m.	The 13th Bn. left REBREUVIETTE and marched to BONNEFAY BOIRE-AU-BOIS	
		1.30 p.m.	Bn. arrived in billets. Dispositions 2 Companies in BONNEFAY 2 Companies in FOSSEUX in BOIRE-AU-BOIS	
	30/10		Operation Order No 7 dated 28th October 1917 is attached. The Bn. spent the day in cleaning up and improving billets. The Commanding Officer inspected billets and Company transport. Major the N.A.G. BOTHER ordered to be attached to the 13th on returning to join the 13th R.R.C.	

M Walthy Seward
Lt Col.
Commdg. 3rd Royal Bucks Regt

SECRET   COPY No. 9

5th. ROYAL BERKSHIRE REGIMENT.

OPERATION ORDER No. 3.

REF : 1/40,000 Map.
     Sheets 51b and c   21st. October. 1917.

INTENTION.

        The Battalion will march to HAUTEVILLE tomorrow.

INSTRUCTIONS.

        Order of march : -

                DRUMS
                Headquarters
                "A" Company.
                "B" Company.
                "C" Company.
                "D" Company.
                1st. Line Transport.
STARTING POINT :   Bridge at G.3.2.d.3.1.
TIME   :   7-30 a.m.

        One section per company will remain behind under 2/Lieut. H.E. Palmer to clean up billets.

TRANSPORT.

Baggage will be stacked ready for loading as under :-

Officer's Kits outside Battalion Orderly Room by
0-30 a.m.
Blankets in bundles of 10 outside Battalion Orderly
Room by 0-30 a.m.
Canteen Stores, Mess Stores, Orderly Room Stores - special instructions will be issued to those concerned.

SICK.

Sick Parade will be at 0-15 a.m.

BILLETING.

        Billeting parties consisting of Company Quartermaster-sergeants under 2/Lieut. J.S. Noble will rendezvous outside H.Q. Mess at 0-15 a.m.
        Bicycles will be provided. The interpreter will accompany the party.

Issued at 12-45 p.m.
   by Orderly

Copy. No. 1.   Filed.
        2.   "A" Coy.
        3.   "B" "
        4.   "C" "
        5.   "D" "
        6.   T. O.
        8.   M. O.   (Sgd) D.E. Ward, Capt.,
        9.   War Diary.   Act/Adjt. Royal Berkshire Regiment.

SECRET   COPY No. 9

5th. ROYAL BERKSHIRE REGIMENT.
OPERATION ORDER No. 4.

Ref : 1/40,000 Map.
    Sheets 51 b and c   22nd, October 1917.

1. INTENTION.

The Battalion will continue the march to BERLENCOURT tomorrow.

2. INSTRUCTIONS.

Order of March :-

    Drums
    Headquarters
    "B" Company
    "C" Company
    "D" Company
    "A" Company
    1st. Line Transport

STARTING POINT : J.35.c.7.5.

Throughout the march the same distances will be observed between Companies as on the march to-day.

TIME : 8-45 a.m.

ROUTE : AVESNES - LIENCOURT - BERLENCOURT.

3. TRANSPORT.

Baggage will be stacked ready for loading as follows :-

Officer's Kits outside the Battalion Orderly Room by 7-45 a.m.

Blankets in bundles of 10 outside the Battalion Orderly Room by 7-45 a.m.

Officer's Mess Kits outside Company Headquarters by 7-45a.m.

4. SICK.

Sick Parade will be at 7-30 a.m. at the Medical Inspection Room.

5. BILLETS.

Billeting Parties consisting of C.Q.M.S's under 2/Lieut. J.S. Noble will rendezvous outside Battalion Orderly Room at 7-15 a.m. Bicycles will be provided. The Interpreter will accompany the Party.

Issued by Orderly at 2 p.m.
    Copy No. 1   "A" Coy.
            2   "B" "
            3   "C" "
            4   "D" "
            5   T.O   (Sgd) D.E. Ward, Capt.,
            6   File   Act. Adjt. Royal Berkshire Regiment
            7   Q.M.
            8   M.O.
            9   War Diary.

SECRET   COPY No. 9

5th. ROYAL BERKSHIRE REGIMENT.

OPERATION ORDER No. 5.

REF : 1/40,000 Map
      Sheet 51c.   October 24th. 1917.

1. INTENTION.

The Battalion will march to MANIN tomorrow.

2. INSTRUCTIONS.

Order of March : -

    Drums
    Headquarters.
    "C" Company.
    "D" Company.
    "A" Company.
    "B" Company.
    Ist. Line Transport.

STARTING POINT : Road Junction H.30.a.40.15.

Throughout the march, 100 yards distances will be observed between Companies and Transport.

TIME : 9-45 a.m.

ROUTE   LIENCOURT - I.34 Central - BEAUFORT.

3. TRANSPORT.

Baggage will be stacked ready for removal as under :-

Officer's Kits and Officer's Mess boxes outside Company H.Q. at 8-45 a.m.

Blankets in bundles of 10 outside Company Billets at 8-45 a.m. Canteen stores and Orderly Rooms' stores - special instructions will be issued to those concerned. Limbers will call for Company Lewis Guns at 9 a.m.

4. SICK.

Sick parade will be at 8-30 a.m.

5. BILLETING.

Billeting parties consisting of C.Q.M.S's Pte. Roader H.Q., and a representative to be detailed by T.O. under Captain. W.C. Adams M.C. will rendezvous outside the Orderly Room at 7-45 a.m.
Bicycles will be provided. The Interpreter will accompany this party.

Issued at 9-45 p.m.
   by Orderly

Copy No. 1   "A" Coy.
         2   "B" "
         3   "C" "
         4   "D" "
         5   Bde. H.Q.
         6   T. O.
         7.   Qr. Mr.
         8.   M.O.   (Sgd) D.E. Ward, Capt.,
         9   War Diary.   Act/Adjt. Royal Berkshire Regiment.

SECRET.   COPY No. 7

5th. ROYAL BERKSHIRE REGIMENT.

OPERATION ORDERS No. 6.

REF : LENS Sheet   SATURDAY 27th.
      1/100,000.   OCTOBER 1917.

1. INTENTION.

The Battalion will march to RIENBUVIETTE tomorrow.

2. INSTRUCTIONS.

Order of march :-

    Headquarters.
    "D" Company.
    "A" Company.
    Drums
    "B" Company.
    "C" Company.
    1st. Line Transport

STARTING POINT : Road Junction at I. 18. c. 9. 3.
                    Ref : Map 1/40,000, Sheet 51c.

(1).   Normal halts will be observed on the march.

(2).   Units will march closed up : only ordinary distances to be maintained.

TIME :   8-40 a.m.

ROUTE :   BEAUFORT - LIENCOURT - ESTREE WAMIN.

3. TRANSPORT.

Baggage will be stacked ready for removal as under :-

Officer's Kits and Officer's mess boxes outside Headquarters at 7-40 a.m.
Blankets in bundles of 10 outside Company billets at 7-40 a.m.
Canteen Stores, Orderly Room Stores - special instructions will be issued to those concerned.

4. SICK.

Sick Parade will be at 7-15 a.m.

5. BILLETING.

Billeting Parties consisting of C.Q.M.S's and representatives detailed by H.Q. and the T.O., under Captain W.C. Adams M.C. will rendezvous outside Battalion Headquarters at 7- 0 a.m.

continued.

Billeting contd.

This party will proceed by lorry to
BUIRE-AU-BOIS ROUGEFAY, and will take over billets
for the Battalion on arrival. They will remain
at BUIRE-AU-BOIS for the night of the 28/29th. inst.
The Interpreter will accompany this Party.

A billeting party consisting of I senior N.C.O.
per Company, representative of H.Q. and Transport
under 2/ Lieut. J.S. Noble will rendezvous at
Battalion H.Q. at o-40 a.m.
Bicycles will be provided for this Party.

Issued at 10-15 p.m.
    By Orderly

Copy No. 1   "A" Coy.
       2   "B" "
       3   "C" "
       4   "D" "
       5   File
       6   T. O.
       7   Qr. Mr.
       8   M. O.   (Sgd) D.E. Ward, Capt.,
       9   War Diary.   Act/Adjt. Royal Berkshire Regiment.

35/12

5 R Berkeley
Jul 30
Nov 7

21

WAR DIARY
INTELLIGENCE SUMMARY.

Army Form C. 2118.

5 R Berks R

Place	Date	Hour	Summary of Events and Information	Remarks and references to Appendices
{BUIRE-AU-BOIS ROUGEFAY Billets	Nov 1st		The Battalion trained during the morning. The R.M.C. awards the D.C.M. to No 5374 Sgt C. MINCHIN on this day	
do	Nov 2nd		The day was devoted to training	
do	Nov 3rd		The morning was spent in training. In the afternoon the Bn. played the 4/5th Suffolk Regt in the Divisional Football Competition and defeated them by 9 goals to 1.	
The Bn. defeated the 9th Essex Regt in this Bgn-club Competition by 13—0.	Nov 4th	10.45 am	The Bn. attended Divine Service in the morning. L:/S.O. BURTON —(T.O) to hospital sick.	
HUMIÈRES	" 5th	8.15 am	The Bn. (less details. Training area marched to ECMMEUX approximately 350 strong, arriving at 3.30 pm, at billets in HUMIÈRES.	
do	Nov 6th	8.0 am	The Bn. paraded at 8.0 am & marched to ECMMEUX for special training, throughout the morning. After lunch the Bn. paraded at 2.45 pm and marched back to billets in ROUGEFAY, BUIRE-AU-BOIS arriving at 7.30 pm. ¾ hour rests were made at 4.45 pm & 6 pm.	
{BUIRE-AU-BOIS ROUGEFAY	Nov 7th		The day was devoted to training.	

WAR DIARY
or
INTELLIGENCE SUMMARY.

(Erase heading not required.)

Army Form C. 2118.

Place	Date	Hour	Summary of Events and Information	Remarks and references to Appendices
ROUGEFAY BUIRE au BOIS	Nov. 8th		Training continued.	
	9th		do:- Football - Final of Bde. Competition - The Bn. played 7th Norfolk Regt at BERNE IVERGNY and won final in 3-1	
	10th	3 p.m.	do:- Battalion Inter-Company Cross Country Run, won by "D" Coy.	
	11th	11 a.m.	Church parade on Rifle Range.	
	12th	10 a.m.	Brigade Assault at Arms held at PAUXX. Following results were achieved by the Bn. 1st Prize:- Alarm Competition (9 platoon "E" Coy.) Fishpond Race (Capt. J.R. WEST) 2nd Prize Tug of War (Transport) Cross Country Run Platoon Competition - Best turn out Gun Mounting Competition	
BUIRE au BOIS ROUGEFAY	13th		Bn. marched to special training with dummy Tanks.	

WAR DIARY
INTELLIGENCE SUMMARY.
(Erase heading not required.)

Place	Date	Hour	Summary of Events and Information	Remarks and references to Appendices
BUIRE au BOIS & ROUGEFAY	14th		Special Training continued.	
	15th		Capt. C.A. HANAH resumed duties of Adjutant do. Orders received for Division to move by train to PERONNE in following days. Transport to proceed there by road.	
	16th	4.30 am	Battalion marched from BUIRE au BOIS and ROUGEFAY to PREVENT. Entrained at PREVENT 7 a.m. - Detrained at PERONNE 3 p.m. - on arriving Company distributed in temporary billets in PERONNE	
	8 p.m.	Battalion marched off to PERONNE to HAUT ALLAINES, where accomodated in tents for the night.	
HAUTE ALLAINES	17th			
	18th	4 p.m.	Moved to SOREL le GRAND where accomodated in bivouacs and shelters.	
SOREL le GRAND			TYLERS GUISLAIN. Co. Adjustment Platoon Commanders proceeded to TYLERS GUISLAIN and reconnoitred Tank assembly points with Tank officers to support attack.	
	19th	4 p.m.	Bn. marched to PEIZIERES where accomodated in bivouacs and huts.	
PEIZIERES			PEIZIERES. Day devoted to fitting out for Battle for the attack, issuing bombs &c.	

Army Form C. 2118.

WAR DIARY
or
INTELLIGENCE SUMMARY.
(Erase heading not required.)

Place	Date	Hour	Summary of Events and Information	Remarks and references to Appendices

	19th/20th	11.30 p.m.	The Battalion plus 1 section M.G. 1 attached and 2 T.M. guns with the teams were of the PEIZIÈRES and moved up in a VICKERS GUISHAN X positions attempting in rear of Tanks which had got into position immediately after dusk, 1000 yds. in rear of front line. Bn. reported in position at 3 a.m.
			
			Following officers and O.R. accompanied the Bn in the attack.
			Lt.Col. E.H.J. NICOLLS M.C. (C.O.)
			Capt. C.A. HALLAM (Adjt.)
			Lt. D. HIKES (signalling officer)
			Capt. W.M. LANSDALE (M.O.)
			
			A.Coy. Major J.L. CARR. B.Coy. Lt. H.K. MAY C Coy Capt N.C. ADAMS M.C. D Coy Capt. J.R. WEST
			  2Lt. T.P. NICKETT. 2Lt. H.M. COOK 2Lt. J. TESTER Lt. H.M. COOK
			  2Lt. A. NATE 2Lt. T.P. HEYRICK 2Lt. J.T. ROSS 2Lt. T.P. HEYRICK
			                          2Lt. F.K. JUDD 2Lt. H.K. de VRIES
			                          2Lt. J. WOODWARD
			
			590 Other Ranks
			
			Operation orders and a recount of attack is attached.
			Casualties:- Officers Killed :- 2Lt. H.K. de VRIES
			  Died of W. :- 2Lt. T.P. NICKETT.
			  Wounded :- Major J.L. CARR Capt. W.C. ADAMS M.C.
			              2Lt. J. TESTER 2Lt. J.T. ROSS.
			
			O.R.
			Killed :- 24
			Wounded :- 121
			Missing :- 16	

Army Form C. 2118.

WAR DIARY
or
INTELLIGENCE SUMMARY.
(Erase heading not required.)

Instructions regarding War Diaries and Intelligence Summaries are contained in F.S. Regs., Part II. and the Staff Manual respectively. Title pages will be prepared in manuscript.

Place	Date	Hour	Summary of Events and Information	Remarks and references to Appendices
	Nov. 21		The Bn. continued to consolidate line taken previous day – shelling very slight – Casualties:- 1 OR Killed, 1 OR wounded.	
	22 } 23 }		Holding line – Casualties NIL.	
	24	5 a.m.	The Battalion was now in conjunction with 7th Suffolk Regt. on left at take and consolidate QUARRY POST and join up with Bn. on left and Pgn. operation orders attached. The attack was carried out by Capt. J.R. WEST and all objectives were taken with 18 prisoners being taken by "D" Coy. The Bn. was apparently complimented by the C.O.C. 35th Infy. Bn. and G.O.C. XIIth Div. in his recognition of this minor operation. Better weather in front systems now less casualties – Bertrelin wounded and experienced a very quiet tour. Casualties NIL 4 O.R. 29th I not other 4 O.R. were wounded. Following details joined in original drafts, Lt. F.L.R. HALL, Lt. H. SCOFIELD, Lt. E.A. WYKES, Lt. E. JONES, Lt. C.F. COLLINS, and Lt. N. ADCOCK, with the other ranks.	
	25) 26) 27) 28) 29)			

WAR DIARY / INTELLIGENCE SUMMARY

Army Form C. 2118.

Place	Date	Hour	Summary of Events and Information	Remarks and references to Appendices
	Nov 30 (cont.)		B" H.Q. had meanwhile withdrawn to a position about 500 yds further N. in original German front line. At 10.30 a.m. the news was received that the enemy were in BOUZENCOURT and that the portion of the Divisional front had been pierced. At 10.45 p.m. the O.C. of the "B" and of the 9th ESSEX Regt. issued orders that all Companies were to withdraw fighting in direction of VILLERS PLOUICH. The situation was very uncertain, but there was however no sign of the enemy in the right flank and the enemy were extremely slow working on left flank. Enemy aeroplanes were cooperating very closely with the infantry flying very low and signalling. The withdrawal was gradually carried out along the old German front line through LA VACQUERIE immediately N. of that village the two Battalions built a breakwork work, but encountered no touch with any troops on their flank. O.C. then sent into VILLERS PLOUICH to reconnoitre the situation and received orders from the O.C. British front line in front of that village. At 3.30 p.m. that no troops were available for the operation. The dispositions then being :- 1 Company (A Coy under Capt. M. Ready M.C.) dug in in R.21 central holding the flank towards GONNELIEU.	

WAR DIARY

INTELLIGENCE SUMMARY

Army Form C. 2118.

Place	Date	Hour	Summary of Events and Information	Remarks and references to Appendices
	30th		Heavy barrage fell on front of Right Division and on our left and on whole Divisional front at 7 am. At 7.15 am the enemy attacked in great force with 55th Division on the Right. This attack was completely successful and the enemy got through in very large numbers at GONNELIEU, GOUZEAUCOURT & VILLERS GUISLAIN, on which line they were held. @ on LATEAU WOOD – North East portion of Divisional front. This attack drove back the 36th and 37th Infy Bdes, who with 3rd Div slowly bombing all the way to the Batalion had not been attacked and did not take in the enemy attack had been launched. At 7.30 a.m. the enemy attacked QUARRY POST under a barrage of heavy T.M.s and simultaneously bombed up NEW TRENCH from the south. The enemy succeeded in getting into the trench and fierce bombing fighting ensued down QUARRY trench and QUARRY support. They were several times driven back and at 9.30 a.m. enemy were still held in line of HD.H.s Trench, though enemy had broken through in both flanks. Owing to difficulty of supply of bombs, we had gradually to withdraw down BLEAK Trench and BREAK support, meanwhile holding the enemy. 1st/9th ESSEX Regt were meanwhile holding the enemy who had come down through line of 7th Norfolk Regt	

Account of Operations carried
out on Nov 20th/1917.

———

According to attended Operation Orders the Battalion was formed
up behind the Tanks at 3 a.m.
At Zero - 10 minutes the Tanks commenced to advance. The enemy
barrage, which was very light and resistance came down at Zero + 12
minutes. The Tanks advanced very slowly at rate of about 50 yards
a minute and a heavy Machine Gun barrage inflicted heavy
casualties on the Right Company (C Coy) - Two out of the 3 Tanks of
"D" Coy broke down, and 2 out of the 4 of "D" Coy.
At Zero "D" HQ was established close in rear of the front line.
The Companies followed close in rear of Tanks. All the Tanks went
too much to the right which caused a certain amount of change of
objective. Such Tanks reached the enemy front line at about Zero + 45 mins,
closely followed by our Infantry. The enemy front line was found
very lightly held and provided very little difficulty, but their support
line was strongly held and prevented any advance of fighting across on
reaching this line.
At 7.45 a.m, Battalion Headqrs got into the 1st objective and
It was then found to be that "D" Coy was occupying
the whole Battalion objective to support line from left Boundary
to junction of BLEAK Support and QUARRY Support, with "A" Coy
on the Right holding QUARRY Support, "B" Coy continues

in ADAHS. French and QUARRY Trench. "C" Coy traversed final objective until nearly 30 otherranks, divided into 2 parties of 14 under Serjt STOKES and Serjt SEYMOUR. Serjt STOKES party with "D" that dash had advanced the line along QUARRY Trench as far as Lt. Harding to QUARRY POST but the bombing offp. his was eventually withdrawn to the Crater on the BANTEUX Rd.

Serjt SEYMOUR's party established a strong point and junction of QUARRY Support and C.T. leading to QUARRY POST.

All objectives had been gained all the objectives of the attack. It was known that all before night it was reported 7th Division had been gained and before night it was reported that our troops were within 2 miles of CAMBRAI.

As result of the attack the Battalion captured about 60 prisoners, 2 m.g.s., 1 Strong T.M., 2 Medium T.M.s, 3 light T.M.s and a large amount of Infantry and engineering equipment, including a number of Flammenwerfer and 'gooseberry' apparatus.

But night the whole position had been consolidated a defensive flank connecting the BANTEUX valley and consolidated.

WAR DIARY

DEC. 2nd (Contd): Remnants of "B" (150 strong) assembled at 5.45 A.M. and marched back to THEIDICOURT where they were accommodated in huts.

Casualties during operations Nov. 30th - Dec. 2nd

Officers: Killed:- 2Lt. E.A.I. NYKES
                  2Lt. F.K. JUDD.

Wounded:- Lt. H.R. MAY.
          Lt. C.N. ADCOCK.

Missing:- Lt. F.E.R. HALL
          Lt. H. SCHOFIELD   } Approximately.
          2Lt. E. JONES

Other Ranks Killed :- 55
            Wounded :- 120   } Approximately.
            Missing :- 120

DEC. 3rd - HEIDICOURT - Battalion reorganized into 2 Companies
           "A" Coy and Composite Coy of A, B + C Coys.

Strength :- Officers. 16.
            O.R.   341

G.H. Shields. Lt. Col.
Commanding "B"
R. Berks Regt.

3/12/17.

WAR DIARY

Nov. 30th (cont.) Remainder of 35th Bde (about 800 strong) holding the British line near POPE ALLEY with a defensive flank down FOSTER LANE, and FUSILIER Reserve. Battalion H.Q. during night at FARM RAVINE.

Dec. 1st At 4:30 am B" H.Q. moved to dugout in NEASH Ra. Attack was confidently expected at dawn. At 9 am the expected barrage came down, but the intended direction from GONNELIEU was repulsed by the guns. Remainder of day spent in shelling very heavily all night, but not by the NEUER PLOUICH and Transport Office drawn under heavy difficulties with Lt. T.B. OXLEY and Transport Office drawn under heavy difficulties with rations which were brought up and attached ourselves under the running thro' evening the 22nd Division. To return to Division we were blind by the 61st Division and the XII R. 13 and 14 Bn to join one third B.C. & remainder of Inner system of Support being immediately to old O.B.1 remainder of Inner system in their B. holding FUSILIER Rsv. Division was collected in its area, their front line being in front of Mr. Rsv with remnants of one Company, area drawn at Rsv. to of POPE ALLEY.

Dec. 2nd Attack hourly expected did not develop. Instructions were received that XIIth Division would be withdrawn at 4 pm and march back to FREUD/COURT. 7th 35th Bde. under command of Lt-Col. E.H.T. MCCOLLIG H.C. were ordered to move at 6 pm.

SECRET.   COPY No. 9

5th. ROYAL BERKSHIRE REGIMENT.

OPERATION ORDER No. 7.

REF. MAP
  LENS 1/100,000.   28th. October. 17.

1. **INTENTION.**

   The Battalion will continue the march to BUIRE-AU-BOIS ROUGEFAY.

2. **INSTRUCTIONS.**

   Order of March :-

   Headquarters.
   "A" Company.
   "B" Company.
   Drums
   "C" Company.
   "D" Company.

   STARTING POINT :   Cross Roads at N.I.b.7.4.
                        (Ref Map : 1/40,000 Sheet 51c.)

   (1).   Normal halts will be observed on the march.

   (2).   Units will march closed up : only ordinary distances to be maintained.

   TIME : 9-15 a.m.

   ROUTE : FREVENT - LIGNY - ROUGEFAY.

3. **TRANSPORT.**

   Baggage will be stacked ready for removal as under :-

   Officer's Kits and Officer's Mess boxes outside Company H.Q. at 8-15 a.m.
   Blankets in bundles of 10, outside Company billets at 8-15 a.m.

   Canteen Stores, Orderly Room Stores - special instructions will be issued to those concerned

4. **SICK.**

   Sick Parade will be at 7-45 a.m. at the Medical Inspection Room.

Issued at
  by Orderly
  Copy No. 1   "A" Coy.
           2   "B" "
           3   "C" "
           4   "D" "
           5   File
           6   T. O.
           7   Qr. Mr.
           8   M.O.   (Sgd) B.E. Ward, Capt.,
           9   War Diary.   Act/Adjt. Royal Berkshire Regiment.

WO 95/1850
PLANA FRAGMENT

Identification Trace for

"C" Batt

Approx. Town

21   22

WO 95/1850
PLAN A

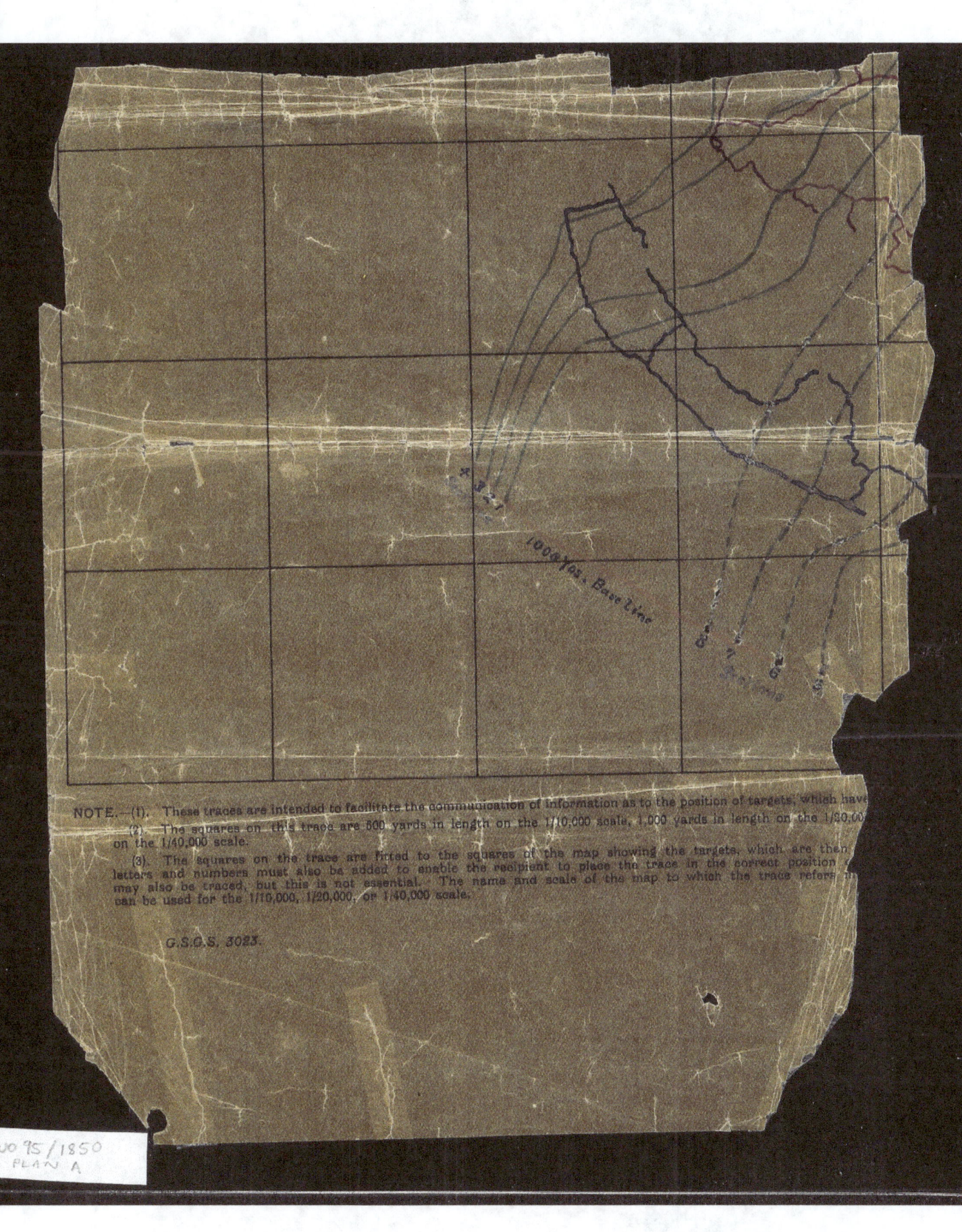

Artillery Maps. **TRACING A**

R.

23

REFERENCE:
No 7 Company. ————
No 8 Company. – – – –

Tracing taken from Sheet ....

of the 1:............ map of ....

Signature .... Date ....

Identification Trace for use with Artillery Maps.

15   17   18   13
      S   O F 6
      P
      Q   E
           D
      22 C 23
         B
R
         A

      28   29

33   36 R M 31

... indicate localities which will
... be consolidated as strong points.

GREEN lines indicate trenches
to be consolidated.

Tracing taken from Sheet 57 c. S.E. 2.

of the 1:   map of

Signature   Date

MESSAGE FORM.

To: .... No. ....

1. I am at.................... { Note :—Either give Map Reference or mark your position by a 'X' on the Map on back.

2. My Line runs..

3. My Platoon / Company is at........................and is consolidating.

4. My Platoon / Company is at........................and has consolidated.

5. Am held up by (a) M.G. (b) Wire at....................(Place where you are).

6. Enemy holding strong point................................

7. I am in touch with....................on Right / Left at............

8. I am not in touch with....................on Right. / Left.

9. Am shelled from................................

10. Am in need of :—

11. Counter Attack forming at................................

12. Hostile (a) Battery (b) Machine Gun (c) Trench Mortar active at................

13. Reinforcements wanted at................................

14. I estimate my present strength at................rifles

15. Have captured................................

16. Prisoners belong to................................

17. Add any other useful information here:—

Name................................
Platoon................................
Time....................m. Company................................
Date................1917. Battalion................................

(A). Carry no maps or papers which may be of value to the Enemy.
(B). Give no information if captured, except the following, which you are bound to give :—
    Name and Rank.
(C). Collect all captured maps and papers and send them in at once.

SECRET

SECRET.   Copy No. 4

35TH INFANTRY BRIGADE ORDER NO. 212.

23rd November 1917.

Map Ref:
Corps Trench Map 214.

1. The 35th and 36th Infantry Brigades will advance tomorrow and establish an outpost line from QUARRY POST to BLEAK QUARRY.
   The 36th Infantry Brigade will capture and consolidate "PELICAN AVENUE" (between R.23.d 7.7 and R.24.a 3.0) and BLEAK QUARRY.

2. A map showing Artillery and Trench Mortar barrages and bombardment is attached.
   The time for the final barrage to cease will be arranged later, in accordance with the situation.

3. The 7th Battalion, Suffolk Regiment will take the HINDENBURG MAIN LINE to the S.E. of their present position as far as:
   Front trench R.29.b 7.2
   Support Trench R.29.b 9.6.
   It will keep in touch with the right of the 36th Infantry Brigade (8th Royal Fusiliers), which will be at the Strong Point R.23.d 8.7. It will threaten QUARRY POST from the N.E. and will get in touch eventually with the 5th Royal Berkshire Regiment on its right.

4. The 5th Battalion, Royal Berkshire Regiment will capture QUARRY POST and the trench running N.E. from it to the HINDENBURG MAIN LINE, where it will join up with the 7th Suffolk Regiment at the trench junction, R.29.b 6.3.
   It will arrange for the two stokes mortars now in action about R.29.c 3.7 and as many captured trench mortars as possible, to take part in the barrage on QUARRY POST.

5. The Company of the 7th Battalion, Norfolk Regiment now with the 7th Suffolk Regiment will remain with it in support.
   The two Companies at CHESHIRE QUARRY will stand by in Brigade Reserve.

6. The 9th Battalion, Essex Regiment, will remain in its present position and be ready to support the advance by fire.

7. The Machine Gun in our Strong Point R.23.c 7.7 will enfilade the objective of the 36th Infantry Brigade during the barrage.
   The remainder of the guns of the 35th Machine Gun Company now in action will stand to, ready to fire on any targets that present themselves.
   The four Reserve Guns of this Company will barrage the western edge of BANTEUX VILLAGE.
   The 235th Machine Gun Company will look out for targets on BANTEUX SPUR, east of QUARRY POST, or in BANTEUX RAVINE.

2.

8. Zero hour will be 8 a.m. on the 24th November 1917.

9. Two watches will be sent round to Headquarters of units between 8 and 9 p.m. tonight (23rd November).

10. ACKNOWLEDGE.

                                                  Captain,
                                          Brigade Major.

Issued at 6.30 p.m.

Copies Nos:-
1. 7th Norfolk Regiment. X
2. 7th Suffolk Regiment.
3. 9th Essex Regiment. X
4. 5th R. Berks. Regiment.
5. 35th Machine Gun Coy.
6. 35th Trench Mortar Battery.
7. 12th Division "G". X
8. 166th Infantry Brigade. X
9. 36th Infantry Brigade. X
10. 37th Infantry Brigade. X
11. 235th Machine Gun Coy. X
12. 36th Field Ambulance. X
13. Staff Captain. X
14. Signals. X
15. War Diary.
16. File.

X MAP NOT ATTACHED

2.

4. **ASSEMBLY.**

Routes will be marked by posts in the ground, as follows :-

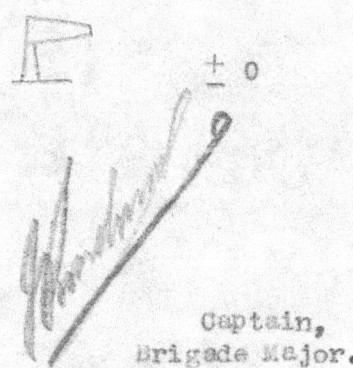

1. Tank Tracks ... ...
2. Artillery Tracks. ...
3. Infantry Tracks.. ...

Captain,
Brigade Major.

Copies to:-
1 7th Norfolk Regiment.
2 7th Suffolk Regiment.
3 9th Essex Regiment.
4 5th N. Berks. Regiment.
5 55th Machine Gun Coy.
6 War Diary.
7 File.

SECRET

Copy No. 4

35TH INFANTRY BRIGADE INSTRUCTIONS NO. 5.

15th November 1917.

Ref. Maps: 1/20,000 GOUZEAUCOURT.
1/10,000 GONNELIEU.

1. **TANKS.**

    (a) All Tanks will be in position at their starting points three hours before Zero hour.

    (b) Tanks will advance followed by Infantry at Zero minus 10 minutes.
    At Zero hour the Artillery barrage will commence.
    At Zero plus 2 hours and 30 minutes troops will advance from the BLUE LINE for the capture of the BROWN LINE.

    (c) Arrangements are being made for Company Section Commanders and Tank Officers to meet their respective Infantry Battalion, Company, and Platoon Commanders at the starting points on X/Y evening, so that the exact spots can be noted.
    Further instructions will be issued as to time and place of meeting.

    (d) The colour of the Tank Battalion flags will be green.

    (e) The following communications between Tanks and Infantry should be made known to all ranks :-

Green Disc;	Wire cut (or crushed down).
Red Disc;	Wire uncut (or uncrushed).
Red, Green or Green, Red;	Have reached my objective.
RD (from Infantry to Tanks);	Bayonet or Rifle waved from side to side, above head.
"Tank wanted" (from Infantry to Tanks);	Helmet on rifle, held above the head.

    (f) A list, showing the names of Section Commanders and Crew Commanders, number on Tank, and name of Tank, is attached as an Appendix (Appendix "A") for No. 7 and No. 8 Companies.

    (g) A tracing showing the approximate Tank routes for each section of Tanks is attached (Tracing "A").

2. **CONSOLIDATION.**

    Communication Trenches from NEWTON POST and SLUSH ALLEY to BLEAK TRENCH will be dug as soon as possible after the BLACK LINE has been taken.
    5th Northants. (Pioneers) will carry out this task, under the orders of the C.R.E.

3. **"S.O.S." Signals.**

    "S.O.S." Signals will be carried as laid down in S.S.135, Chapter XXXI (iv), viz: 12 per Company.

SECRET

SECRET.
Copy No. 4

AMENDMENT NO. 2 TO
35th INFANTRY BRIGADE INSTRUCTIONS NO. 1.

17th November 1917.

The following alterations and additions will be made to 35th Infantry Brigade Instructions No. 1 :-

PART I.

Para. 8.   Add:
"58th Division will co-operate by a machine gun barrage across the BANTEUX RAVINE, to deal with any counter-attack from the direction of BANTEUX against the right of the 35th Infantry Brigade."

PART II.

Para. 24, Crossing Places for Tanks.

Line 4.   Delete: "For a distance of 8 feet each side of the tape."

Add: "Where the tape crosses the trenches it should be left two feet clear on the right (facing the enemy) of the cleared track. The width of the crossings will be 16 feet."

PART III.

Para. 33.   Tracing "A", showing daylight line, should be adjusted to run from Q.32.a 0.0 to Q.5.d 0.0.

Captain,
Brigade Major.

Copies Nos:-
1 7th Norfolk Regiment.
2 7th Suffolk Regiment.
3 9th Essex Regiment.
4 5th R. Berks. Regt.
5 35th Machine Gun Coy.
6 War Diary
7 File

SECRET.   Copy No. 4......

5th Royal Berks.

35TH INFANTRY BRIGADE INSTRUCTIONS NO. 1.

13th November 1917.

Ref. Maps: 1/20,000 GOUZEAUCOURT.
1/10,000 GONNELIEU.

PART I - GENERAL.

1. **SECRECY.**

    Information contained in these and subsequent Instructions should only be communicated to those immediately concerned.

2. **OPERATIONS.**

    An attack will be carried out by the III Corps, in conjunction with other troops on the Left. The 12th Division will be the Right Division of the III Corps. On the Left of the 12th Division will be the 20th Division.
    On the immediate flank of the 12th Division, the 166th Brigade, 55th Division, VII Corps, will advance 3 or 4 small posts from FIFE TRENCH and GARDINER'S BANK, so as to overlook STICK and BANTEUX RAVINES, and a stronger post will be established about R.35 central.
    There will also be a discharge of gas projectors into HONNECOURT WOOD at zero - 2 hours, followed by bursts of Machine Gun fire.

3. **OBJECT.**

    The object is to break the enemy's line by a coup de main between the CANAL DE L'ESCAUT at BANTEUX and the CANAL DU NORD near HAVRINCOURT, and to pass the Cavalry Corps through the gap on the first day.
    The success of the operation will depend on secrecy, surprise and rapidity.

4. **THE ENEMY.**

    The enemy's strength on the Divisional Front is reported to be 3 Battalions in the Front System and 1½ Battalions in Support. The 9th Reserve Division to which they belong fought recently in FLANDERS and was withdrawn at the end of September.
    The total enemy Infantry at present opposite the III Corps available for defence and counter-attack, amounts to 15 Battalions. His Artillery on this front is weak.

5. **METHOD OF ATTACK.**

    The attack will be made in co-operation with Tanks as laid down in the training memoranda issued.
    There will be no preliminary bombardment and practically no preliminary wire cutting by Artillery.
    Artillery and Smoke Barrages will start at Zero hour and lift from objective to objective as the attack progresses.
    If the wind is favourable a smoke barrage will be put on the CANAL DE ST. QUENTIN VALLEY to screen our Right Flank.
    There will be a large concentration of our guns, but they will not register beforehand.

6. ROLE OF THE 12TH DIVISION.

The role of the 12th Division is to make good its objectives in the BLUE and BROWN LINES and at the same time to form a Defensive Flank facing East.

In occupying the latter it is essential to have observation of the approaches from the ST. QUENTIN CANAL VALLEY so as to guard against counter-attack.

7. DISTRIBUTION OF 12TH DIVISION.

The 12th Division will attack on a two-Brigade front up to the BLUE LINE, 35th Brigade on the Right and 36th Brigade on the Left. The 36th and 37th Brigades will continue the attack up to the BROWN LINE, the 37th Brigade carrying out the extension of the Defensive Flank.

The 35th Brigade will consolidate the Defensive Flank South of the BLUE LINE.

The 36th Brigade will consolidate Strong Posts successively in support of the Defensive Flank, and will act eventually as Divisional Reserve at the same time holding the Left Sector of the BROWN LINE facing N.E.

The 36th Brigade will be prepared to co-operate in the capture of LA VACQUERIE and will establish communication with the 20th Division about R.21.b 8½.6, R.16.b.9.2, and R.5.c 9½.4.

The 37th Infantry Brigade will move W. of the crest of the GONNELIEU - BONAVIS RIDGE to a position of assembly in the BLUE LINE on the Right of the 36th Brigade. After capturing its Sector of the BROWN LINE it will continue the Defensive Flank from the BLUE LINE to the BROWN LINE and subsequently to about M.2.d 9.7.

The 35th and 36th Brigades will have a preliminary objective, the BLACK LINE, where their second waves will pass through their first waves.

There will be a pause on the BLUE LINE during which a Smoke Barrage will be placed beyond it to cover the forming-up for the attack on the BROWN LINE.

8. MACHINE GUNS.

The 235th Machine Gun Company will cover the Right Flank during the advance to the BLUE LINE and co-operate by barrage fire.

Brigade Machine Gun Companies will be with their Brigades. The 36th Machine Gun Company will cover the advance on the Left to the BLUE LINE by barrage fire.

9. INFANTRY CO-OPERATING WITH TANKS.

Infantry will be prepared to improve gaps made by Tanks in wire, and to make others for passage of R.F.A. They will also supplement the covering fire of the Tanks, and assist them when in difficulties with their tools.

10. MOPPING-UP PARTIES.

The objectives captured will be thoroughly searched to ensure that no parties of Germans are unaccounted for. The HINDENBURG MAIN LINE is reported to contain numerous dugouts. Mills and "P" bombs will be carried in order to clear them.

Precautions will be taken beforehand to ensure that dugouts within the Brigade area are not unnecessarily destroyed or burnt out, as they will be required afterwards.

11. **CONSOLIDATION.**

All objectives, when gained, will be consolidated immediately, and the defences strengthened by Vickers Guns disposed as far as possible chequerwise and in depth.

The defence will be organised in depth, and special "counter-attack" troops told off to meet hostile counter-attacks.

All posts should be sited at least 20 yards from any existing road so as not to impede future traffic.

12. **ADVANCE OF CAVALRY.**

The following road is reserved for the use of Cavalry and is not to be used by other troops till the Cavalry have passed through :-

GOUZEAUCOURT - BARRICADE (R.21.d.3.4) - LA VACQUERIE.

The repair of this road and of the BARRICADE - BONAVIS Road will be carried out by the 5th Northants. Regt. under the orders of the C.R.E.

13. **A.A. MACHINE GUNS.**

From "W" day onwards, each Brigade will organise a scheme of anti-aircraft machine gun defence. These will be located in three echelons as follows :-

   (a) The trench system to be mainly found by Lewis Guns.

   (b) The remainder of the forward area back to the daylight line.

   (c) Throughout the Central Area for the protection of refilling points, dumps, camps, billets, etc.

Battalions and the Machine Gun Coy. will also take forward with them during the advance anti-aircraft Lewis and Machine Guns to deal with low-flying aeroplanes during the operation.

14. **DISPOSAL OF HOSTILE GUNS.**

In the event of the capture of hostile guns, information should be sent immediately to the nearest Brigade Headquarters for transmission to the Artillery, giving exact location of guns, nature of gun and whether ammunition is at hand.

This information should be passed on to the nearest 6" Trench Mortar Detachment, who will arrange to send up personnel to man the gun. On no account will spare parts, sights, etc., be removed as souvenirs from captured guns.

15. **COUNTER-ATTACK PLANE.**

An aeroplane will be up continuously from daylight onwards whose sole mission will be to detect the approach of enemy counter-attacks.

Whenever this plane observes hostile parties of 100 or over either assembling or moving to counter-attack, it will drop a Smoke Bomb over that portion of the front against which the enemy is moving. The Smoke Bomb will burst about 100 feet below

15. COUNTER-ATTACK PLANE (Continued).

the machine into a white parachute flare, which descends slowly leaving a trail of brown smoke about 1 foot broad, behind it. On seeing the above signal, Artillery and Machine Gun barrages will be opened immediately without further orders on all hostile approaches in that vicinity.

16. CONTACT PLANE.

A Contact Aeroplane will fly over the Corps front from Zero on "Z" day at hours to be notified later. Flares will be lit by the leading troops only when demanded by the contact 'plane either:

    (a) by Klaxon Horn.
    or
    (b) by a series of white lights.

The necessity for lighting flares will be impressed on all concerned, and sufficient flares for this purpose issued to the troops. If troops have exhausted their stock of flares, they should indicate their position to the aeroplane by waving their helmets.

Brigade and Battalion Headquarters will be marked by ground sheets of authorised shape, with the code letters of the unit laid out with white strips (9 feet in depth) alongside.

17. "S.O.S.".

The following flares and 'S.O.S.' signals will be used :-

Flares.

    Cavalry will use RED Flares.
    Infantry will use WHITE Flares.

'S.O.S.' signal.

    III Corps)
) Rifle Grenade bursting into
) 2 GREEN and 2 WHITE.
    VII Corps)

18. CONCENTRATION.

The following is a forecast of the move of the Division to the Forward Area :-

Detraining Area.	Staging Area.	Forward Area.
V/W	W/X	X/Y nights.

PART II - SPECIAL.

19. **DISPOSITIONS.**

The Brigade will attack on a front of two Battalions: 5th R. Berks. Regiment on Right, 9th Essex Regiment on Left. The 7th Suffolk Regiment will leapfrog the Left Battalion and take the HINDENBURG MAIN LINE.
The 7th Norfolk Regiment will be in Brigade Reserve.
The boundary line between Battalions is shown on attached Map.

20. **RELIEFS.**

On X/Y night, the 7th Norfolk Regiment will take over the front line from the 20th Division within the Brigade boundary, as shown on Map, with the exception of a screen of sentries in the front line. This screen will be relieved on Y/Z night. The 7th Norfolk Regiment will only send forward sufficient men to garrison the trenches.

21. **ASSEMBLY.**

On Y/Z night, Battalions will assemble in rear of the Tanks approximately in the position shown on attached map. These positions are to be carefully reconnoitred beforehand. No talking or smoking is to be allowed.
From these positions the two leading Battalions will follow the Tanks in the organisation laid down. No. 8 Coy. C. Battalion, Tank Corps, will work with the 5th R. Berks. and No. 7 Company with the 9th Essex Regt.

22. **TANKS.**

The leading Tanks will advance at intervals of about 125 yards, and cross the German wire at approximately the positions shown on attached Map. The average speed of the Tanks may be taken at fifty yards per minute.
As soon as the HINDENBURG OUTPOST LINE has been mopped up by the two leading Battalions (who will remain and consolidate), all the Tanks, except the Right Section, will, after a pause of 15 minutes, advance straight ahead to the HINDENBURG MAIN LINE. The Left four Tank Sections will be followed by the four companies of the 7th Suffolk Regiment who will time their advance so as to be able to go on with the Tanks from BLEAK SUPPORT.

23. **FLANK-GUARD TANKS.**

No. 1 Tank Section on the extreme right will remain on BANTEUX SPUR as flank guard to cover the consolidation work by the Infantry, and to exploit the situation (See para. 25 below).
No. 2 Tank Section (right but one) on reaching the HINDENBURG MAIN LINE, will also remain as flank guard to the 7th Suffolk Regiment.
The remaining six Tank sections, after completing their work on the HINDENBURG MAIN LINE, will pause for 15 minutes on the BLUE LINE and then move on in support of the attack by the other brigades on the HINDENBURG SUPPORT LINE.

24. CROSSING PLACES FOR TANKS.

Crossing places for Tanks in our present front trenches will be marked out beforehand by the Tank Corps, and at those points the parapet and parados should be cut down and the spoil thrown into the trench, for a distance of 8 ft. each side of the tape.

This work and the preparing of trench boards as ladders and bridges to assist the Infantry out or over the trenches will be carried out by the 7th Norfolk Regiment as soon as they take over the line.

25. RIGHT BATTALION.

The Right Battalion will turn BLEAK SUPPORT into a front line facing N.E. and wire it as soon as possible.

As it is all-important to command the approaches along the BANTEUX SPUR, this Battalion, with the help of its flank guard section of Tanks, will push its outposts without delay Eastwards along the Spur, and will gain and consolidate the most commanding position it can find. If it is found that the enemy is demoralised, it should push down the Spur and mop up, possibly as far as QUARRY POST, but the distance they can go in safety depends on our Artillery programme, which will be notified later.

BLEAK TRENCH should be made into a support line and wired.

This Battalion should consider the question of possible counter-attacks by the enemy from the S.E., as well as the N.E. or along the BANTEUX SPUR, and arrange its defences accordingly.

26. LEFT BATTALION.

The Left Battalion will consolidate BARRACK SUPPORT at once as a fire trench to face N.E., and wire it as soon as possible. It will also consolidate BLEAK WALK and portions of BLEAK TRENCH, as support lines.

As soon as the Tanks, followed by the 7th Suffolk Regiment, have proceeded onwards from BLEAK SUPPORT towards the HINDENBURG MAIN LINE, mopping up the Machine Gun Posts shown on Map in R.28.b on the way, the 9th Essex Regiment will push out parties to take over and consolidate these posts into a "strong point". Judging from the map, this strong point will be of great importance and will form the nucleus of a front line approximately along the line of the road (CHESHIRE STREET) as indicated on attached map.

27. LEAPFROG BATTALION.

(a) The 7th Suffolk Regiment, advancing from the BLACK LINE behind the left four Sections of Tanks, and mopping up the enemy's machine gun emplacements en route, will attack and consolidate the HINDENBURG MAIN LINE, including the buildings at R.23.a 8.5.

It will be the duty of this Battalion to select and consolidate a defensive position (front and support lines) astride of the HINDENBURG MAIN LINE, facing E. The exact positions to be taken up can only be determined when the ground has been captured, but it is thought that it may be approximately as indicated on attached map, strong points being first of all made at :-
    (a) Sunken road, R.23.c 2.5
    (b) Cross roads, R.23.c 5.9
    (c) Buildings, R.23.a 8.5
with supporting points about the trench junctions :-
    R.23.a 3.6
    R.23.a 1.4½
    R.23.a 2.0.

27. **LEAPFROG BATTALION (Continued).**

(b) At the same time that the 7th Suffolk Regiment advance with their four sections of Tanks, the other three sections of Tanks (Nos. 2, 3, and 4) will also proceed to the HINDENBURG MAIN LINE.

The sunken roads may necessitate detours by the Tanks but the Infantry should make short cuts across them, rejoining their respective Tanks on the other side.

(c) No. 2 Section of Tanks will remain as flank guard when the others go on. This section will cover the consolidation by the Infantry and will exploit the situation in the HINDENBURG MAIN LINE. If it is found that the enemy shows signs of demoralisation and a willingness to surrender, this section of Tanks accompanied by at least a Company of Infantry will proceed South-Eastwards along the HINDENBURG MAIN LINE and mop up, but the distance they can go in safety will depend on our Artillery programme, which will be notified later.

28. **RESERVE BATTALION.**

The 7th Norfolk Regiment will follow the advance as far as our old front and support lines, where it will remain in reserve. It will take immediate steps to join up NEWTON POST with the German line by a fire trench along the sunken road running N.E. from NEWTON POST. This is to be wired.

It will also form a support line approximately along the line indicated on attached map, utilising the other sunken road (BANTEUX ROAD) running East from GONNELIEU, as far as possible.

This Battalion will hold itself in readiness to move off at short notice.

29. **MACHINE GUN COMPANY.**

(a) The duty of the Machine Gun Company is to arrange for machine gun defence as soon as possible after the objectives have been taken. It will pay particular attention to being able to fire direct, if possible, otherwise indirect, into all portions of the ST. QUENTIN CANAL VALLEY where the enemy is likely to assemble by day or night for counter-attack, and on all bridges over the Canal. (See photographs).

(b) During the first advance, one section Machine Gun Company will be attached to the 5th R. Berks. Regiment, and be under the orders of the Battalion Commander.

This section will come into action on BANTEUX SPUR to cover the advance by the 7th Suffolk Regiment on the HINDENBURG MAIN LINE, and to fire on the latter S.E. of our advance at any targets that present themselves.

One half section of the Machine Gun Company will accompany the 9th Essex Regiment and its role will be similar to the above.

Another half section will accompany the 7th Suffolk Regiment to the HINDENBURG MAIN LINE.

All the above will assemble with the Battalions and will move forward in rear of them, in touch with Battalion Headquarters.

The remainder of the Machine Gun Company will be in Brigade Reserve, in a position to be notified later.

29. **MACHINE GUN COMPANY (Continued).**

(c) As soon as the Brigade moves into the forward area previous to the attack, the O.C. Machine Gun Company will arrange for Anti-Aircraft fire in depth (See para. above).

He will also arrange for A.A. Mountings (one per Section) to accompany the Advance.

In making out his scheme for Machine Gun Defence he will allow for A.A. fire along the whole defensive flank.

30. **STOKES MORTARS.**

For the first advance, Stokes Mortars will assemble with, and follow in rear of, each of the three leading Battalions as follows. They will be under the orders of Battalion Commanders and will be provided with ten carriers per mortar by the Battalion to which they are attached :-

5th R. Berks. Regt. ... 2 Mortars.
9th Essex Regt. ... ... 1 Mortar.
7th Suffolk Regt. ... ... 2 Mortars.

As soon as the objectives have been taken, the O.C. Trench Mortar Battery will see that the above five Mortars are in the best possible positions for dealing with counter-attacks from the East. He will arrange reliefs so that they are constantly ready night and day, and arrange through Brigade Headquarters for the supply of ammunition.

As soon as the Trench Mortars are in action, the Infantry Carriers may rejoin their units, by order of the Battalion Commanders.

31. **BRIGADE SNIPERS.**

As soon as the objectives have been taken the Brigade Sniping Officer will get in touch with Battalion Commanders who will give him every assistance in posting Snipers with telescopic sights in the best positions that can be found. Reliefs of snipers will be arranged for.

PART III - MISCELLANEOUS.

32. **LIGHTS.**

(a) No fire or light is to be lighted in any camp, bivouac, hut or shelter unless the light is screened from ground and aerial observation.

(b) All cooking for troops in the open will be done in cookers only and not in open fires, unless these are properly screened.

(c) Electric torches, when used to aid movements, must only be flashed, and not used as a continuous light.

(d) No lights will be used on any vehicles in the area, except motors and lorries.

(e) In every unit, officers and N.C.Os. will be specially detailed to patrol their lines periodically during the night to see that no lights are showing.

The A.P.M's of the Corps and Divisions will also visit camps.

(f) Arrangements are being made for a balloon or aeroplane to be up at night, whose sole duty will be to locate and report naked lights.

33. **MOVEMENT: CONCEALMENT OF.**

(a) The III Corps area will in future be divided into the three following Zones, which are shown on attached tracing, marked "A" :-
    (i)   Front Zone   - In front of the daylight line, and under direct observation of hostile O.Ps.
    (ii) Central Zone - Where movement and roads can be observed by hostile balloons on fine days.
    (iii) Back Area   - Which can only be observed by hostile aircraft.

(b) In the Front Zone, movement by day in the open will be restricted to the following :-
    (i)   No party to exceed 2 men.
    (ii) Parties of 2 to move at 100 yards distance.
    (iii) Working parties not exceeding 10 may proceed to the front line at intervals of 100 yards by the special routes selected by the 20th Division.

No horse or vehicle will be permitted beyond the Daylight Line without a pass signed by the A.P.M. of the 20th Division. All routes crossing the Daylight Line are to be posted immediately with notices forbidding all movement exceeding the above. These roads will be picquetted from November 5th to ensure these instructions being obeyed.

33. MOVEMENT: CONCEALMENT OF. (Continued).

The above notices should be placed in positions which will enable motor cars and other vehicles to be properly screened from balloon observation. Where necessary vehicles should be sent back to wait under cover.

(c) In the Central Zone, on a "clear day", all movement by day will be restricted to the following :-
   (i) No party to exceed 32 foot men and 16 mounted men.
   (ii) All parties to move in single file along the edges of the metalling. No troops to move in the centre of the roads.
   (iii) Intervals of 100 yards between parties and convoys. Convoys to be limited to 10 vehicles.

(d) When any day is sufficiently clear for observation by hostile balloons, O.C. No. 41 Balloon Section will inform Corps Headquarters who will notify all concerned by wire.
On ordinary dull days the restrictions applicable to the Back Area will apply.

(e) In the Back Area movement will be subject to the following restrictions at all times :-
Parties of men and transport not larger than the equivalent of one Company at intervals of 200 yards.

(f) Special precautions will be taken to prevent an excessive movement of motor cars in the Balloon Zone by arranging for Officers to share cars as much as possible, and fit in their inspections so as to go out and return in the same car.

(g) The hours of daylight will be defined weekly by orders from Brigade Headquarters.

(h) All tents are to be struck in the daytime.

(i) Men are to avoid walking about near any camouflage.

(j) Officers visiting the Corps front for any purpose will report at 20th Division Headquarters.

34. PERSONNEL LEFT OUT OF ACTION.

Reference S.S.135, Section XXX (Amended). All officers and other ranks undergoing Courses or on leave, and other ranks selected for Commissions, may be included in the 108 left behind.
Besides the above, only the best N.C.Os. or men should be left behind.

35. DRESS.

Reference S.S.135, Section XXXI. In addition :-

(a) Each man will carry an entrenching tool, three shovels to one pick.

(b) Packs, with greatcoats, will be dumped in the forwarding area.
Jerkins will be carried, rolled on the back.

(c) A large proportion of wire cutters and wire breakers are being arranged for.

36. MARCHING.

Special attention is directed by the Third Army to the following points :-

(a) Punctuality from the starting point - no main traffic routes to be blocked by troops waiting to march off.

(b) 200 yards interval will be maintained in rear of Battalions.

(c) No 'double banking'.

(d) All units will observe the regulation clock hour halts, i.e., 10 minutes before each clock hour.

(e) In the event of a vehicle breaking down, it will at once be cleared from the road.

(f) An Officer will march in rear of each Company or similar unit.

(g) A free passage for traffic moving in the opposite direction will be kept.

(h) On arrival at destination, main traffic routes will at once be cleared.

37. SPECIAL PARTIES FOR TANKS.

Battalions will detail special parties to look for any of our wounded that may be lying in the track of the Tanks, and remove them. This is especially necessary after the leading wave has gone forward.

38. GENERAL.

Special attention is drawn to the following points :-

(a) No orders are to be sent by wire or telephone.

(b) All letters are to be carefully censored.

(c) Importance of every man using his rifle when possible during the advance, once sections have extended.

(d) The importance of covering the movement of neighbouring platoons by fire, especially while crossing the wire.
Attention is called to the coloured diagrams already issued.

(e) Importance of proper section control and discipline on the battlefield, especially control in the dark without verbal orders.

(f) The vital importance of absolute silence while forming up with the Tanks. At least one night practice per Battalion.

(g) Importance of visual signalling and of having runners properly organised. Also, selecting reliable men as guides for ration parties, etc.

38. **GENERAL.** (Continued).

(h) All officers and N.C.Os. to know how to use the standard message pad.

(i) On reaching final objective, see that all Lewis Guns and rifles are clean and in proper order, ready to repel counter-attacks.

[signature]
Captain,
Brigade Major.

```
Copy No.  1 to  7th Norfolk Regiment.
          2     7th Suffolk Regiment.
          3     9th Essex Regiment.
          4     5th R. Berks. Regiment.
          5     35th Machine Gun Coy.
          6     35th Trench Mortar Bty.
          7     File.
          8     War Diary.
          9     do.
                C. Battalion, Tank Corps (Part II only).
                36th Infantry Brigade.   ( do. )
                37th Infantry Brigade.   ( do. )
                12th Division "G".       ( do. )
```

Map and Tracing "A" not attached.

Specialists, contd.

Bombers.

12 bombs in buckets with R.G. rods.
120 rounds S.A.A.

Orderlies.

75 rounds S.A.A.
2 bombs and R.G. rods
Note book
wire cutters.

Signallers.

75 rounds S.A.A.
2 bombs
message books
wire cutters.

Pioneers.

Axe
Saw
nails (assorted.)
20 notice boards as detailed.

S.A.A.

German rifles and ammunition will be used as far as possible in captured trench, so that our own may be saved for a counter attack.

Care of arms.

As soon as objective is taken, section commanders will at once inspect all rifles and ammunition and see that everything is clean and in working order.

Souvenir Hunting.

Company Commanders will take special precautions that any souvenir hunting is under proper supervision.

Communication.

There will be no telephone lines, and all signalling will be visual.
Messages can be sent by

(a). Visual signalling
(2). Runner
(3). Pigeon
(4). Dog

No. 3 and 4 are not to be used unless for emergency.

15/II/17.

Capt.
Adjt. Royal Berkshire Regiment.

Consolidation contd.

If there are any dug-outs in the captured trench, Strong Points should be made to protect them and wired.

Dress.

All ranks.

Fighting Order : with waterproof sheets and jerkins : extra rations.

Officers.

Platoon Commanders will be dressed as the men, with rank on their shoulders. Other Officers may ware their own kit if they like, but will not shew field boots or ties.

All Officers will carry : -

6 Very Light Cartridges
S. O. S. Signal
Note Book
Blue and red pencil
Compass
Map message sheets
wire cutters
Periscope (vigilant)

N.C.O's (Sergeants)
----

6 Very lights
S. O. S. Signals
Note Book
Periscope
Map message sheets
Blue and red pencils
Watch.

N.C.O's (Section commanders)

Flares
Note Books
Map message sheets
Periscope
Cleaning rod for rifles

Other Ranks.

Pick or shovel (1 pick to 3 shovels)
4 sandbags
2 bombs with R.G. rods
170 Rounds S.A.A.
Periscope

Specialists.

Lewis Gunners

Each Team to carry 27 Lewis Gun Discs
70 Rounds S.A.A.
2 bombs and R.G. rods

The Tanks will start at about Zero minus 10 and should reach the German trench at about Zero plus 10.

At Zero, a barrage will open on German trenches, and smoke will be sent over German line to the South.

On reaching the objectives, a defensive flank will be formed roughly on the following lines

BLEAK SUPPORT will at once be consolidated by "A" Company, from Battalion boundary on left to R.28.d.60.90.

"B" Company from right of "A" to R.28.d.70.35.

"D" Company BLEAK TRENCH from Battalion boundary on left to R.28.d.30.45.

No. I Tank section will remain behind at the disposal of O.C. "A" Company, when, as soon as barrage has lifted, will work along QUARRY TRENCH and its SUPPORT LINE and consolidate a line commanding the low ground by BANTEAU. From the map, a good line seems to run along R.29.a.50.20. - R.29.b.50.99. - R.29.c.25.75. - R.29.c.30.40.

O.C. "C" Company may exploit as far as QUARRY POST but NOT further.

"C" Company will consolidate as soon as they have taken their objectives, and will form Battalion outpost line.

The Main line of defence will be BLEAK SUPPORT, with SUPPORT LINE BLEAK TRENCH

The 9th. Essex are consolidating the same lines to our left.

Company limits in the objectives will be from their gap in the wire to the next gap on the left.

Special.

The Battalion will form up behind the Tanks, approximately as per diagram .

They will move in section blobs as far as possible, and then extend into line.

Instructions.

Each Platoon will arrange to be close up to its Tank when it goes through the German wire, but during the advance, it will move independently to the Tank, and when under hostile fire, by short section rushes, covered by fire. At end of rush, sections will lie down, - all crowding is to be avoided, and when section is going through the wire, other sections will bring a heavy fire on the German trench to keep the enemy's heads down.

When Tanks are working down trenches, the bombers only, will enter the trench, the others will follow the Tank and mop up the trench from the outside.

The Stop Platoons will form stops in the trenches, points to be stopped will be notified later in Operation Orders. They will also improve gaps in the wire made by Tanks.

The special mopping up sections will remain in German front trench and complete the mopping up.

Consolidation.

Trenches to be consolidated will be consolidated previously, by a series of Strong Points, with cross fire between them. Full use will be made of Lewis Guns. Firesteps will at once be made. The trench will be wired as soon as possible, if wire is available. Wire will be put out at once in order to take advantage of smoke screen on our left. Right

SECRET.   SECRET

ROYAL BERKSHIRE REGIMENT.

PRELIMINARY INSTRUCTIONS.

The attack will be carried out as follows :-

General.

There will be no preliminary bombardment or wire cutting.
The Battalion will attack behind Tanks as follows :-

Four Tank sections are allotted to the Battalion, each consisting of an advance guard Tank and the main body Tanks. The advanced guard Tank goes on ahead through the German wire - it works along German parapet, mopping up the trench, until it reaches the next gap in the wire to the left; this Tank is not followed by Infantry.
The two main body Tanks, move about 100 yards behind, each followed by a Platoon of Infantry in Tank formation., i.e. small-section blobs. These Tanks go through gap made by A.G. Tanks, go straight over the German Front Line. The leading Tank works along parades of front trench cleaning it up; it then goes on to 2nd. trench and joins No. 2 M.G. Tank in last Battalion objective; they cruse up and down the trench, mopping it up, and finally leave Battalion and go off to help further objectives.
The advance guard Tank in this time has wheeled round, gone over the front trench in the same place as the others, and joined them.

The Tanks will form up somewhere about R.34.c.o.o under cover of darkness.
The Battalion will form up in Tank formation as follows :-

    No. I Tank Section   Right   "C" Company.
    No. 2   -do-   "B" Company.
    No. 3   -do-   "A" Company.
    No. 4   -do-   "D" Company.

The Points in the German Line that each Tank section will make for, are :-

    No. I Tank Section   ....   R.28.d.75.35.
    No. 2   -do-   ....   R.28.d.50.35.
    No. 3   -do-   ....   R.28.d.22.30.
    No. 4   -do-   ....   R.28.c.99.70.

The Objective of the Battalion is as follows :-

BLEAK TRENCH   from   R.28.c.80.70 to R.28.d.75.35.

BLEAK SUPPORT   from   R.28.b.25.20 to R.28.d.75.35.

                                                                                 continued.

55th Infantry Brigade

The attack was carried out
was to get into [illegible] opposite
of the platoon in action as
a self supporting body.
Whilst [illegible] captured
10 prisoners, killed 8 Germans
also [illegible], no casualties
[illegible] captured about 400 of
trench line about [illegible] dugouts

The attack was carried out as
follows [illegible] whilst [illegible]
attacking
two platoons of B coy were
detailed to carry out [illegible]
attack from [illegible]

[illegible] Patrols from the
companies holding sector R
and [illegible] sector sent out
reconnoitring patrols along their
trenches to get in touch with
the enemy which they did on
all occasions. A party [illegible]
in map [illegible] was also carried
out [illegible] last night

At 7.30 last last night I
ordered company forming
support in Quarry Support
to make good a sergeant
and 6 men & carry bags for
ammunition carrying dump
about 100x from our store
and a telephone line were
laid and 25 D coy formed
an advanced [?]
At zero minus 1 hour the
two platoons of D coy advanced
to support in Quarry Support
by [?] slow rushing and
forward through [?] our own
bombing stop in British
Trench. Two [?] [?]
bombers and rifle grenaders
had been formed up in A and
B coy [?] during
night.
At zero the artillery opened
a barrage on enemy [?]
lifted at zero +5 to [?]
just in front of [?] [?]
The heavy artillery firing on
Pozieres — our own artillery
[?] 5 heavy [?] fired on
Sunken road at points marked

- lifting at zero +5 to
  further down the sunken
  road
- Another group (?) fires at
  fourteen & waits for QUARRY
  post & QUARRY trench till
  zero +5 and then after
  about 30 further down the
  sunken
  road

The machine guns were told
to hold their covering positions
and were not to expose themselves.
Not move forward themselves.

The platoon in QUARRY trench
was told to move forward
and establish a block about
50 yards beyond NORTHERN
post below the ridge from
[QUARRY] also [make?] a
[?] post & [launch?] [?] towards
QUARRY post and to [work?]
around the post in the truck

The platoon in QUARRY valley? T
was told to push along trench
to QUARRY post work round
to the left & [keep?] [communication?]
trench leading to NORTHERN
MAIN post and [also?] truck

1/11 The Suffolks

The whole of quarry Post
was heavily fired upon
so it was impossible to
take it from anywhere
but up the trenches.
The following method was
adopted.
a) continuous rapid rifle fire
b) a crawl up to [?] as
far as possible as soon as
opposition was met a
barrage of the No 20 Rifle
grenades howitz a barrage
of about 120 [?] the
barrage was continued and
put down a heavy [?]
No 23 Rifle grenades making
a barrage [?] to see
under this [?] the bombers
crept forward and if necessary
[?] out of the trench & got
round behind the enemy
Lewis guns were used
[?] out to a flank
The company was also
that if they [?] [?]

serious opposition we
made like in the trenches
as far as they had got
and as well the help of
the supports working down
communication and a dump
from [...]
[...] without [...]
would be absolute and if
go the mine being [...] the
the enemy to [...] of [...]
away by [...] buying all I
did [...] think to be [...]
The attack was entirely
successful and I consider it
was due to the good [...]
and the goodwill [...] by the
men [...] from [...]
[...] this was [...]
we practice [...] [...] the care
[...] [...] [...] [...] saw
the enemy

The casualties of the [...] have
held the line were [...]
[...] a few [...] and
[...] gunners [...] [...]
[...] [...] [...] [...] [...]
We had no casualties

E.J.C. [...] Lt Col
24.11.17.   Commdg 6th Royal [...] Reg

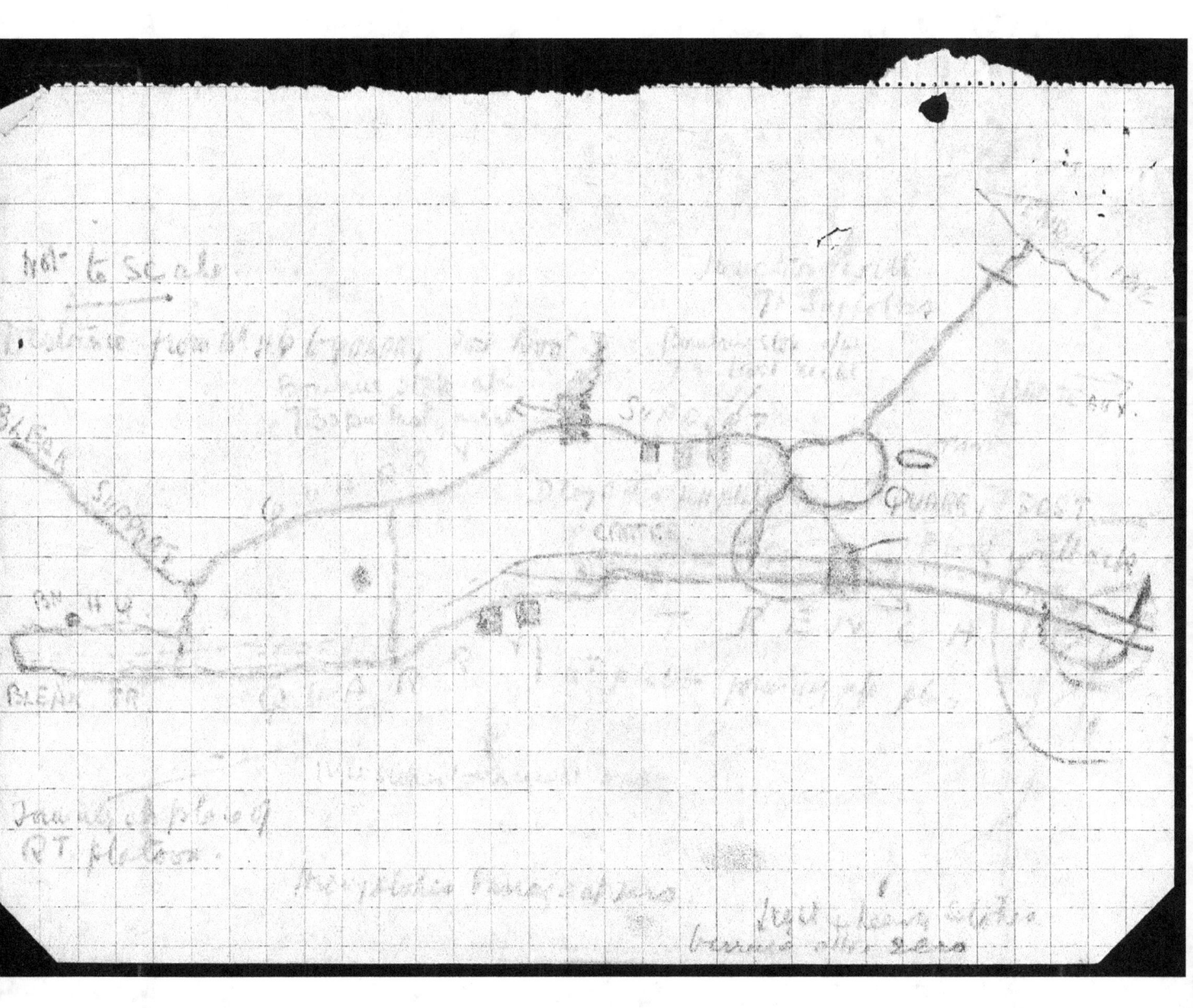

Royal Berkshire Regt.

Order No. 2.

Ref Trench Map 6007 & 6201 ??

1. The 35th and 36th Bdes. will advance simultaneously and establish an outpost line from QUARRY POST to BLEAK QUARRY.

The 36th Bde. will capture consolidate PELHAM AVENUE between R.23.d.8.2. and R.24.c.3.0. and BLEAK QUARRY.

The 7 Suffolks will take the HINDENBURG line to R.28.b.7.2. & R.29.b.0.8.

This Battalion will capture QUARRY POST and trench leading to HINDENBURG line junction inclusive.

II. The attack will be carried out as follows:

(a) Artillery - The Artillery will put a barrage on QUARRY POST from Zero to Zero +5 min. At Zero +5 barrage will lift to trenches in front of Battalion. A.H. + ?

(b) Heavy T.M. will fire from Zero to Zero +5 on R.30.a.05.05. and R.29.a.80.50.
from Zero +5 to ? all on R.29.d.80.50

(c) Stokes Mortars from Zero to Zero +5 on R.29.d.0.7. from Zero +5 to ? on R.29.d.80.50.

(b) Machine Guns will cooperate as much as possible in attack and deal with enemy targets.

(c) Smoke barrage will be placed on EMMOUTRETTES.

d. "B" Coy will carry out the attack as follows:

(i) Zero - 1 hour, 1 platoon will assemble in dugout in QUARRY Support at R.29.c.70.90. and 1 platoon in support at R.29.c.50.50.

(ii) Zero both platoons will advance along QUARRY Trench into QUARRY Support.

A bombing block will at once be formed at R.29.d.1.7.

The platoon in QUARRY Support will take the N portion of QUARRY Post and then work along C.T. leading to HINDENBURG LINE and gain touch with 7th Bn. Sher. Foresters.

Other platoon will work round QUARRY Post to the S. and hold portion as far as C.T.

If the attack is held up by bombing, more bombing blocks will be formed as far as possible so that the Post will be cut off & eventually have to surrender.

A Platoons will advance protected
by R.E. covering.

2 x Coy. and HQ men will be
placed at disposal of O.C. "D"
for carrying up.

Mr... will report to O.C. "D"
Coy at 6 am tomorrow.

O.C. "A" & "B" Coys will arrange & form
dumps of bombs & S.A.A. near
front line as possible.

O.C. "D" Coy will establish his H.Q.
at R.20.c.50.90. by two men 30 hours.

B H.Q will not move
D will ... at the ... of O.C.
D Coy.

There will be at 8 am
O.C. A & B Coys will be enough
to get all their men in dugouts before
this time, only sentries and L.G.
in position.

VII Where the position is taken the
following redistribution will take
place.

D Coy will hold from R.39.b.6.5
... to 29.6.9.7 (inclusive) with
2 platoons.

1 Platoon in support in C trench
opposite between ADMS to CARTER Post

A Coy will hold old German Front Line
from R.29.c.9.7. to B.H.Q. i.e. 2
platoons, 1 platoon in ADAMS Tr.

B Coy in Reserve in BEEAR
Support from R.28.b.2.3 to
R.28.b.7.4 (inclusive)

The word RABBIT will be
sent from B.H.Q. when relief
will take place.

Issued at 11p.m.
23/1/17

A. Miller
Capt & O.C.
5/R Berks Regt

Copy No 1. A. Coy
" 2. B. Coy
" 3. to Coy
" 4. Bde
" 5. T. Hollis
" 6. File

the journal before
cooperated with the attack
by at once going forward
from the captain's position
and smothering escaping
down the customary stopping
of the end [illegible]
[illegible] ratchet [illegible]
to the conclusion

[signature illegible]

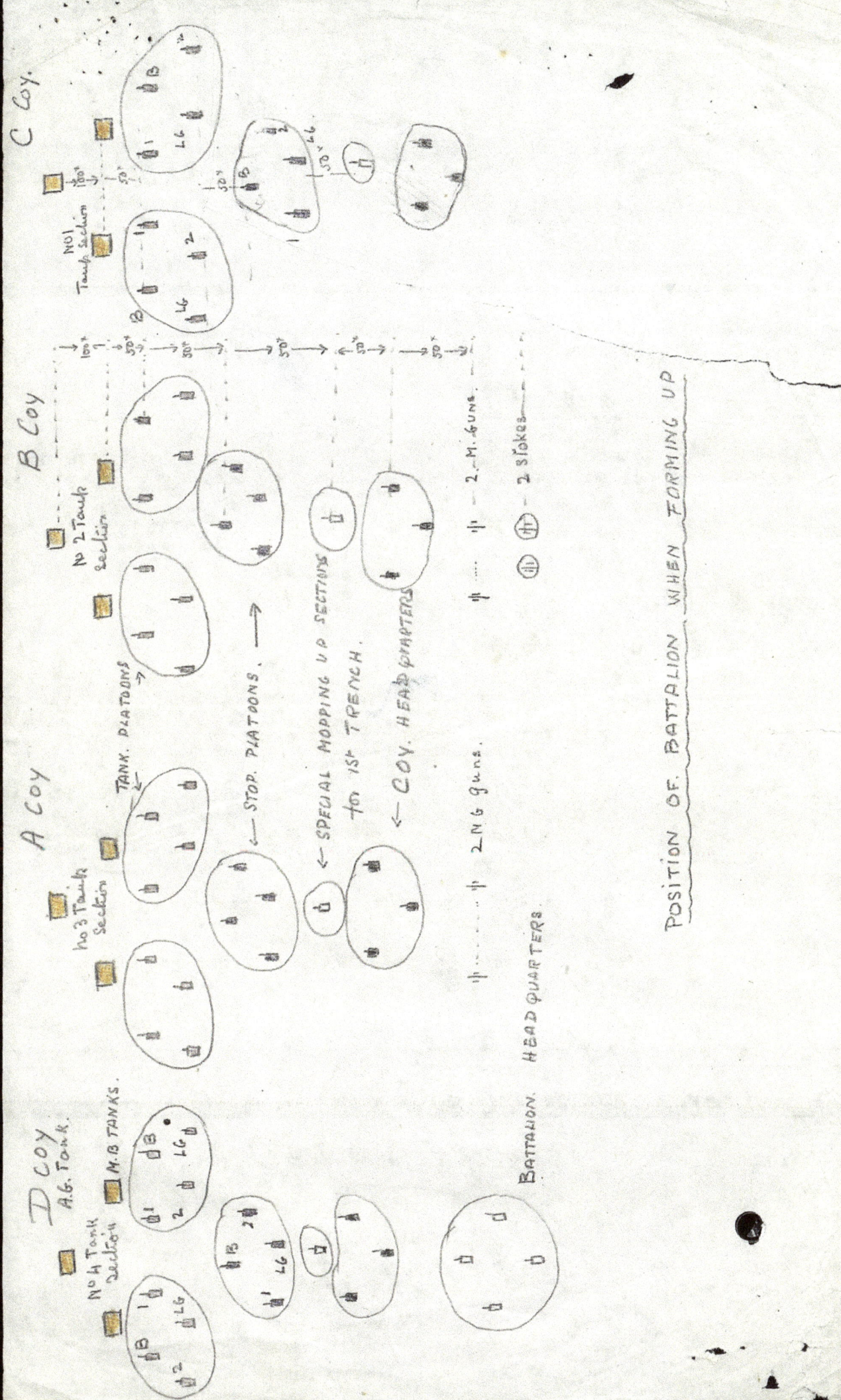

Section Commanders.	Crew Commanders.		Crew Number.	Manufacturers No.	Name of Tank.

No. 8 Company (Continued).

Section Commanders.	Crew Commanders.		Crew Number.	Manufacturers No.	Name of Tank.
No. 6 Section					
Lieut. E.R. SANDERS	Lieut.	J.H.LIST	C.26	2898	"CELERITY II"
	2/Lt.	E.C.WOOD	C.27	2385	"CENTAUR II"
	"	H.H.CALCUTT	C.28	2842	"CORNCRAKE II"
	"	C.W.ROBERTS	C.29	8089	"CURIOSITY II"
No. 7 Section					
Capt. H.M.JOHNSTON	2/Lt.	W.P.WHYTE	C.32	2882	"CRAB II"
	"	W.ROBINSON	C.33	8042	"CRUSTACEAN II"
	"	R.J.REW	C.34	2877	"CROCODILE II"
	"	A.D.ADAMS	C.31	2400	"CATERPILLAR II"
No. 8 Section					
Capt. W.E. SILVER	2/Lt.	F.M.BOXALL	C.37	8033	"CALIBAN"
	"	F.L.A.FIELD	C.38	2839	"CANNIBAL II"
	"	E.J.ROLLINGS	C.39	2059	"CYCLOPS"
	"	G.RITCHIE	C.S.1	6003	"CLOWN"

APPENDIX A.

TO ACCOMPANY 35TH INFANTRY BRIGADE INSTRUCTIONS NO. 3 OF 15TH NOVEMBER 1917.

No. 7 Company.

Section Commanders.	Crew Commanders.	Crew Number.	Manufacturers No.	Name of Tank.
No. 1 Section.				
Capt. A.V. MONK.	2/Lt. W.E.DREEN	C.5	4007	"CHINA"
	" R.C.McNICOL	C.3	2852	"CAPE COLONY II"
	" P.H.O'DOWD	C.4	2788	"CYPRUS II"
No. 2 Section.				
Capt. L.V. SMITH, M.C.	2/Lt. E.H.ARUNDEL	C.2	2724	"CEYLON"
	" J.M.WADDINGTON	C.16	2816	"CA' CANNY"
	" L.E.MINCHIN	C.17	8015	"GUIDICH N'RIGH II"
No. 3 Section.				
Capt. R.A. YOULL	Lieut. A.V.COLEMAN	C.11	2784	"CARSTAIRS II"
	" E.P.READMAN	C.12	2726	"CUMBRAE"
	2/Lt. L.F.MASTERS	C.13	2053	"CAITHNESS"
No. 4 Section.				
Lieut. F.S. PARSONS	2/Lt. A.H.MARTIN	C.14	2883	"CULLODEN II"
	" V.S.MADHAM	C.18	2044	"CELTIC"
	Lieut. H.PROPHETT	C.19	2381	"CLYDE II"
RESERVES.		C.1	2085	"CANADA"
		C.15	4008	"CASA"
WIRE PULLING TANKS.				
2/Lt. C.M. LeCLAIR	2/Lt. M.G.R.ELLIOTT		4515	
	Sergt. HUNT, J.		4568	
	2/Lt. M.McBEAN		4559	
	" J.T.YEOMAN		4514	

No. 8 Company.

Section Commanders.	Crew Commanders.	Crew Number.	Manufacturers No.	Name of Tank.
No. 5 Section				
2/Lt. E.M. WOLF	2/Lt. H.L.M.COBBAN	C.21	2061	"CURMUDGEON II"
	" D.F.BRUNDRIT	C.22	2731	"CYNIC"
	" H.M.ASHFORTH	C.23	2021	"CRUSTY"

Army Form C. 2118.

WAR DIARY
or
INTELLIGENCE SUMMARY.
(Erase heading not required.)

5-R Bucks /31

Place	Date	Hour	Summary of Events and Information	Remarks and references to Appendices
HEUDICOURT	Dec. 4th		Battalion Resting.	
	5th	9.30 a.m.	Battalion marched from HEUDICOURT (about 350 strong) to BRUSLE, where were billeted in huts.	
	6th	5.45 a.m.	Battalion marched from BRUSLE to TINCOURT & the Transport with rations by road & thence to BOUZINCOURT. Battalion entrained at TINCOURT and detrained at DERNINCOURT, marched through ALBERT to a very comfortable camp of huts between BOUZINCOURT and AVELUY.	
	7th		Rest Camp at BOUZINCOURT and marched ATHENOP when the Battalion plus Transport entrained.	
	8th	11 pm	Detrained 11 a.m. at BERGUETTE and marched to & confortabl billets in FONTES, when the Battalion has not met in January 1916.	
FONTES	9th 10th 11th		Training commenced.	
	12th	9am	The Battalion left FONTES and marched to BUARBECQUE where again very comfortably billeted.	
H(Row)D Bn R.Bucks Regt BUARBECQUE			BUARBECQUE – Following Officers joined for duty from the Lt. C. E. CROUCH Lt. H. H. PAGRAM. Lt. J. L. THOMSON 2nd Lt. J.G. DEWAR 2nd Lt. P. WILMSHURST	
	13th		BUARBECQUE – Training –	

Army Form C. 2118.

WAR DIARY
or
INTELLIGENCE SUMMARY.
(Erase heading not required.)

Instructions regarding War Diaries and Intelligence Summaries are contained in F. S. Regs., Part II. and the Staff Manual respectively. Title pages will be prepared in manuscript.

Place	Date	Hour	Summary of Events and Information	Remarks and references to Appendices
	DEC. 14.		BUARBECQUE - Training Continued	
	15.		do. Draft of 20 OR joined	
	16.	9.30am	B returns left BUARBECQUE and marched to ROBECQ	
	17.		ROBECQ - 2Lt. J.G. RENE and Lt. J.E. RICK NORD joined for duty	
	18.		do. Training	
	19.		do. do.	
	20.		do. do.	
	21.	9.15am	Left ROBECQ and marched to billets in HERVILLE. Lt. Col. E.H.T. NICOLLS in command of 35th Inf.Bde. Major T.V. BLAKELEY DENNISS in command of the Battalion	
	22.		HERVILLE Training Continued	
	23.		do. do.	
	24.		do. do. 2/Lt. T. LODHAM joined for duty.	
	25.		do. Christmas day spent very comfortably in billets. Christmas dinners in Company billets.	
	26.		do.	
	27.		do. Following NCOs and NCOs returned to Battalion 825- R.Q.M.S. PIKE.C. 16mmo Sergt TRINDER. H.E.	

Army Form C. 2118.

WAR DIARY
INTELLIGENCE SUMMARY.
(Erase heading not required.)

Instructions regarding War Diaries and Intelligence Summaries are contained in F. S. Regs., Part II. and the Staff Manual respectively. Title pages will be prepared in manuscript.

Place	Date	Hour	Summary of Events and Information	Remarks and references to Appendices
MERVILLE	Dec 28.		Training Continued.	
do	29.		do	
do	30.		Church Parade MERVILLE hall at 11" a.m.	

McArthur Oeunit
Major Commdg "D"
R. Bucks. Regt.

30/12/17.

35th Brigade.
12th Division.

5th BATTALION

ROYAL BERKSHIRE REGIMENT.

JANUARY 1918

Battalion transferred to 36th Brigade 6.2.18.

Army Form C. 2118.

WAR DIARY
INTELLIGENCE SUMMARY.

Transferred to 1/1/R 36th Bde (Phrase heading not required.)
1/1/R 36 J 32

Instructions regarding War Diaries and Intelligence Summaries are contained in F. S. Regs., Part II. and the Staff Manual respectively. Title pages will be prepared in manuscript.

Place	Date	Hour	Summary of Events and Information	Remarks and references to Appendices
	Dec. 31st			
	Jan 1st		MERVILLE - Training continued during the week. Hard frost.	
	2nd			
	3rd			
	4th			
	5th		Battalion marched from MERVILLE to billets in VERTE RUE and CAUDESCURE. Following Offrs joined for duty; 2/Lt E.A.MACHIN, 2/Lt GREGORY, D.H. BETTS, G.F. CONNING	
	6th		VERTE RUE and CAUDESCURE.	
	7th		The Commander in Chief made the following awards for gallantry in 11th, 20th and 30th.	
	8th		D.S.O. - Lt. Col. E H J NICOLAS M.C. M.C. Capt. J.R WEST	
	9th		Capt. J H REMDY M.C. Bar to M.C. J.R. HAY	
	10th			Hon. Lieut. & Q.M. J.R. OXNEY.
	11th		D.C.M. 11268 Sergt. C SEYMOUR. 16095 " P. LEPPARD.	
			Following are extracts from list of New Years Honours	
			M.C. Capt. C. A. MALLAM.	

Army Form C. 2118.

WAR DIARY
or
INTELLIGENCE SUMMARY.
(Erase heading not required.)

Place	Date	Hour	Summary of Events and Information	Remarks and references to Appendices
	Jan 12 13 14		The Corps Commander awarded M.M.'s and stars following gallantry on Nov 20th and Nov 30th. 9309 Sgt Epsley G. (2nd bar) 7410 Pte Towell G. 10580 " Burton J. (Bar) 9306 L/Cpl Rusher J 10499 L/Cpl Hinton J 10355 Pte Bate A. 10153 A/Sgt Trundle M. 11173 L/Cpl Cookson A. 13035 L/Cpl May F. 10529 Sgt Nicolson N.	
	15		CAUDESCURE and VERTE RUE.	
			Moved to billets in and around DOULIEU. Transport and country forms DOULIEU - Lt G. CAPES joined for duty.	
	16.		"	
	17		"	
	18		" Following Officers joined for duty at attendance at Army Worcester Agr School. 2 Lt. N BARKER " Lts HANDLEY " R. GEE GONEY	
	19			
	20			

Army Form C. 2118.

WAR DIARY
INTELLIGENCE SUMMARY.
(Erase heading not required.)

Place	Date	Hour	Summary of Events and Information	Remarks and references to Appendices
	Jan 21	9.15 am	Left DOUVIEU in Transport and relieved 9th R. Sussex Regt in right Battalion sector of Right Brigade sector, in FLEURBAIX Sector Boundaries NEW BOND St – BROMPTON Rd: both inclusive. Portuguese Right Q"ERSUX on left. Dispositions:- Right front Coy A Coy " " " B " Left " " C " Support " " D Coy (at WINDY POST). Reserve " "	
	22		Relief complete at 11.45 am.	
	23		⎫	
	24		⎪ Front line Trenches. Very quiet sector and great	
	25		⎬ accommodation for all ranks.	
	26		⎪ Casualties. 2 O.R. wounded.	
	27		⎭	
	28		Lt A.G. PUNNETT joined for duty.	
	29	11 am	Relieved by 7th Norfolk Regt and moved into Brigade Reserve – B"Hq ROUSE du BOIS, Companies billeted round RUE	
	30		⎫ Bn Reserve.	
	31		⎭	

E.E. Stephens
Lt Col.
Comdg 9/B/
R. Sutherlin Regt
31/1/18

...idgeshire Regiment

Re-inforcements during January 19..

6. 1. 19   4 ORs
7. 1. 19   1 ORs
8. 1. 19   4 ORs.
16. 1. 19   36 ORs
22. 1. 19   3 ORs.

[signature]
Lieut Col.
Commdg 1st Camb Reg.

1850/2

1st Batallion
Cambridgeshire
Regiment.

12TH DIVISION
35TH INFY BDE

1-1ST BN CAMBRIDGESHIRE REGT

MAY 1918 - MAR 1919

From 39 DN 118 BDE

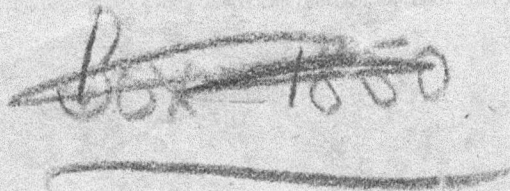

35th Brigade.
12th Division.

1/1st BATTALION

CAMBRIDGESHIRE REGIMENT.

MAY 1918

Battalion joined 35th Brigade from 39th Div. Composite Brigade 9.5.18 and absorbed 7th Suffolk Regt. 19.5.18.
66

Vol 234

War Diary
1/1st Cambs
May, 1918

Absorbed 7" Suffolk 19.5.8

12 Sis
55. Bde

CONFIDENTIAL

Army Form C. 2118.

WAR DIARY or INTELLIGENCE SUMMARY

1/1 Camb.B.R.

(Erase heading not required.)

Fighting Strength 1st May 1918
37 off. 574 o.r.

Place	Date 1918	Hour	Summary of Events and Information	Remarks and references to Appendices
DICKEBUSCH	MAY 1.		The 39th Divisional Composite Brigade was reorganized into two Battalions — No II Batt. consisting of 1/1 Camb.B.R. 1/1 Herts.R. 1/6 Chesh.R and 4/5 Bl.Watch under the command of Major M.C. Clayton DSO 1/1 Camb.B.R. The remainder of the Battalion belongs to the 39th Divisional opening as I Batt.	M.C.C.
		5pm.	Batt. marched from Dominion Camp to a position of readiness at H19a (sheet 28)	
		8.30pm	Batt. returned to Dominion Camp.	
	2	4am.	Batt. moved again to same position and bivouacked there until 10pm on 3rd when orders were received to withdraw to huts at G.10a (Sheet 28) between Busseboom and Poperinghe.	
BUSSEBOOM	3			
	4	3.30am	Batt. arrived. Huts at G.10a (Sheet 28)	
		3pm	Marched to School Camp N.W. of Poperinghe.	
POPERINGHE	5	2pm	Marched to Rouxbrugge	
		11pm	Entrained - less transport which proceeded by road	
RUMINGHEM	6	7pm	Detrained at Watten Station. Here the 39th Divisional Composite Brigade ceased to exist, the various details returning to their own Battalions. The remainder of the Composite Brigade during its time in the line amounted to 46 officers and 1996 o.r. On detrainment 1/1 Camb.R. proceeded to billets at Ruminghem, where a large draft of officers and a number of o.r. awaited them.	
	7 8		Two days were spent in refitting and bathing.	
	9	9.15pm	Batten, less 1/4/5 Bl.Watch marched to Audricques Station.	

Army Form C. 2118.

WAR DIARY
or
INTELLIGENCE SUMMARY   1/1 CAMB. R

(Erase heading not required.)

Instructions regarding War Diaries and Intelligence
Summaries are contained in F. S. Regs., Part II.
and the Staff Manual respectively. Title Pages
will be prepared in manuscript.

Place	Date 1918	Hour	Summary of Events and Information	Remarks and references to Appendices
AUDRICQUES.	May 9	Noon	Bn entrained & proceeded to join 12th Division.	Appendix 77
LEALVILLERS.	10	3pm	Detrained at RINCHEVAL and marched to LEALVILLERS arriving into Divisional Reserve 12th Division.	
	11 12 13 14 15 16 17 18		Continued with refitting and training. Reconnoitred front and made preliminary arrangements with O.C. 7th Suffolk Regt for absorbing approximately 10 offs and 420 O.R.	
ACHEUX.	19	2pm	Marched to ACHEUX into billets, and 11 offs and 408 O.R of 7th SUFFOLK REGT. Battalion was reorganised into 4 companies each of 2 infantry platoons of 3 sections and two LG platoons of two sections each. In addition two HQ LG platoons each of four sections were formed.	Appendix 78.
			A Coy commander Capt A. JOHNSON B " " Capt H.W. BAYNES SMITH M.C C " " Capt U.T. SAVILLE M.C D " " Lt. C.H. BOWERS	
			The above regiments was experienced and under instructions of VII CORPS. Battalion became reserve Battalion of 35th Inf. Bde.	MCC

Army Form C. 2118.

WAR DIARY
or
INTELLIGENCE SUMMARY
(Erase heading not required.)

1/1 Camb. R.

Place	Date 1918	Hour	Summary of Events and Information	Remarks and references to Appendices
MAILLY-MAILLET	MAY 20	8pm	Moved into intermediate line "Jeff" MAILLY SECTOR, east of AUCHONVILLERS RIDGE. Batt HQ in MAILLY MAILLET.	Op. Order 79
	21 22		Summary intermediate line. Wiring parties employed carrying, wiring and deepening the line. No situation though two quiet except for gas shelling and M.G. fire at night. One Officer (2/Lt RUNNE) and 1 NCO were hit by high explosive by E.A. on the centre company HQ.	
	23.		Continued work on trenches. A company who were working through the night camped the centre company.	
	24 25		2/Lt E.O. Saunders proceeded to leave in Engl. and resumed command of the Battn. Continued work on trenches. Wired in front of an enemy strong points in the trenches. Carrying parties and wiring parties appeared to trouble. Enemy artillery active all day damaging horse road as Batt HQ becoming no casualties	
	26	7pm	Moved back HQ to reserve edge of AUCHONVILLERS RIDGE taking over those erected by us b/f from Batt.	
	27	2pm	Relieved by 6/2 DORSET R. of 17th Division. Relief was much impeded by heavy gas barrage and several casualties were caused through "mustard gas."	Op. Order 80
		5am	left ACHEUX WOOD and marched to RAINCHEVAL arriving in billets at 9 pm.	

Army Form C. 2118.

WAR DIARY
or
INTELLIGENCE SUMMARY

(Erase heading not required.)

1/1 Comb K

Place	Date 1918	Hour	Summary of Events and Information	Remarks and references to Appendices
RAINCHEVAL	MAY. 28 29 30 31		In billets. Refitting, training. Commenced individual training and range practice. Fighting Strength May 31st. 43 off. 999 o.r. Appendix - list of Casualties and reinforcements during May 1918.	

McCaw? Major
R.L. H Court?

SECRET.   Copy No. 8

1/1st CAMBRIDGESHIRE REGIMENT.

Operation Order No. 97.

Ref. Map.   In the Field.
HAZEBROUCKE 5A.   8/5/18.

INFORMATION. 1. The 1/1st Camb. Regt will be transferred to the 18th Division. Third Army. Where it will absorb the 7th Suffolk Regt.

INTENTION. 2. The Battalion will entrain at AUDRUICQ and detrain at CANDAS EXCHANGE.

DETAIL. 3.(a) Order of March:- H.Q. A. Band. B. C. D.

(b). Starting Point:- Battalion H.Q. Mess.

(c). H.Q. will pass the Starting point at 8.15 a.m. followed by Coys at one minute interval.

(d). Route:- via POLINCOVE.

(e). Dress:- Full marching order. Box respirators over both shoulders. Steel helmets on packs.

(f). Entraining. Lieut. D. Orbell is detailed as entraining Officer and will proceed with the Transport.

(g). Loading Party. O.C B. Company will detail 1 Sergt. and 20 other ranks to act as loading party. They will report to the Transport Officer at 7.30 a.m.

TRANSPORT. 4. Transport will march independently and will arrive at AUDRUICQ Station at 8.0 a.m.

BAGGAGE. 5. Officers valises, blankets and Medical Stores will be stacked at the Q.M. Stores ready for loading by 7.30 a.m. Mess Stores by 8.0 a.m.

RATIONS. 6. The Q.M. will issue rations for the 10th at the Station.
Breakfast will be at 6.45 a.m. to-morrow.

REPORTS. 7. O.C. Coys will certify the cleanliness of vacated billets, and report the completion of entrainment to Battn. H.Q., on the train.

A C K N O W L E D G E.

(sd). C.H. Mellis. Lieut.
Actg. Adjt. 1/1st Cambridgeshire Regiment.

Copies issued at 8 p.m.
No. 1.   A Company.
 " 2.   B   "
 " 3.   C   "
 " 4.   D   "
 " 5.   H.Q.
 " 6.   Q.M.
 " 7.   T.O.
 " 8.   War Diary.
 " 9.   "   "
 " 10.   Lieut. D. Orbell.
 " 11.   File.

SECRET.
Copy No.

1/1st CAMBRIDGESHIRE REGIMENT.

Operation Order No.75.

In the Field.
16th May 1918.

INTENTION. 1. The 1/1st CAMB. REGT. will move to ACHEUX and take over billets from the 7th SUFFOLK REGT.

DETAIL. 2. (a). Order of March:- Band, A, B, C, D, H.Q.

(b). Starting Point:- H.Q. billet at Eastern End of LEALVILLERS.

(c). A Company will pass the starting point at 2 p.m followed by Coys at 1 min interval.

(d). Dress:- Full marching Order, box respirators over both shoulders. Steel helmets on packs.

BILLETS. 3. Orders have already been issued.

BAGGAGE. 4. Orders have already been issued. Mess stores to be stacked at Q.M.Stores by 1.30 p.m.

DETAILS. 5. The details of the 7th SUFFOLK REGT. will be marched to their respective Company billets at 2 p.m., under arrangements to be made by O.C.7th SUFFOLKS.

REPORTS. 6. O.C.Coys. will certify the cleanliness of vacated billets and report arrival in billets to New Battn. H.Qrs.

ACKNOWLEDGE.

(sd) C.H. Hollis. Lieut.
Actg.Adjt.1/1st Cambridgeshire Regiment.

Copies issued at 11.30 p.m.
No.1. A Coy.
2. B "
3. C "
4. D "
5. H.Q.
6. Q.M.
7. T.O.
8. 7th Suffolks.
9. War Diary.
10. " "
11. File.

SECRET.   Copy No. 8

1/1st CAMBRIDGESHIRE REGIMENT.

Operation Order No. 79.

Ref. Map.   In the Field.
Sheet 57 d. S.E.   29th May 1918.

INFORMATION.   1. Inter-Battalion reliefs will take place on night 30/31st May 1918. in the MAILLY Sector.

INTENTION.   2. The 1/1st CAMB. REGT. will relieve the 9th ESSEX REGT and 1 Company of the 8th BUFFS in Close Support.

Detail.   3. (a). Relief.   Coys will relieve as follows:—

1/1st Camb.R.	9th Essex R.	
Battn.H.Q.	Battn.H.Q.	
A Company.	B Company.	(Left Front)
B "	1 Coy.of h Buffs.R.	(Right Front).
C "	D Company.	(Left Rear).
D "	C "	(Right Rear).

Two H.Q. Reserve Lewis Gun Platoons with C Company.

(b).
        Time.   The Battn. will pass the Starting Point (Battn.H.Q.). at the following times:—

        H.Q.   8.30 p.m.
        C Company   7.30 p.m.
        B "   7.40 p.m.
        D "   8.0 p.m.
        A "   8.10 p.m.

200 yards interval between Platoons.

(b). Guides.   N.C.Os of advance parties will act as Guides under Company arrangements.

(c). Dress.   Full Marching Order.

ADVANCE PARTIES.   4. Advance Party of 1 Officer per Company and 1 N.C.O. per platoon and the R.S.M. will proceed to the Support Line at 3.30 p.m. to take over stores etc.

LEWIS GUNS.   5. Lewis Guns, Magazines etc., will be carried on the Company Lewis Gun Limbers which will move in rear of their respective companies.

Blankets & VALISES.   6. Blankets rolled in bundles of 10 and labelled will be stacked at the Q.M.Stores by 3 p.m. Officers' valises will be stacked at Q.M.Stores by 2 p.m.

MESS STORES.   7. Mess Stores, dixies etc., required for the line will be taken up on Company Lewis Gun Limbers.

RATIONS.   8. Rations for to-morrow will be taken on L.G. Limbers.

DETAILS.   9. Instructions as to number of details to be left out of the line will be issued later.

REPORTS.   10. (a). O.C.Coys will report relief complete to Bn H.Q.   Code Words "RUM UP".

(b). Lists of Trench Stores taken over and certificates of cleanliness of vacated billets will be sent to Battn.H.Q., by 12 noon 31:5:18.

ACKNOWLEDGE.   (sd). C.H. Hollis. Lieut.
Copies issued at   Actg.Adjt. 1/1st Cambridgeshire Regiment.
  No.1. A Coy.   No. 6 Q.M.
  " 2. B "   "   7 T.O.
  " 3. C "   " 8 & 9 War Diary.
  " 4. D "   " 10. File.
  " 5. H.Q.

SECRET   Copy No. 16

1/1st CAMBRIDGESHIRE REGIMENT.

Operation Order No. 80

Ref. Map.   In the Field.
Sheet. 57d. 1/40,000.   26th May 1918.

INFORMATION.   1.(a). The 12th Division (less Artillery) will be relieved in the MAILLY SECTOR on May 25th and the following days.

(b). The 35th Infantry Brigade will be relieved by the 50th Infantry Brigade in the MAILLY LEFT SECTOR on the night May 26/27th 1918.

INTENTION.   2.(a). The 1/1st CAMB. REGT. will be relieved by the 6th DORSETSHIRE REGIMENT in CLOSE SUPPORT.

(b). After relief the battalion will proceed to billets at RAINCHEVAL.

INSTRUCTIONS.   3.(a). <u>Relief.</u> Coys will relieve as follws:-

1/1st Camb.R.	6th Dorsetshire Regt.
Battn. H.Q.	Battn. H.Q.
A Company.	A Company.
B "	B "
C "	C "
D "	D "

(b). <u>Time.</u>   6th Dorsets may be expected about 12.30 a.m.

(c). <u>Guides.</u>   1 guide per Platoon and 1 per Battn. H.Q., will report to an Officer to be detailed by O.C. C Company, at junction where "C" Track cuts Railway Line (MAILLY MAILLET) Station at 12.15a.m.

(d). <u>Route.</u>   "C" Track to O.12. Track to O.9.d.2.2. road to AR QUEVES - RAINCHEVAL.

(e). <u>Advance Parties.</u> Instructions have already been issued.

(f). <u>Lewis Guns and Mess Stores.</u> Limbers will report to Company ration dump for Lewis Guns and Mess Stores.

(g). <u>Rations.</u> The battalion will halt West of ACHEUX for tea. Breakfast on arrival in billets.

REPORTS.   4.(a). All defence schemes, trench stores and detail of work in hand will be handed over on relief. Reserve of water will be handed over and seperate receipt taken. Receipts to be forwarded to Battn. H.Q. by 4.0 p.m. May 27th. 1918.

(b). Completion of relief will be notified to these H.Qrs. by the Code Word "MAUD".

ACKNOWLEDGE.

(sd). C.H. Hollis. Lieut.
Actg. Adjt 1/1st Cambridgeshire Regiment.

Copies issued at p.m. 25th instm
No. 1. C.O.
" 2. A Coy.
" 3. B "
" 4. C "
" 5. D "
" 6. H.Q.
" 7. Q.M.
" 8. T.O.
" 9. War Diary.
" 10. " "
" 11. File.

1/1st Cambridgeshire Regiment.

Casualties during May, 1918.

May 14th.	1 O.R.	Killed.	
" 21st.	Lieut. J.E.Ruane.	Wounded.	
	2 O.R.	Wounded.	
" 23rd.	1 O.R.	"	
" 24th.	1 O.R.	"	
" 25th.	2 O.R.	"	
" 26th.	3 O.R.	"	
" 27th.	12 O.R.	"	(1 at duty).
" 28th.	2 O.R.	"	

Reinforcements during May, 1918.

May 8th.   Capt. ~~H.H.Hadden~~ U.J.Saville. Rejoined from 118 TMB

May 19th.
- Capt. E.J.Greene. M.C.)
- Lieut. V.N.Rawes.)
- " F.M.Wilson.)
- " H.C.Crosher.)
- " C.J.Webb.)
- 2/Lt. F.M.Bond.)   Joined from 7th Suffolks.
- " G.G.R.Nock.)
- " H.L.Pedley.)
- " R.J.Lawler. M.M.)
- " E.L.Hope.)
- " H.A.Aldrich. M.C.)

408 O.R.   ditto.

35th Brigade.
12th Division

1/1st BATTALION

CAMBRIDGESHIRE REGIMENT.

JUNE 1918

No 25

Ivan Berry
11th Cambs
Regt

June, 1918.

WAR DIARY or INTELLIGENCE SUMMARY

Army Form C. 2118.

1/1st CAMBRIDGESHIRE REGT

Place	Date	Hour	Summary of Events and Information	Remarks and references to Appendices
RAINCHEVAL	1/6/16 to 15/6/16		During this period, the Battalion was at rest and training in the village of Raincheval. The nature of training was chiefly (open fighting), and the Batt. also acting as G.H.Q. reserve.	Bt. Orders
HEDAUVILLE	16.6.16		The Battalion, less "Battle surplus" personnel, marched to HEDAUVILLE and bivouacked along a track in P.33.b (Ref. Sheet 57.D.S.E) where it was acting as reserve battalion of the 35th Brigade. Bns. were entrained to DONQUER (detailed) under Major L.C. Clayton D.S.O.	Bt. Orders Mills No 31
	19.6.16		Remained in position in that area until the 19th June, when the Batt. moved to another position in area V.2.d, where bivouacs were constructed behind a steep bank.	
	19.6.16 to 21.6.16		This period was spent in building and improving new shelters, and in Physical training, bayonet fighting, games and inter platoon competitions. Large working parties were sent each night to the front line "Purple" lines. Officers reconnoitred all sectors of the front line which the Batt. was about to take over.	P.S.

WAR DIARY
or
INTELLIGENCE SUMMARY

(Erase heading not required.)

Army Form C. 2118.

1/1st CAMBRIDGESHIRE REGT

Place	Date	Hour	Summary of Events and Information	Remarks and references to Appendices
22.6.18.			On the night of the 22/23rd June, the Battalion relieved the 6th Queens Regt. in the Front Line position of the left Sub-sector of the 12th Divisional Front, in positions E. and S. of MARTINSART, as follows:— HEATHCOTES BANK, LOTHIAN TRENCH, SAUCHIEHALL FRONT, SUPPORT, and RESERVE TRENCHES, OLDHAM STREET, and one Company in reserve in BOUZINCOURT TRENCH. (N.E. of BOUZINCOURT.)	Ref. Operation Order No 82. (attached).
23.6.18			Capt. E. Walker, M.C., joined the Battn. detail.	
26.6.18			Lieut A Jackson " " " " "	
29.6.18			Lieut. E. Hay " " " " "	
{30.6.18 / 1.7.18}			On the night of the 30th June – 1st July, a minor operation was carried out by 2 Officers (2.Lt. B. L. Hope and 2.Lt. R. G. Francis), and 32 O.R. 30 enemy were encountered & enemy machine gun party was interfering m.g. and T.M. fire, and after causing at least 3 enemy casualties, was forced to retire. Casualties – 2 Lt. Francis and 3 men wounded	

Battn. Strength June 30th 3 Offrs 999 ORs
"   "   "   "   "   "   "   "   40   " 1044 ORs

[signatures]

SECRET   Copy No 9

1/1st CAMBRIDGESHIRE REGIMENT.

Operation Order No. 81.

Ref. Map.
Sheet 57 D.   In the Field.
                                                              18th June 1918.

INFORMATION.   1.   The 12th Division (less Artillery) will
                  relieve the 38th Division (Less Artillery) in the
                  right (AVELUY) Sector of the VTH Corps Front
                  between June 18th and 19th.
                  The 36th Infantry Brigade will relieve the 115th
                  Infantry Brigade.

INTENTION.   2.   The 1/1st CAMB. Regt will relieve the 4th
                  N.STAFFS Regt in the Area about P.33, b.c.d.

INSTRUCTIONS.   3 (a) Dress.   Full Marching Order.

                  (b) Order of March A, B, H.Q., D, C.

                  (c) Starting Point. The starting point will be
                  the level crossing N.19 d.3.0. Coys will pass the
                  point as follows:-
                       A Company.   2.55 p.m.
                       B   "   3.1 p.m.
                       H.Q.   3.3 p.m.
                       D Company.   3.5 p.m.
                       C   "   3.8 p.m.
                  A distance of 200 yards will be maintained between
                  Coys.
                  (d) Advance Party. 1 N.C.O. per Company and 1 for
                  H.Q., will report to Lieut. C. WARREN at Battn. H.Q.
                  at 11 a.m.
                  (e) Guides. Guides will meet the Battalion AT
                  P.27. central.
                  (f) B.S.Personnel. The Battle Surplus Personnel will
                  move under orders from Major. H.C.CLAYTON. D.S.O.
                  (g) Officers Kits, Mess Stores. These will be
                  stacked ready for loading in the yard of the Officers
                  mess by 1 p.m.
                  (h) L.G.Stores. Stores to be loaded on Company
                  L.G.Limbers will be stacked ready for loading in the
                  Company billet yard and a small loading party detailed
                  by 11 a.m.
                  (i) Transport. As per instructions already issued
                  to the Transport Officer.

REPORTS.   4.   O.C Coys will certify in writing the cleanliness
                  vacated billets at RAINCHEVAL to Battn. H.Q., by 2 p.m
                  tonight.
                  Relief will be reported by the code word "7,000.
                       Complete

                                  (sd). A.Johnson. Capt.& Adjt.
Copies issued at a,m,   1/1st Cambridgeshire Regiment.
No 1.   C.O.
 " 2.   A Coy.
 " 3.   B "
 " 4.   C "
 " 5.   D "
 " 6.   H.Q.
 " 7.   T.O.
 " 8.   War Diary.
 " 10.   "   "
 " 11. Lieut.C.Warren.
 " 12. Major.H.C.CLAYTON.D.S.O.
 " 13. File.

SECRET.   Copy No. 11
                    1/1st CAMBRIDGESHIRE REGIMENT.
                    NNN----------------------------

Ref. Map.   In the Field.
Sheet. 57D. S.E.   Operation Order No. 82.   21st June 1918.
==

INFORMATION.   1. There will be an inter-Brigade relief in the Left
               Sub-Sector of the Divisional Front on the night
               22/23rd June 1918.

INTENTION.   2. The 1/1st Cambridgeshire Regiment will relieve
               the 6th Queens Regt in the Front System.

INSTRUCTIONS. 3. (a). Dress:- Full Marching Order.
                  (b) Order Of March:- A, B, C, D, H.Q.
                  (c). Starting Point:- V.8.d.6.6.
               Companies will pass this point as follows:-
                  A Company.   9.55 p.m.
                  B   "   10.10 p.m.
                  C   "   10.25 p.m.
                  D   "   10.40 p.m.
                  H.Q.   10.55 p.m.
               Companies will march 200 yards between platoons.
                  (d). Guides. 1 guide per Company and 1 for Battn. H.Q.,
               will be at P.34.b.6.0., at 10.30 p.m. Platoon and
               Post guides will be at Battn. H.Q., at Q.32.d.3.0.
               Up to this point rear platoons of Companies must arrange
               for keeping conection with leading platoons.
                  (e). Relief. A Coy. will relieve the Left Front Company
                               B "   "   "   "   "   Right "   "
                               C "   "   "   "   "   Support Company.
                               D "   "   "   "   "   Reserve Company.
               Battn. H.Q., will relieve Battn. H.Q.
                  (f). Advance Parties. Advance Parties consisting of
               C.S.M's and 1 N.C.O. per platoon will precede the
               Battalion, starting at 2.0 p.m.
                  (g). Lewis Guns. Lewis-Guns will be man-Handled up
               to the line.
                  (h). Officers valises. etc.. Officers valises, and all
               Company Stores to go back to the Transport will be
               dumped at the Battn. salvage dump by 8.30 p.m.
                  (i). Rations. Rations for the 23rd will be brought
               here, issued and carried on the man.
                  (j). Cooks. etc.. Cooks and others not to go up the
               line will go back to the Transport at 8.30 p.m. with
               stores etc..

REPORTS.   4. Lists of Trench Stores, documents. etc., to be taken
               over, and reports of cleanliness of vacated billets will
               be forwarded to Battn. H.Q. by 12 noon 23rd inst..
               Relief complete will be reported to Battn. H.Q. by runner
               by Code Words as follows:-
                   A Company. ARE WE DOWNHEARTED ?
                   B   "   THE BING BOYS ARE HERE.
                   C   "   CALL ME EARLY MOTHER DEAR
                   D   "   DON'T GO DOWN THE MINE DAD DY.

ACKNOWLEDGE.
                                       (sd). A. Johnson. Capt. & Adjt.
Copies issued at   p.m.   1/1st Cambridgeshire Regiment.
No. 1.   C.O.
 "   2. A Company.
 "   3. B   "
 "   4. C   "
 "   5. D   "
 "   6. H.Q.
 "   7. Q.M.
 "   8. T.O.
 "   9. O.C. 6th Queens Regt.
 " 10. & 11. War Diary.
 " 12. File.

"Reinforcements" during June 1918.

June 2nd   4 other ranks
"   5th   32   "   "
"   6th   11   "   "
"   7th   1   "   "
"   8th   9   "   "
"   9th   3   "   "
" 11th   8   "   "
" 13th   1   "   "
" 14th   1   "   "
" 15th   1   "   "
" 18th   22   "   "
" 20th   2   "   "
" 23rd Capt. C.Walker M.C & 2 other ranks
" 25th   1   other rank.
" 26th Lieut A Jackson & 1 other rank.
" 29th Lieut E. Hay & 1 other rank.

Casualties during June 1918.

June 4th wounded 1 other rank.
 "   5th   "   1   "   "
 " 26th   "   1   "   "
 " 27th   "   2   "   "
 " 28th   "   4   "   "
 " 30th   "   2nd Lt C.G Francis
                and 3 other Ranks.

35th Brigade.
12th Division

1/1st BATTALION

CAMBRIDGESHIRE REGIMENT.

JULY 1 9 1 8

War Diary
for
July - 1918.

1/1 st Cambs Regt

WAR DIARY or INTELLIGENCE SUMMARY

Army Form C. 2118.

1/1st Cambridgeshire Regt.

Place	Date	Hour	Summary of Events and Information	Remarks and references to Appendices
Martinsart	July 1st 1916		The Battalion was in the line on the left sub-sector of the AVELUY sector, in position N. and E. of MARTINSART. The situation was quiet except for occasional shelling of the support companies & slight shelling and gas at night.	
"	2nd		Fairly quiet — continued work on trenches and wiring ahead of wiring parties in front and support system.	
"	3rd			
"	4th			
"	5th	2.0 p.m.	The General Officer made a tour of inspection of the line.	
		2.30 p.m.	40 O.R's (reinforcements) arrived under R.S.M. Burtt, who took over the duties of R.S.M. in the Battalion.	
		6 p.m.	Major Blake arrived from School to assume command of Battalion while the Brigadier was on leave, during which period Lt. Col went with Major Clay to return to 118th DONCIER.	
	6th			

WAR DIARY
or
INTELLIGENCE SUMMARY 1/1st Cambridgeshire Regt

Army Form C. 2118.

Place	Date	Hour	Summary of Events and Information	Remarks and references to Appendices
MARTINSART	July 7th		Everything quiet. 2nd Lt Lawler arrives from details	
	8th		At 4.40am enemy put down a barrage on MARTINSART and our left front company lasting for 1½ hours, but no infantry action followed.	
		10.30am	A party of officers of the 10th Cheshires about to reconnoitre line, present to taking over from us.	
		9.30pm	A strong patrol of 1 officer (2nd Lt S. Taylor) and (R28.d.O.75) 2nd Lt 14 O.R.s went from H.9.2.5.4 (R4.5YD.SE) to a point from waterlifarm from the purpose. Patrol proceeded in an easterly direction down the EMBANKMENT. After reconnoitring the EMBANKMENT patrol was divided & 1 officer & 14 O.Rs proceeded to the E. end of EMBANKMENT —(H.9.d.55.) & from there 1 NCO & 10r. proceeded to ascertain the position of enemy post and and round same. These posts were located within 100x. and the enemy wire was found to be a concertina obstacle, 30x in depth attached to the EMBANKMENT, and cut for its	B.S.

WAR DIARY or INTELLIGENCE SUMMARY

Army Form C. 2118.

11th Cambridgeshire Regiment

Place	Date	Hour	Summary of Events and Information	Remarks and references to Appendices
MARTINSART	July 8th	Cont	remainder of the party, the patrol being then disposed as follows:- 1 section (1 NCO + 6 men) approached enemy post at W.9.b.5.4 from the left and another section from the right, at about 20' interval. The officer + 7 ORs remained at E. end of EMBANKMENT to cut post off from above + also had out the wire. One section waited the approach of patrol from W.9.b.4.5. when the right section had penetrated about half way through, they were discovered and fired upon at about 20 rounds very accurately, and this section had to withdraw. Meanwhile the left section, seeing what was happening, and finding themselves entangled with a thick belt of wire, vigorously bombed the post, several bombs being seen to explode in the trench, and the M.G. that was apparently put out of action, as it did not fire again. The whole unit being then thoroughly alert, the patrol withdrew to our own lines (at 2.5 am)	
"	"	9ᵃ	Very quiet. Preparations made for relief. Battn. was relieved by the 10th Sherwoods at 11 am and marched back to HERISSART, arriving in billets at 7 p.m.	Appendix " 9

Army Form C. 2118.

WAR DIARY
or
INTELLIGENCE SUMMARY

1/1st Cambridgeshire Regiment

(Erase heading not required.)

Instructions regarding War Diaries and Intelligence Summaries are contained in F.S. Regs., Part II. and the Staff Manual respectively. Title Pages will be prepared in manuscript.

Place	Date July	Hour	Summary of Events and Information	Remarks and references to Appendices
HERISART	10th & 11th		Spent in resting and cleaning up.	
	12th		Orders received to be ready to move at 6.0 a.m. on the 13th. Details for DOMQUER arrive.	Appendix III
	13th		Batt⁰ left HERISART at 9.0 a.m. and marched past the Div¹ General, getting into buses and lorries at 11.45 a.m. Route through AMIENS to RUMIGNY where Batt⁰ was billeted in the village.	
RUMIGNY	14th to 29th		Training from 9 a.m. to 1 p.m. Football and sports each afternoon.	
	30th	9 a.m	Battalion leaves RUMIGNY and entrains for CANAPLES, arriving there at 4.0 p.m. and is billetted in the village.	Appendix 4
	31st		A holiday is granted by the C.O. in commemoration of the attack by the Batt⁰ at ST JULIEN on the 31st July, 1917. Water sports are held in the afternoon. Strength of Batt⁰ on 1/7/18. 40 Offrs & 1044 ORs. " " " " 31/7/18. 42 " & 1055 ".	BO

W Waugh Major
Comdg 1/1 Camb⁵ Regt

2449 Wt. W14957/M90 750,000 1/16 J.B.C. & A. Forms/C.2118/12.

SECRET.   Appendix 1.
                                                              Copy No. 12.

1/1st CAMBRIDGESHIRE REGIMENT.

MINOR OPERATION.

Ref. Map. 57d. S.E.   July 8th 1918.

INFORMATION.   1. An early enemy attack is anticipated on this
                   front. An identification is urgently needed.
                   The 1/1st Camb. Regt. will secure a prisoner
                   to-night. 7th Norfolk Regt. are also raiding posts
                   in AVELUY WOOD to-night.

INTENTION.   2. A strong patrol of 1 Officer, 4 N.C.Os. and 24
                   men will raid the enemy post W.9.b.5.4. to-night.
                   Failing capture of prisoner at this point, patrol
                   will push along enemy trench until one is secured.

INSTRUCTIONS. 3.(a). 2nd Lt. S.TAYLOR will command patrol.
                   Full instructions have been issued to him.
                   (b). 35th Stokes Mortar Battery will fire 50
                   shells on targets between W.4.c.3.5. and W.10.a.4.7.
                   (West edge of AVELUY WOOD) at Zero hour.
                   (c). 6" NEWTONS will fire 10 shells on W.3.d.9.2
                   10 on W.9.b.9.8. and 10 on W.9.b.3.3. at same hour.
                       Should a prisoner be captured before Zero
                   hour, instructions contained in (b) and (c) above
                   will be cancelled, Code Word "CLOSE DOWN" being
                   used.
                       In this case Stokes will fire one round per
                   mortar only. 6" NEWTONS will not fire.
                       In addition to Code Word mentioned above a
                   green Very Light will be fired from SAUCHIEHALL
                   TRENCH, immediately a prisoner reaches our lines

ZERO HOUR.   4. Zero Hour will be 1.30 a.m.

REPORTS.   5. O.C. D Coy. is responsible for sending Code Word
                   to 35th T.M. battery by runner, and 6" NEWTON
                   Battery by wire direct. This message will be
                   repeated to Battn. H.Q. immediately.

                                   (sd) Edward. T. Saint. Lt. Col.
                              Comdg. 1/1st Cambridgeshire Regiment.

Copies to
No. 1.   2nd LT. S.TAYLOR.
 "   2.   A Coy.
 "   3.   B Coy.
 "   4.   C Coy.
 "   5.   D Coy.
 "   6.   35th T.M.Batty.(In the Line).
 "   7.   6" NEWTONS.
 "   8.   35th Inf. BDE.
 "   9.   7th Norfolks.
 " 10.   5th R.Berks.
 " 11.   War Diary.
 " 12.   "
 " 13.   File.
 " 14.   C.O.

SECRET.   Copy No. 9

1/1st Cambridgeshire Regiment.

Operation Order. No. 88.

Ref. Map. 57d.   In the Field.
                                    8:7:18.

INFORMATION 1. (a). The 18th Division (less artillery) will be relieved in the AVELUY Sector on July 9th and following days.
(b). The 35th Infantry Brigade will be relieved by the 51st Infantry Brigade, in the AVELUY Left Sector on the night July 9th/10th.

INTENTION. 2. (a). The 1/1st CAMBRIDGESHIRE REGIMENT will be relieved by the 10th SHERWOOD FORESTERS (NOTTS & DERBY REGT.) in the Right Front sub-sector.
(b). After relief the Battalion will march to HERISSART.

INSTRUCTIONS. 3. (a). RELIEF. Coys. will be relieved as follows:-

1/1 Cambs.	10th Sherwoods
Battn H.Q.	Battn. H.Q.
A. Coy.	A. Coy.
B. Coy.	B. Coy.
C. Coy.	C. Coy.
D. Coy.	D. Coy.

(b). TIME. 10th SHERWOOD FORESTERS may be expected about 11 p.m.
(c). GUIDES. 1 guide per platoon and 1 for Battn. H.Q. will report to an Officer, to be detailed by O.C. A.Coy. at Battn. H.Q. at 7.30 p.m.
(d). CONCENTRATION. The Battalion will form up at head of valley V.2.d.
(e). ROUTE. "A" Track to HEDAUVILLE - road to V.3.d. - Track to V.2.c. - Track to HERISSART.
(f). DISTANCES. East of WARLOY 200^x will be maintained between companies.
(g). ADVANCE PARTIES. Instructions have already been issued.
(h). RATIONS. The Cookers will be at V.2.d.3.3. where tea will be taken. Breakfasts on arrival at billets.
(i). L.Gs. MESS STORES, etc., L.G.Limbers will be at usual company ration dumps at 12 midnight (i.e. A.C.&H.Q at Battn. HQ B.& D Coys. at B Coy H.Q.) for L.Gs. and Mess Stores.

REPORTS. 4. (a). All Defence Schemes, Trench Stores, details of work in hand, maps etc., will be handed over on relief. Reserve water will be handed over and separate receipts taken. Receipts to be forwarded to Battn. H.Q. by 4 p.m. 10th inst.
(b). Relief complete will be notified to Battn. H.Q. by wire, by Code Words "SENDING SALVAGE

ACKNOWLEDGE.

Copies. at... t o
No.1 C.O.   No 7. T.O
" 2 A.Coy.   " 8. 10th Sherwoods.
" 3 B.Coy.   " 9. War Diary.
" 4 C.Coy.   " 10. "
" 5 D.Coy.   " 11. File.
" 6 Q.M.

                              (sd) A.Johnson. Capt. & Adjt.
                                 1/1st Cambridgeshire Regiment.

SECRET.

Appendix III

1/1st CAMBRIDGESHIRE REGIMENT.

Copy No. 11

Operation Order No. 89.

Ref. Map.
LENS.11. 1/100,000.

In the Field.
13:7:18.

INFORMATION.   1.   35th Infantry Brigade will move by bus to-morrow.

INTENTION.   2.   The 1/1st Cambridgeshire Regiment will embus on the RUBEMPRE - PUCHEVILLERS road.

INSTRUCTIONS.   3. (a). Starting Point.   Cross roads 300 yards West of HERISSART CHURCH (6.E.97.34).

(b). Order of March:- D, H.Q., A, B, C.
(c). Times of passing starting point:-

D Company.   8.58 a.m.
H.Q.   8.59 a.m.
A Company.   9.0 a.m.
B "   9.1 a.m.
C "   9.2 a.m.

On the march to the embussing point 50 yards will be maintained between Companies.

(d). Mess stores. Mess boxes to be at Q.M.Stores by 8 a.m. Stores not there by that time will not be loaded.

(e). Transport. Under orders already issued to T.O. Cookers will return to Transport to-night. 1 cook will accompany each cooker.

(f). Camp kettles. Companies will carry camp kettles for use on arrival.

(g). Loading party. D Company will detail two platoons complete (total strength 2 Officers and 50 other ranks) as loading party for transport. They will report at Town Major's Office HERISSART at 7.20 a.m., whence lorries will take them to ROSEL.

(h). Organization. The Battalion will be told off in 12 parties of 20 and 23 parties of 25 on arrival at embussing point.

(i). Billeting parties. C.Q.M.S's will report to 2nd.Lieut. R.J. LAWLER. M.M., at starting point at 8.55 a.m., bringing embussing states with them.

(j). Billets. Particular care will be taken that the vicinity of billets is kept scrupulously clean.

REPORTS.   4.   Certificates of cleanliness of billets to the Adjutant at Embussing point.

ACKNOWLEDGE.

(sd). A. Johnson. Capt. & Adjt.
1/1st Cambridgeshire Regiment.

Copies issued at 12.15 a.m.
Copy No. 1.   C.O.
" " 2.   A Company.
" " 3.   B "
" " 4.   C "
" " 5.   D "
" " 6.   H.Q.
" " 7.   Q.M.
" " 8.   T.O.
" " 9.   2nd.Lieut. R.J. Lawler. M.M.
" " 10.   War Diary.
" " 11.   " "
" " 12.   File.

SECRET.

Appendix IV

1/1st CAMBRIDGESHIRE REGIMENT.

Copy No. 9.

Operation Order. No. 90.

Ref. Maps.
AMIENS 17. & LENS 11. 1/100,000.

In the Field.
30th July 1918.

INFORMATION. 1. The 35th Infantry Brigade will move to the VIGNACOURT AREA to-day by march route and train.

INTENTION. 2. The 1/1st Cambridgeshire Regiment will proceed by march route to PROUZEL STATION and entrain there

INSTRUCTIONS. 3. (1). Parade. The Battalion will move in column of route in the following order:-
Band, A, B C, D, H.Q.
The Head of the column will pass Battalion Headquarters at 9.0 a.m.
A distance of 100 yards will be maintained between Coys throughout.

(2). Dress. Full marching order.

(3). Route. Point 133. ½ mile West of RUMIGNY — ST SAUFLIEU — PROUZEL STATION.

(4). Lewis Guns. Each Company will send 4 Lewis Guns and 20 drums per gun to the Q.M. Stores by 8.30 a.m. Remaining Lewis Guns and Ammunition will be conveyed on the Lewis Gun Limbers.
1 N.C.O and 3 men per Company will report to the Transport for A.A. Duties.

(5). Baggage. Mess stores. etc.. This will be conveyed by lorry, and will be dumped at the Q.M. Stores by 8.30 a.m.

(6). Transport. Transport will proceed by march route. Cookers. Lewis Gun limbers and Officers Chargers will accompany the Transport.
Starting Point for Transport:- Cross Roads ½ mile North of Church at HEBECOURT.
Transport will be in position at this point at 11.30 a.m.

REPORTS. 4 (1). Billets. Billets will be left in a scrupulously clean condition.
Certificates to this effect will be handed in at the starting point.

(2). Report of arrival and location of new Billets will be sent to Battn. H.Qrs. on arrival.

(sd). E. Walker. Capt. & A/Adjt.
1/1st Cambridgeshire Regiment.

Copies issued at   a.m.
No.1. C.O.
 " 2. A Company.
 " 3. B   "
 " 4. C   "
 " 5. D   "
 " 6. H.Q.
 " 7. Q.M.
 " 8. T.O.
 " 9.& 10. War Diary.
 " 11 File.

1/1st Cambridgeshire Regiment.

Reinforcements during Month of July, 1918.

5:7:18.
                    1 O.R.

7:7:18.
                    1 O.R.

8:7:18.
                    2 O.R.

9:7:18.
                    3 O.R.

20:7:18.
                    Capt. B.H.Wallis. (A.S.C.)
                    Lieut.A.M.Fison.
                        "   K.H.Clayton.
                    63 O.R.

23:7:18.   1 O.R.

1/1st Cambridgeshire Regiment.

Casualties during Month of July, 1918.

Date	Name	Casualty
1:7:18.	2/Lt. E.G.Francis.	Wounded.
	3 O.Rs.	"
2:7:18.	7 O.Rs.	Wounded. (1 accidentally & 1 since died)
3:7:18.	2/Lt. H.L.Finding.	Wounded.
	1 O.R.	Killed.
	3 O.Rs.	Wounded.
4:7:18.	3 O.Rs.	Wounded. (1 since died).
8:7:18.	2 O.Rs.	Wounded.
9:7:18.	3 O.Rs.	Wounded.

35th Brigade.
12th Division.

1/1st BATTALION

CAMBRIDGESHIRE REGIMENT.

AUGUST 1 9 . 1 8

35/7 1/1 Cambridge
War Diary Vol 27
for
August 1918

1/1st Camb Regt

Sheet 62d NE.
61c N.W.
57c S.W.

WAR DIARY or INTELLIGENCE SUMMARY

Army Form C. 2118.

1/1 Camb. R.

(Erase heading not required.)

Place	Date 1916 AUG.	Hour	Summary of Events and Information	Remarks and references to Appendices
CANAPLES.	1		Reconnaissance carried out of support lines at BUIRE-SUR-ANCRE & RIBEMONT	
	2	12.30pm	Entrained at 12.30pm - detrained at CONTAY - FRANKVILLERS Road and marched via ROUND WOOD to FRANKVILLERS to supports in RIBEMONT	9 Other ranks 91.
RIBEMONT.	3 4 5 6		Manual head work - wiring and improving Trenches.	
	7	6pm	Batt. moved to BALLARAT & BENDIGO lines south of RIVE ANCRE	
MORLANCOURT	8	4.20am	Batt. attacked and captured enemy front line W of MORLANCOURT.	9 Other ranks 2. Appendix I
	9	5.30pm	Batt attacked and captured MORLANCOURT.	Appendix II
	10.		In reserve in trenches sunken road in K 8 c.	
	11 12 13 14 15		ditto Reorganised & reequipped	
	16	10pm	Relieved 5 A.R. Berks in line of supports vicinity K 4 b & K 5 S.E. of MORLANCOURT	9 Other ranks 93.
	17 18		In line night working.	
	19	10pm	Relieved by 9 A. Essex R. and moved into Div. Reserve in K 1 c.	9 Other ranks 94.
VILLE-S-ANCRE				

Sheet 62d NE
62 c NW
57 c SW
57 c SW

Army Form C. 2118.

WAR DIARY
or
INTELLIGENCE SUMMARY

1/1 Camer R

(Erase heading not required.)

Place	Date 1916	Hour	Summary of Events and Information	Remarks and references to Appendices
VILLE S/ANCRE	20		In reserve in K.1.C. Coy HQs & reconnaissance carried out	
	21	9pm	Moved into position in trenches in E.41 - E.5 a r c Infantry trenches.	
MEAULTE	22	4.15am	Move was completed at 4.30am on 22nd. Capt Edmondson & Lt C.W. Warren. Moved was most difficult owing to continual sniping by the enemy & several casualties were caused during the jump. At 4.45 am the barrage opened & the advance commenced with objective the BRAY-MÉAULTE road from F.19d 3.0 to F.19 a 2.2. There was a thick mist & the smoke from the barrage made it most difficult to maintain direction. Considerable opposition was met with from machine guns in shell holes. The objective was reached at 6.20am and consolidated. About 15-20 M-Gs were captured and two 77mm guns. There was considerable hostile shelling throughout the day and on the 1st line on our left became active a the right flank and on the ½ brigade on our right. The situation on the [?] became obscure & Bn HQ was moved into a strong point. The situation was eventually cleared up by the reserve brigade which came up supported by tanks. There were 12 Officer casualties during the day a diligent attn [?]	McC

Sheet 62d N.E.
62c N.W.
57c S.W.

Army Form C. 2118.

WAR DIARY
or
INTELLIGENCE SUMMARY   1/1 Camb R

(Erase heading not required.)

Instructions regarding War Diaries and Intelligence Summaries are contained in F. S. Regs., Part II. and the Staff Manual respectively. Title Pages will be prepared in manuscript.

Place	Date 1918	Hour	Summary of Events and Information	Remarks and references to Appendices
MORLANCOURT	AUG 22 (cont)		The remaining Officers the battn. also suffered a severe loss through the death in action of CSM H. BETTS. This warrant Officer had been serving in France since Feb 1915. He proved himself one of the gamest leaders the battalion has ever had. Although many times recommended he did not receive his DCM until Sept 1917, he won a bar to this DCM in March 1918 and was recommended for the Military Cross for his great work at MORLANCOURT on 9/8/18 - where he single handed attacked and captured 30 prisoners.	
	23.		Consolidating position	
	24.	2pm	Relieved by 1/4 R.W. Kent R — moved back to position in reserve road at E.24.d (MORLANCOURT — MEAULTE road) Reorganised & reequipped	
MEAULTE	25	2.30am	Moved to a position about 500 yds S.E. of MEAULTE in support of 36 & 37 Bde	
		11am	Information received that enemy was withdrawing. In Liezer 36 & 37 Bdes were following him up. Battn. moved forward in K.15d. until C.O. advanced & was	
		3.25p	Battn. pushed through troops in front was ordered to seize L. & ridge in A.5 & C. Four Hally trenches were occupied. Chg for MC

2449 Wt. W14957/M90 750,000 1/16 J.B.C. & A. Forms/C.2118/12.

WAR DIARY or INTELLIGENCE SUMMARY

Army Form C. 2118.

Sheet 62d NE
62c NW
57c SW

1/1 Comb R

Place	Date 1916	Hour	Summary of Events and Information	Remarks and references to Appendices
MAMETZ	25 (cont)		Having advanced spasmodically. Heavy barrage was put down by the enemy and considerable fire was brought to bear from M-Gs on the forward slope and summit of the ridge. Stokes rifle and 18 pdrs on the occasion L Gs being first brought to bear over the crest for the final advance. The ridge was cleared up to within 100 yds of the summit by snipers who continued to engage by bursts of fire the enemy M-Gs in the crest. A post was therefore established about 100 yds short of the crest.	
	26	8am	Coy withdrawn B5&7+R at F10.1 & 2.	
		3 pm	Enemy noticed forming up and A+B being put to summit.	
MARICOURT	27	10am	Further advance in artillery formation. HW Barges [?] someone in sight. On left Chain river. No sig[n] of Cls - the MARICOURT - LA BRIQUETERIE road was opened & consolidated.	
MONTAUBAN	28	4.50pm	Attack with barrage from LA BRIQUETERIE on MALTZ HORN RIDGE Position consolidated Posts 53 etc belong to three different regiments taken prisoners.	
			Heavy shell fire throughout the day	

Sheet 62d NE.
62c NW
57c SW

Army Form C. 2118.

WAR DIARY
or
INTELLIGENCE SUMMARY 1/1 Camb R

(Erase heading not required.)

Place	Date 1916 Aug	Hour	Summary of Events and Information	Remarks and references to Appendices
MONTAUBAN	28	9pm	Heavy shelling of Batt HQ. Lt Col ET SAINT DSO. enemy wounded, Lt H F DRIVER killed. Capt & Adjt E. WALKER M.C. slightly wounded.	
		10p	Battalion relieved by 2nd R Welsh. Major M C Clayton DSO assumed Command. Battalion moved to bivouac A 4 b 10 in Brigade reserve	
	29	1.30p	Batt moved to MALTZ HORN RIDGE in support of 37th Brigade — the bullet pulverise in the of the whole MAUREPAS RE FOREST	
	30	9am	47th Division passed through 12th Division which remained in its present area to support and refit.	
	31		Reorganising. Batt HQ in FAVIERES WOOD. Capt E Walker rejoined in addition. Strength at end of month 28 off/s 896 OR	

M<unclear/> E Major
Cmdg 1/1 Camb R

1/1st Cambridgeshire Regiment. Appendix F.
Report on Operations. August 8th 1918.

The first information regarding the proposed attack was received at a conference at Brigade H.Q at 2.30 p.m on 6th August. In the scheme then discussed the 1/1st Camb. Regt were to be in Brigade Reserve.

At 3.30 p.m on the 7th, the C.O. was sent for to Brigade H.Q and informed that the Divisional front was to be extended southwards, and the 1/1st Camb. Regt would attack on the right, objective being from K.8.a.8.3 to K.13.b.7.7. The time available for reconnaissance was practically nil, all that was possible was for one officer per company to reconnoitre assembly positions. The unsettled condition of the line on our right also presented difficulties.

At 6 p.m. Battalion moved to positions in the BALLARAT and BENDIGO LINES, and was fully occupied in equipping for the attack until midnight. Battalion H.Qrs were established for the night at J.11.a.7.7 and the whole area was subjected to heavy mustard gas shelling from 10.0 pm to 12.30 am.

At 12.30 am Companies commenced to move to Assembly positions, A & B Coys in BURKE LINE, C & D Coys in CLARE RESERVE and COPPER TRENCH, positions which had been hastily reconnoitred on the preceding evening. Battalion HQ moved to J.12.d.4.7 at 4 am. It was then very foggy and movement slow and difficult on that account.

At 4.20 am the barrage opened and the attack of the Divisions on the right commenced.

Bombardment of our objectives continued until 6.20 am, when it became intense and A & B Companies commenced the assault.

A message was received at 7.0 am from O.C "B" Coy (Capt H.W. BAYNES-SMITH, M.C) stating that objectives were taken and patrols out in front, and at 7.5 am a message from O.C "A" Coy (Lt. E. HAY) reported that he had failed to reach objective having been held up on the line K.8.a.0.0 - K.7.d.9.0. Later information stated that heavy casualties occurred in this line and that both Companies were back in our old front line.

The situation was immediately reported to Brigade, and a scheme for a fresh attack by the remaining two companies approved by the Brigadier.

At 10.15 am C & D Coys were ordered to assemble in our old front line preparatory to a fresh attack, and A and B Coys ordered to return to reserve positions in CLARE RESERVE and COPPER TRENCH, and at 10.30 am orders for the attack were issued. C Coy to attack on right, D on left. Zero 12.15 pm.

A Barrage had been arranged with Brigade as follows:- 10 minutes on road from K.8.d.2.9 - K.8.c.0.3, lifting at 12.25 pm to enemy trench K.8.c.9.6 - K.14.a.5.6, and lifting again at 12.35 pm to road K.8.d.6.3 - K.14.b.2.0.

At 12.15 pm the barrage opened according to programme, and at the same hour C & D Coys left their assembly positions. It was necessary for the leading waves to change direction half right in order to get parallel to the objective, and this movement was carried out in perfect order, and the attacking troops moved up to the barrage, and lay down waiting for it to lift. The shooting was very accurate and heavy, which greatly assisted the operation.

At 12.28 pm the barrage having lifted, the attacking waves rose and charged the position, killing those of the defenders who offered resistance.

At 12.35 pm the second wave went on to the second objective which was the enemy trench K.8.c.9.6 - K.14.b.2.0.

From the two positions 316 wounded and unwounded prisoners were taken, and upwards of 30 enemy dead were counted. 14 Machine Guns and 8 light and 2 medium Trench Mortars were captured.

At 12.50 pm reports were received from O.C. "C" Coy (LT. C.H. HOLLIS, M.C.) and O.C. "D" Coy (CAPT. B.H. WALLIS) that the position was captured and being consolidated, and A & B Coys. were moved up into CULGOA TRENCH and K.7.d central in support.

Total Casualties during the operations were:-

A. Coy.	Killed	2 Officers	2 ORs.
	Wounded	2 "	72 ORs.
B. Coy.	Killed		70 ORs.
	Wounded		76 ORs.
C. Coy.	Killed		2 ORs.
	Wounded		11 ORs.
D. Coy.	Killed		2 ORs.
	Wounded	1 Officer	8 ORs.
Total		5 Officers	183 ORs

This attack, though hastily conceived, was carried out particularly well, all movements being made in very good "parade" order, and great credit is due to L^T C.H. HOLLIS. M.C and CAPT B.H. WALLIS for their excellent handling of the operation.

(Sd) Edwd. T. Saint
Lt. Col
Commanding 1/1st Camb. Regt.

8 8 18

1/1st Cambridgeshire Regiment.
Report on Operations. 9/8/18. Appendix II

In conjunction with the attack of the 37th Brigade, the 1/1st CAMB. REGt were ordered to find two Companies to take and clear the village of MORLANCOURT, the 37th Brigade operating against a more distant objective on either flank.

Orders were accordingly issued for C and D Companies to carry out the operation, C Coy on the left to clear the NORTH of the village, D Coy the SOUTH, the dividing line being the road from the Church to cross roads K.8.b.4.5 inclusive to C Coy.

After clearing the village companies were ordered to occupy the line CRUCIFIX in K.3.c – CRUCIFIX at K.9.b.1.0 (C.Coy), thence to CRUCIFIX in K.3.d (D Coy) remaining there until objectives of 37th Inf Bde were taken.

Zero was at 5.30 pm, and three tanks were to co-operate.

At 5.15 pm the Tank detailed for the Southern portion of the village crossed the sunken road at K.8.c.1.3 and on reaching the high ground just SOUTH of the road, was seen by the enemy who immediately put down a heavy barrage on our assembly positions and knocked out the Tank.

As the remaining Tanks had not arrived at Zero, after waiting until 5.40 pm the attack was launched without them under cover of the artillery barrage.

The attackers were immediately fired on by several M.Gs from the village and by T.Ms from K 9. b & c, and it was necessary to deal with the M.G's before the village could be entered. They were quickly put out of action by Lewis Gun fire, and by the gallantry of individuals, who charged them and killed the crews. The clearing of the village then proceeded quickly and the two tanks arrived in time to follow the infantry through. Both Companies arrived at the positions detailed for them E. of the village, before the units of the 37th Brigade had come up to them, and they therefore took up a defensive position until 8 pm when the objectives of the 37th Brigade were reported taken and the two companies, less two platoons, withdrew in accordance with their orders.

O.C. 6th BUFFS ordered 2 platoons, under Lt. A JACKSON to fill a gap on his right flank, and these two platoons did not rejoin until 5.30 am, the following morning.

47 Prisoners, wounded & unwounded, 19 M.G.s and 4 T.Ms were captured during the operations.

Our casualties were:-
Killed 1 Officer 1 OR
Wounded 1 Officer 14 ORs

(Sd)
Edwd T Saint
Commanding 1st Lt Col
11th Camb Regt

14/8/18.

Note: 30 unwounded prisoners were handed over to an escort of the 6th BUFFS, their ultimate fate is unknown.

SECRET.   1/1st CAMBRIDGESHIRE REGIMENT.   Copy No. 8

Operation Order No.81.

Ref. Map.   In the Field.
LENS.11. 1/100,000 & Sheet 62D.N.W.   2nd AUG. 1918.

INFORMATION. 1. The 35th Infantry Brigade will relieve the 173rd. Inf an try Brigade to-night 2/3rd Aug.1918.

INTENTION. 2. The 1/1st Cambridgeshire Regiment will relieve the 2/4th LONDON Regt. in LEFT SUPPORT Section.

INSTRUCTIONS. 3. (1).Parade. The Battalion will move in column of route in the following order:-
H.Q., D, A, B, C, Battle Surplus under Capt. G.H.DOWNES. Harvesting Party under Lieut. C.Baldwin Hannant TAYLOR.
Dress:- Full Marching Order.
Route:- CANAPLES CHATEAU - and along CANAPLES-RAVENSAS Road. to embussing point 500 yards N.W. of RAVENSAS.
A distance of 50 yards between Coys.
Head of the Column will pass CANAPLES CHATEAU at 11.15 a.m.

(2). Embussing. At the embussing point men will be drawn up in groups of 6 parties each in columns of 25 with distance of 50 yards between each group.

(3) Assembly Point. On arrival at the assembly point Battalion will occupy Western Side of ROUND WOOD C.30.B. the lorry conveying Lewis Gun Stores etc. will be there and Coys will draw their material from it.

(4) Advanced Party & Relief. Instructions will be issued at ROUND WOOD.

(5). Battle Surplus. This will assemble on parade at Battn. H.Qrs at 10.30 a.m. It will assemble at the embussing point in rear of the buses each train with all necessary cooking utensils and Officers baggage. Battle Surplus will detrain at FIENVILLERS and receive instructions there.

(6) Harvesting Party. This will parade at Battn. H.Qrs. at 10.30 a.m. and will embus in rear of the Battalion and proceed with it to the assembly point, where it will receive instructions.

(7).Lewis Guns.Baggage.Tools. As per instructions already issued to Coys.
(8).Transport. As per instructions issued.

REPORTS. 4. Reports of cleanliness of billets at CANAPLES will be handed to head of column at embussing point.
Reports on arrival at assembly point R.W. will be handed in at ROUND WOOD.
Relief complete will be sent to Battn. H.Qrs &
Code Word:for relief complete " RAIN".

ACKNOWLEDGE.

(sd) E. Walker. Capt.& A/Adjt.
1/1st Cambridgeshire Regiment.

Copies issued at a.m.
No.1. C.O.
" 2. A Coy.   No.7. T.O.
" 3. B "   No.8. War Diary.
" 4. C "   No.9. "   "
" 5. D "   No.10.File.
" 6. H.Q.   No.11. Q.M.

SECRET.   Copy No. 10

1/1st CAMBRIDGESHIRE REGIMENT.

Operation Order No. 92.

Ref. Map.
Sheet. 6 2D. N.E. 1/20,000.

In the Field.
7th Aug. 1918.

INFORMATION. 1. (1). On "Z" Day at Zero hour the 18th and 58th Divisions on our right will attack with the object of consolidating a line from K.13.b.central along the crest of the ridge to K.17.c., and thence to K.24.central.
There will be no preliminary bombardment. Tanks will co-operate.

(2). In conjunction with this operation the 35th Infantry Brigade will attack and will consolidate a line across the Valley on our front, with a view to forming jumping off ground for a further attack, 24 or 48 hours later, to capture the spur N. and N.E. of MORLANCOURT.

(3). The line to be consolidated will be from Brigade Southern Boundary at K.7.d.0.8. to CRUCIFIX K.2.d.0.2., and thence Northwards along the road (inclusive) to E.26.d.0.5. Patrols will be pushed out forward of this line to ascertain the position of the enemy and give warning of counter-attack. The further up the spur we can establish posts on the first day the better.

(4). The attack will be carried out by the 7th. Norfolk Regt. on the right and the 9th Essex Regt. on the left.

INTENTION. 2. The 1/1st Cambridgeshire Regiment will be in Brigade Reserve and will take up assembly position South of the ANCRE by Zero hour. Battalion headquarters at J.11.a.7.7.

INSTRUCTIONS. 3. (1). On the night 6/7th August 1918, C Company will move to BALLARAT TRENCH (Right half) Company Headquarters J.11.a.7.7.

(2). On the night 7/8th August 1918, following moves will take place commencing at 8.0 p.m. by Platoons every precaution being taken against observation.
 A Company. to BENDIGO SWITCH.
 B   "   "   BENDIGO TRENCH.
 H.Q.   "   J.11.a.7.7.
A and B Coy H.Qrs. at J.11.a.7.7.

(3). <u>Overcoats</u>. These will be buttoned with haversacks in pockets in bundles by Sections (Lewis Gun Sections in 2 bundles) labelled with Platoon and Section, and will be stacked by 10.00 as follows:-
 A, B and H.Qrs. at J.5.c.3.7.
 C and D Coy.   at J.4.d.1.4.
A and C Coy. will find Guards over them until collected by the T.O.

(4). <u>S.A.A.</u> Each man will carry extra 50 rounds.

(5). <u>Bombs</u>. One Rifle Section per Platoon will carry 4 No.36 Grenades per man (in pockets).

(6). <u>Tools</u>. One Rifle Section per Platoon will carry 2 picks and 4 shovels as per Fighting Order.

(7). <u>Ground Flares</u>. will be carried 10 per Platoon These will be lighted only in the most forward position and whenever called for by Aeroplane with KLAXON HORN.

(8). <u>Very Lights</u> 1 per man will be carried.

(9). <u>Rations</u>. 1 Days rations will be carried in the pack in addition to Iron Rations.

(10). <u>Water Bottles</u>., will be filled tonight and all ranks warned to use them sparingly.

Sheet 2. Operation Order No.92.

INSTRUCTIONS. 3. (contd).

(11). Stretcher Bearers. Each Company will be provided with 2 stretchers and will use 8 stretcher bearers The 4 reserve will return their rifles to the Battalion Dump.
(12) R.A.P. At Brigade Headquarters at J.5.d.7.5.
(13). Battalion Dump at Battn. H.Wrs. J.11.a.7.7. from which all stores will be drawn by Coys which they are not able to issue from the Trench.
(14). Communication. All possible information will be supplied to Battalion Headquarters. Signallers will carry all signalling equipment including lamps, Shutters, and Flags. Visual will always be used where possible and runners saved.
(15). Watches. Watches will be synchronized by Lieut. C. WARREN. at midnight tonight.
(16). Zero Hour. Zero hour will be notified later.

REPORTS. 4. All reports to Battalion Headquarters.
Arrival in Assembly Positions, as soon as possible. Code Word. "CIGARETTE".

(sd). E. Walker. Capt.
Actg.Adjt. 1/1st Cambridgeshire Regiment.

Copies issued at p.m. to:-
No.1. C.O.
" 2. A Company.
" 3. B "
" 4. C "
" 5. D "
" 6. H.Q
" 7. Q.M.
" 8. T.O.
" 9 M.O.
" 10 and 11. War Diary.
" 12. File.

SECRET.   Copy No. 5

1/1st CAMBRIDGESHIRE REGIMENT.

Operation Order No.93.

Ref. Map.   In the Field.
Sheet 62.D. or Message Map.   16th August 1918.

INFORMATION.   1.   The 35th Infantry Brigade will relieve the 36th
               Infantry Brigade in the Line on the night 16/17th
               August 1918.

INTENTION.   2.   The 1/1st Cambridgeshire Regiment will relieve
               The 5th R.Berks.Regt. in the RIGHT SUB-SECTOR.

INSTRUCTION.   3.(1). Companies will relieve as follows:-
               A Coy. 1/1st Camb.R. will relieve A Coy. 5th R.Berks.R
               B   "   "   "   "   B   "   "   "
               C   "   "   "   "   C   "   "   "
               D   "   "   "   "   D   "   "   "
               H.Q.   "   "   "   H.Q.   "   "
                  (2). Companies will move in the following order:-
                        B, D, A, C, H.Q.
                  (3). There will be an interval between each platoon
               of 2 minutes, the leading platoon passing present
               H.Q. at 8.30 p.m.
                  (4). Route:- Cross Country to K.9.c.2.7. thence
               along track to K.9.d.60.98. where they will meet
               guides (1 per Platoon).

REPORTS.   4.   Lists of Trench Stores taken over will be
               sent to Battn. H.Q. by 12 noon 17th inst.
               Relief complete by Code Word " MAPS"
               All trenches evacuated will be left clean..

 Copies issued at 6 p.m.   (sd). E. Walker. Capt. & A/Adjt.
No.1. A Company.   1/1st Cambridgeshire Regiment.
 " 2. B   "
 " 3. C   "
 " 4. D   "
 " 5. H.Q.
 " 6. Q.M.
 " 7. T.O.
 " 8. War Diary.
 " 9. "   "
 " 10. File.

SECRET.   1/1st. CAMBRIDGESHIRE REGIMENT.   Copy No. 8

Ref. Map.   Operation Order No 94.   In the Field
Sheet 62. D. N.E. 1/20,000.   19:8:18.

INFORMATION. 1. The 9th ESSEX REGT. will relieve the 1/1st
CAMB. REGT, in the RIGHT SUB-SECTOR tonight
August 19/20th. 1918.

INTENTION. 2. A Company 1/1st Camb. R. will be relieved by B Coy
9th. Essex R. B Coy 1/1st Camb. R. will be relieved
A Company. C Coy 1/1st. Camb R. will be relieved
by C Company. D. Company 1/1st Camb R will be relieved
by D. Company. H.Q. 1/1st Camb. R. will be
relieved by H.Q. 9th Essex. R.

INSTRUCTIONS. 3. (1) Guides for 9th Essex R. will be at CRUCIFIX
K.3.c.4.8. at 9-30 p.m. 1 per Platoon and 1 for
Company H.Q.
   (2) Trench stores, Aeroplane Photos, Defence
Schemes and details of Work in hand will
be handed over on relief and receipts forwarded to
this Office by 12 noon 20th inst.
   (3) Patrols O.C. B. Company and D Company will
leave 3 men to act as guides to patrols of the
9th Essex R. These men will rejoin their Coys one
hour before daybreak.
   (4) Stores. 1 Limber will be at K.4. a. 7.2 at
10.0.p.m. to convey dixies, mess stores, petrol cans
food containers to new location.
   (5) New Location. upon relief Companys will proceed
to new area in K.1.c. K.1.d. K.7.a & K.7.b. as
disposed in my X.17. para 9.
   (6) Rations and Water. These will be brought
to new location tonight.
   (7) Movement. Movement in connection with relief
will be restricted before dark as much as possible.

REPORTS. 4. Relief complete to present Battn H.Q. Code Word
"CHALE"
Arrival in new location to new Battn. H.Q.
by hand.

COPIES ISSUED AT 6-30 p.m.   (sd) E. Walker. Capt. & A/Adjt.
No.1. A. Coy.   1/1st. Cambridgeshire Regiment.
" 2   B "
" 3   C "
" 4   D "
" 5   HQ "
" 6   QM "
" 7   TM
" 8 & 9 War Diary.
" 10   File.

SECRET.   1/1st CAMBRIDGESHIRE REGIMENT.   Copy No. 9

Operation Order. No.945

Ref. Map.   In the Field.
Sheet 6 BD. N.E. 1: 20,000.   21st AUGUST 1918.

INFORMATION.   1.   In conjunction with the 47th Division on
                the Right and the 36th Infantry Brigade on the
                Left (the 18th DIVISION being on their Left) the
                35th Infantry Brigade will on "Z" Day attack
                and capture the enemy positions shown as first
                and second Objectives on attached map.

INTENTION.   2.   The 1/1st Cambridgeshire Regiment and 7th.
                Norfolk Regt. will attack on the right and left
                respectively the First Objective, after which
                the 9th Essex Regt and the 6th E.Kents will pass
                through and take Second Objectives.
                3 Tanks will co-operate on the Brigade Front.

INSTRUCTIONS.   3.(1). The 1/1 Camb.R. will attack on a Three
                Company Front. B Coy. on the Right. C Coy. in
                the Centre and A Coy on the Left. Each on a
                Three Platoon Front.
                Each Platoon will be in Two Lines at 25 paces
                distance. Support Platoon of each Company
                will be 100 paces in rear.
                D Company will be in Battn.Reserve and will move
                in accordance with orders from Battn.Commander.
                   (2). Boundaries between Coys as marked on Map
                attached.
                   (3). Flanks O.C. B Company is responsible for
                keeping touch with the 19th LONDON R. on the
                Right and O.C. A Company an with the 7th NORFOLKS
                on the Left at the Points marked with cross on
                attached map.
                   (4). Direction. Right Company 62 Magnetic.
                                   Left Company 61   "
                        Right of Centre Company 62   "
                   (5). Barrage. The Artillery Creeping barrage will
                start at Zero and lift at Zero plus 4.
                It will move at a uniform rate of 100 yards in
                4 minutes until it is 300 yards in advance of the
                First Objective. It will pause there until Zero
                plus 118 and will then move forward at the rate of
                100 yards in 4 minutes till it is 300 yards
                beyond the Second Objective where it will form
                a protective barrage for half-an-hour.
                   (6). Assembly Points shown on the map attached.
                   (7). Success Grenades will be fired from the
                objective as soon as taken.
                   (8). Zero Hour will be notified later.
                   (9). Battn. H.QRS. at K.5.a.5.0. (Old Right
                Platoon H.Qrs.) will move when First Objective is
                taken to about K.30.c.0.4.)
                   (10).R.A.P. K.4.d. 7.7. (Old B Coy.H.Qrs.)
                   (11).Watches. will be synchronized from Bn.H.Q.

Sheet 2. Operation Order No.94. 21st August 1918.

INSTRUCTIONS. 2. (12). **Relief.** The 1/1st Camb.Regt. will relieve
(contd). the 9th Essex Regt in the Line 21st/22nd August
1918.
(13) Coys will be ready to move at 6.0 p.m. but
will not before they get orders from Battn.H.Q.
(14). <u>Order of Move</u> B, E, C, A, D, H.Q.
Usual Platoon Intervals.
(15). Battn. H.Qrs. at K.5.a.8.0.Reports will
be sent back by 1st Company at K.22.d.3.2.
(16). Code word for Relief of 9th Essex.R.
will be "GOON".
(17). Code word for arrival in Assembly Positions
will be "DRIVER".
(18). Special vigilance will be exercised at all
times against Gas Shelling.

(sd). E. Walker, Capt. & A/Adjt.
1/1st Cambridgeshire Regiment.

Copies issued at p.m.
No.1. C.O.
No.2. A Company.
" 3. B   "
" 4. C   "
" 5. D   "
" 6. H.Q.
" 7. Q.M.
" 8. T.O.
" 9.&10. War Diary.
" 11. File.

1/1st Cambridgeshire Regiment

Re-enforcements for August 1918.

Lieut. G. H. Keating	} Rejoined from Hos.	10.8.18
2/Lieut. R. MacDonald		
64 O.Rs joined for duty		16.8.18
Lieut. P. H. Winfield joined for duty		19.8.18
Lieut. E. A. Pearce	— — —	— — —
48 O.Rs	— — —	— — —
2/Lieut. E. Gibbons	— — — from Hos	— — —
2/Lieut. G. Mack	— — —	20.8.18
2/Lieut. H. F. Woor	— — —	— — —
Captn. J. H. H. Harding-Newman	— —	21.8.18
Lieut. A. F. Gray	— — —	— — —
— F. E. Spicer	— — —	— — —
— E. A. Banyard	— — —	— — —
14 O Rs joined for duty		— — —
34 — — —	— —	25.8.18
Lieut H. J. Unwin —	— —	28.8.18
50 — O Rs	— — —	— — —
175 — — —	— —	— — —
2/Lieut H. W. Huckle	— —	29.8.18
2/Lieut B. Carter	— —	— —
2/Lieut W. G. Linsey	— —	— —
Captn H. D. Boyd	— —	— —
30 — ORs	— —	— —

1/1st Cambridgeshire Regiment
Casualties for August 1918.

Aug 6th.   1. O.R. Wounded   (Died 7/8/18)
Aug 8th.   Lieut. F. G. B. Cobham Killed.
            2/Lieut. E. D. Twelvetrees —
            Lieut. E. Hay. Wounded.
            2/Lieut. H. A. Aldrich —
            Lieut. F. M. Wilson. —
            13 O.Rs. Killed.
            44 — Wounded.
            —   — Missing.
            141 — (W) Gas.
            1   — NYDN

Aug. 9th   Lieut D. Rayner Killed
           2/Lieut. H. Chambers. Wounded (Deced 11/8/18)
           1. O.R. Killed
           3 — Wounded
           3 — (W) Gas.

Aug. 10th 9 — Wounded.
           7 — (W) Gas.

Aug. 11th 2 — Killed
           1 — Wounded
           6 — (W) Gas.

Aug. 12th 3 — Wounded.
           3 — (W) Gas.

Aug. 13th 1 — Wounded

Aug. 14th 2nd Lieut E. L. Hope. Wounded
           1 O.R. Wounded

Aug. 16th 2 — (W) Gas.

Aug. 17th 1 — Killed
           2 — Wounded

Aug. 18th 1 — Wounded.
           4 — (W) Gas.

(1)

Casualties for August (Cont'd)

Aug: 21st 2. O.Rs. (W) Gassed.
- 22nd Captn. H.J. Saville M.C. Wounded
  Lieut. A.S. Joyner —
  Lieut. F.E. Spicer. —
  Lieut. G.H. Singleton —
  Lieut. A. Jackson. —
  Lieut. E.A. Pearce —
  Lieut. P.H. Winfield —
  2/Lieut. R. MacDonald —
  2/Lieut. R.J. Lawler M.M —
  2/Lieut. J. Mack. —
  22 O.Rs. Killed
  10 - O.Rs. Missing
  114 - O.Rs. Wounded
  9 - O.Rs. (W) Gas.
  2 - O.Rs. NYDN.
  23rd Lieut. K.H. Clayton. Killed
  2/Lieut. C. Hewer. Killed
  1 - O.R. Killed
  3 - O.Rs. Wounded.
  2 - O.Rs. (W) Gas.
  24th 1 - O.R. Killed
  4 - O.Rs. Wounded.
  25th 1 - O.R. Killed
  1 - O.R. Missing
  5 - O.Rs. Wounded.
  26th Lieut. A.H. Gray. Killed
  3 - O.R's. Killed.
  3 - O.R's. Missing.
  34 - O.R's. Wounded.
  2 - O.R's. (W) Gas.
  4 - O.R's. NYDN.

Casualties for August (Contd)

Aug. 27th   2 - O.Rs   Killed
             6 - O.Rs   Wounded

28th Lieut. H. F. Driver. M.C.   Killed
      Lieut. Col. E. F. Saint D.S.O.   Wounded
      Captn. E. Walker. M.C.   Wounded (Duty)
      Lieut. V.N. Lumsden   Wounded
      2/Lieut. E. Gibbons   Wounded
      Lieut. S. Taylor   Wounded
      4 - O Rs   Killed
      24 - O R's   Wounded
      3 - O Rs   NYDN

12th Division
35th Brigade.

1/1st CAMBRIDGE REGIMENT.

SEPTEMBER 1 9 1 8

WAR DIARY or INTELLIGENCE SUMMARY

Army Form C. 2118.

1/1 CAMB R.

(Erase heading not required.)

Instructions regarding War Diaries and Intelligence Summaries are contained in F.S. Regs., Part II. and the Staff Manual respectively. Title Pages will be prepared in manuscript.

Place	Date Sept 1918	Hour	Summary of Events and Information	Remarks and references to Appendices
MONTAUBAN	1.		Batt. resting and reorganizing in FAVIERE WOOD	
	2.		ditto. News was received of the death from wounds received in action of Lt. Col. E.T. Saint D.S.O. which occurred on 29th ult. The news was received with the greatest regret. The Col. of C.H. Saint is to Henry Ellis who installed which he had so successfully commanded since October 1917.	
			Tedden at company training	
	3.	3.30pm	Entrained & proceeded to FRICOURT	
SAILLY	4.	6.30pm	Relieved R.W.K. reg't 12th Division in Bray de Reserve near GOVERNMENT FARM	
SAILLISEL		11.30pm	C.O. returned from Bde HQ with orders	
	5.	12.30am	C.O. returned from Bde HQ. Orders issued to attack NURLU	
		3.15am	Batt. formed up & were guided to position along VAUX wood to canal bridge below RIVERSIDE WOOD. The marsh through VAUX WOOD was rather difficult owing to heavy shelling. Both HE & mustard gas. It's Batt. was very strong but as day increased we reached betwixt batteries	
NURLU		7.45am	A/B Coys reached the ran of night flight of 7th Norfolk Regt. D Coy attached to S. of NURLU in the direction of QUESSA TRENCH. A Coy operated with Capt A. Johnson made steady progress until they were held up by machine gun fire W. of ATAX TRENCH	

			Army Form C. 2118.

WAR DIARY
or
INTELLIGENCE SUMMARY
(Erase heading not required.)

1/1 Comb R.

Place	Date	Hour	Summary of Events and Information	Remarks and references to Appendices
NURLU	16/18 Sept 5		B Coy advance unopposed - successful French prisoners were sent back. On reaching the ridge immediately W. of NURLU they came under intense M-G fire & suffered heavy casualties. LT ORBELL OC Coy was instantaneously killed likewise 2/LT. HUCKLE & LT BANYARD was severely wounded. 2/LT G.G.R NOCK (Suffolk Regt att 1/1 Camb R) led the remnants forward in a most gallant way until he reached a trench about 100 yds W. of the village on the opposite side of the road. his few S were all killed or wounded. D Coy meanwhile had advanced in a S.S.E direction across several tracks VER, a TRENCH - they attacked about 20-30 prisoners let a m-g to the ridge found their way obstructed by wire & entered their field of fire and by their m-g fire & trench gun obtained route E of NURLU. PERONNE Rd. C Coy remained in reserve under CAPT BOYD at RIVERSIDE WOOD. Owing to all these front companies being held up & no o fire they were compelled to consolidate where they were. Casualties amount to reall & numerous element of Bdg.	Nec
		9p 5.15 a	Orders received to attack at 5am.	

Army Form C. 2118.

WAR DIARY or **INTELLIGENCE SUMMARY**
(Erase heading not required.)

3 / 1/1 Cam E.R.

Instructions regarding War Diaries and Intelligence Summaries are contained in F. S. Regs., Part II. and the Staff Manual respectively. Title Pages will be prepared in manuscript.

Place	Date 1918 Sept	Hour	Summary of Events and Information	Remarks and references to Appendices
NURLU	6		D Coy withdrawn to Batt Reserve	
	7		C Coy moved up to left of A Coy at FAUCON TRENCH.	
	8	8 AM	Aby attacked but repulsed abt front at V 28 a & I C by followed through. Whole entire attacks in swing then Objective the ground east of NURLU - FIN's road not aft but a NE end of NURLU. Owing to the heavy hvy withdrawn most of his fire the casualties were insignificant. The Batt met left y Stockers m as soon as our men advanced - Batt remained in captured trenches - Companies withdrawn as one tire by battery in CANAL DU NORD.	
			The division being relieved Batt concentrated in RIVERSIDE WOOD + moved bivouac.	
RIVERSIDE WOOD (NURLU)	9 10 11 12 13 14 15 16		Reorganising, training, musketry. Special attacks were given to learn gunnery. Fuel was being made of the range.	
	17	3:30p	Instructions received that Batt would be next employed in the attack on EPÉHY. Batt by ment road to S.W. corner of NURLU where they rested and had tea	Off-r b for Curtis R.96 mc

2449 Wt. W14957/M90 750,000 1/16 J.B.C. & A. Forms/C.2118/12.

Army Form C. 2118.

WAR DIARY
or
INTELLIGENCE SUMMARY

(Erase heading not required.)

1/1 CAM. B.R.

Place	Date 1915 SEPT.	Hour	Summary of Events and Information	Remarks and references to Appendices
	17	7p	Lup NORLU - met note R. reservefaction A Coy ESt. B " ESA (in Battlezone) C " E 1rd D " E 12a B IHQ ESd O 3.	
EPÉHY	18	1am		
		5.20am	Battalion attacked. All companies met with stiff opposition. ENEMY was garrisoned by troops of 52R BAVARIAN ALPINE Corps who offered strenuous resistance. A Coy had lost all officers - the remainder of the company retired - entered village N. of FISHERS POST but was unable to maintain themselves in the position owing to company of 7th Norfolk not being able to proceed. C+D Coys owing to the E noted of village to another east of EPEHY C+D Coys were unable to make much progress owing to the village. ENEMY was defeated by M.G. posts + groups of melee & Summer who ran up the trees without making the flank and flanks were located. D Coy however made considerable progress and captured over 60 prisoners.	
		10.30am	D Coy reinforced by two platoons of B Coy under LT BOND without... Commencement M.G. posts hy were unable to advance at this object. Captured could not hold. At the night. One person was wounded DCO	All

2449 Wt. W14957/M90 750,000 1/16 J.B.C. & A. Forms/C.2118/12.

Army Form C. 2118.

WAR DIARY or **INTELLIGENCE SUMMARY**
(Erase heading not required.)

1/1 CAMB'K

Place	Date 1916 Sept	Hour	Summary of Events and Information	Remarks and references to Appendices
EPEHY	18	10.30am (cont)	The remaining Platoons were also in the railway in F.I.C. Here the Bn were kept by [?] N.C.Os but managed to dig cover [?] in the crump holes to the side.	
		3pm	Two coys of R. Berks came up in a wave & their and the entrenge no [?] men through to FISHER'S KEEP. My thanks to the CAM.M.G. garrison the ravine chung [?] sent out a & company here the CAM.M.G. garrison the ravine chung [?] sent out a & company of a large party of the [?] were cleaned of [?] CROPPER POST and some from the occupied of [?] trenches were cleared of [?] & Room FRENCH. PRINCES RESERVE was organised OCKENDEN & Room FRENCH	
	19	11pm	Bn attached to [?] [?] went over in splendid style but the Allmng is there were tired out & though wrong to make the hostile M-Gs open out upon hint the carys halted about 100-150 yds short of the trench. Two batteries (12rdm) D.A arrived that Room TR. but first night of Confereures outfits.	
		3pm	Be freshide [?] Bangamer [?] and instead but it was all thus. been running between Pickden? [?] by and Curtis but Rocken Den Trench. [?]	
		5.30pm LEFT	[?] of Bn leapt into front [?] received...orders to stand to. The owo [?] of a certain [?] of [?] but the dues of interest [?] were established in Eyechy and ClathingYou carried out.	
	20		Held OCKENDEN & Room TRs to protect line	
	21		Do. Posts established in front of line.	
	22		Side-stepped to the north establishing posts in POPLAR TR - OCKENDOVER line	
	23	10pm	Overtaken R. Sussex Rest. Relieved by R. Berks & Booth [?] command march on to march in F.I.C.	

MMc

Army Form C. 2118.

WAR DIARY
or
INTELLIGENCE SUMMARY.
(Erase heading not required.)

1/1 Camb. R.

Place	Date 1915 SEP	Hour	Summary of Events and Information	Remarks and references to Appendices
EPEHY	24		Reorganising. Four companies each of three platoons formed. Battle order. Inlying Picket in set trench. Spent out Brigade operational wing.	
	25		River of captured Villers. Batt. in Brigade reserve.	
	26		Relieved 7 Norfolks and 6 and Essex in trenches PR 16 to PR 20 ? sector.	Appu. 2. Op. Order No 97.
	27		B sapped. Heavy shelling causing several casualties to C Coy.	
	28		ditto	
	29		B division reserve	
	30		Brigade reserve	
			8am Villeaux left the ? and concentrated in W 27 b. as ordered. Orders to stay day.	

Lieut Col
C.O. 1/1 Camb R

SECRET.   1/1st CAMBRIDGESHIRE REGIMENT.   Appendix 1
                                                                Copy No. 1

                       Operation Order No. 96.

Ref. Maps.   In the Field.
Sheet 62c.N.E. 1:20,000. &   17th September 1918.
Sheet 57c.S.E. 1:20,000.

INFORMATION.   1.(a). At Zero hour on "Z" Day the 12th Division
                   will attack EPEHY and PEIZIERES and the trenches
                   East of them up to and including LITTLE PRIEZ FARM
                   and then exploit to SWALLOWS and LARK Trenches;
                   The 18th Division attacking on our right and the
                   58th Division on our Left.
                     (b). The 36th Infantry Brigade will be on the
                   right and the 35th Infantry Brigade on the Left,
                   with as first main objective EPEHY and PEIZIERES
                   villages and the trench lines East of them running
                   through F.8.a.5.6, F.2.c, F.1.d, F.1.b, and
                   second objective the GREEN Line from F.2.d.7.8,
                   through F.2.b.4.9. thence along ROOM Trench to its
                   junction with POPLAR Trench, whence Posts will be
                   pushed out as far as the protective barrage permits
                   to cover consolidation.
                     (c). The Boundary Line between the 35th and 36th
                   I.B.s will be from E.12.d.5.7, through F.7.a.1.0
                   and thence to Railway at F.1.d.8.6, F.2.c.0.8,
                   F.2.d.6.8. The Boundary between the 35th I-B and
                   the 58th Division will be from E.6.a.4.3, E.6.b.4.5,
                   North Point of FISHERS KEEP, Railway at F1.a.9.9.
                   thence to X.26.c.1.8, thence to Junction of POPLAR
                   and ROOM Trenches. Joint Posts will be established
                   with 36th Infantry Brigade at Railway F.1.d.95.80,
                   trench F.2.c.6.6 and on GREEN Line F.2.d.7.8,
                     (d). The 36th I.B. will attack with the 7th NORFOLKS
                   on the right and the 9th ESSEX Regt on the left,
                   Boundary line between them being as follows:-
                   Road at M.F.12.b.6.7. (inclusive) 9th ESSEX REGT.)
                   road junction F.1.c.6.5. (inclusive) to 7th NORFOLKS),
                   road junction F.1.d.0.8. (inclusive to 7th NORFOLKS),
                   Railway at F.1.b.5.3,- F.1.b.8.5, thence to X.26.d.2.2.

INTENTION.   2.(a). A Company 1/1st Camb.R. will attack on the
                   Left of 9th Essex.R, its lleft moving from E.6.b.7.9
                   on to the North end of FISHERS KEEP and 50 yards
                   North of WEEDON Post, and its right from E.6.b.7.4.
                   on to the centre of FISHERS KEEP which will then be
                   mopped up from North to South: a special party being
                   sent on to deal with WEEDON POST.
                     (b). C Company 1/1st Camb.R. will be formed up behind
                   2nd Wave of 7th Norfolks and D Company behind 2nd Wave
                   of 9th Essex R, and will follow the abovementioned
                   waves and mop up posts in and around EPEHY.

Sheet 2. Operation Order No. 96.   17th September 1918.

DETAIL.
3. (a) A Company will assemble on tape in front of wire on the line E.5.b.7.4 to E.5.b.7.9. Compass bearing for left of A Company 108° Magnetic. and right of A Company 103° magnetic.

(b). On reaching trench West of village in E.6.b. one platoon of A Company will occupy it, make a stop on its left flank and work down to the right to join with the 9th ESSEX Rr. at E.6.d.8.7.
To Platoons will attack and mop up FISHERS KEEP the remaining platoon will be used for attacking and mopping up WEEDON POST.

(c). Whilst advancing A Company will keep clear of the valley in E.6.b. & d, but its right boundary in the village will be the line from E.6.d.8.6. to F.1.a.9.6.

(d). Boundary line between C and D Coys will be SUNKEN ROAD running from E.12.b.1.1. to F.1.c.0.1. thence road running round Southern edge of CRESCENT to F.1.d.1.6, thence line to F.1.b.5.3. Road inclusive to D Company.

(e). Right boundary of C Company will coincide with right boundary of 7th NORFOLKS and left boundary of D Company will coincide with left boundary of 9th ESSEX REGT.

(f). C Company will detail platoons to deal with SHARPE POST, CROPPER POST, ROBERTS POST and the triangle formed by railway tracks in A.1.d.

(g). D Company will detail two platoons to attack and occupy CRESCENT, one platoon for CULLEN POST one platoon for PACKERS POST.

(h). B Company will be in reserve in present front line in E.5.d.

MOPPING UP. 4. O's C Coys C, D and A Coys will detail parties for mopping up Posts and buildings in their areas. Any cellars or deep dug-outs which cannot be conveniently cleared at once will have sentries posted over them.

LEWIS GUN POSTS. 5. L.G. Posts will be established in according to plan issued to Company Commanders. These posts will not be withdrawn until orders are received from Battn. H.Qrs.

TANKS. 6. One tank will accompany A Company and will attack FISHERS KEEP, another tank will attack on right of C Company.

CONSOLIDATION. 7. On the village being reported clear of the enemy C, D and A Coys less L.G. Posts mentioned in para. 5 will consolidate in depth and in fron of PRINCE RESERVE.

ASSEMBLY 8. Orders will be issued for Coys to move to West of their assembly positions where Coys will rest and be isued with Tea and Rum.
C and D Coys will assemble on tape under instructions from Major. R.G.ROYLE. D.S.O.
O.C. A Company will be responsible for laying out tape and assembling on his position.

BARRAGE. 9. (a) Barrage for the 35th I.B. will move 100 yards in 4 minutes for the first three minutes; it will then move at 100 yards in 5 minutes for 6 lifts; after which it will move at 100 yards in four minutes until it reached the line about 200 yards East of PRINCE RESERVE where it will remain for 15 minutes.

(b). The protective barrage for the GREEN LINE will remain until Zero plus 199 minutes and will then move forward at the rate of 100 yards in 4 minutes.

It will thicken up 3 minutes before the advance to warn troops of the lift.

Sheet 3 Operation Order No. 96.   17th September 1918.

COMMUNICATION. 10. Company Signallers will not join their Companies until Company H.Qrs have been established when they will be sent from Battn. H.Qrs. to open communication.

APPROACH MARCH. 11. Separate orders for the approach march will be issued.

BATTN. REAR H.QRS. & FORWARD TRANSPORT. 12. After Zero hour these will be in SUNKEN ROAD X.X.X.X.X.X.X. at E.8.d. 7, 8.

SYNCHRONIZATION. 13. Watches will be synchronized during the approach march.

PRISONERS. 14. These will be marched down to Battn. H.Qrs. by escorts detailed by Company Commanders and handed over to the Regimental Police.
Escorts will if possible be found from slightly wounded men.
No unwounded N.C.O. will be used as escort.

R.A.P. 15. R.A.P. will be established as in SUNKEN ROAD near Battn. H.Qrs.

REPORTS. 16. Reports to Battalion Headquarters at E.8.c.8.6.

                                        (sd). E. Walker. Capt & Adjt.
                                        1/1st Cambridgeshire Regiment.

Copies Issued at   a.m.
No. 1. C.O.
 " 2. 2nd in Command.
 " 3. A Company
 " 4. B   "
 " 5. C   "
 " 6. D   "
 " 7. H.Q.
 " 8. Q.M.
 " 9. T.O.
 " 10. War Diary.
 " 11.   "   "
 " 12   File.

SECRET.
EXTRACT.   1/1st CAMBRIDGESHIRE REGIMENT.

Supplement to Operation Order No. 96.

In the Field.   17th September 1918.

APPROACH MARCH.

1. The Battalion will assemble in area at D.9.b. at 4.30 p.m. where all available trenches and banks will be used to give cover from aircraft.

2. Company limbers will report to their Companies at 3.0 p.m. to carry Lewis Guns, Material, bombs, tools and unecessary stores.
   Each Company will detail a N.C.O. to accompany its limber and limbers will be guided to the above area under Company arrangements.

3. Two cookers will proceed in advance and tea will be served at D.9.b.

4. Each Company will post A.A. Observers during this period and the utmost vigilance will be exercised.
   Immediately our A.A. guns open fire all movement must cease at once.
   This point is most important and must be impressed on all ranks.

5. The Battalion will cross main MORLU - PEIZIERE Road at 7.0 p.m. in the following order C, D, B.C, A and B. Companies at 150 yards distance.
   Lewis Gun limbers and pack ponies with hot tea and rum will proceed in rear of their Companies.

6. The Adjutant will guide the Battn to road in E.14.a. and b where Coys will rest till guided up to 'hot tea' area.

7. Whilst resting alongside road in E.14.a. and b, Lewis Guns tools and bombs will be distributed from limbers, but great care must be taken that Stores are properly distributed.

8. C.S.M's of A, C and D Coys will go with their Companies to the final assembly point, whence they will report to Battn. H.Qrs.
   They will not rejoin their Coys until orders are given from Battn. H.Qrs.

9. The Band will report to the Adjutant at 2.30 p.m.

10. Battle Surplus will proceed to Transport lines under Capt. T.H.H.Harding-Newman.
    They will parade at H.Qrs. at 3.0 p.m.

11. All Company Signallers will march with A.& H.Qrs

12. **EQUIPMENT.** Each man will carry one sand bag.
    Tools.   50 per Company (40 and 10.)
    Bombs.   6 per rifleman.

Copies issued at 1245 p.m. to
All recipients of Operation   (sd). E. Walker, Capt.& Adjt.
Order No.96.   1/1st Cambridgeshire Regiment.

SECRET.   1/1 CAMBRIDGESHIRE REGT   No 81

In the field - Operation Order no. 97   26/9/18
Ref: ST EMILIE 1/20.000.   Appendix 2.

1. INFORMATION.
The 7th NORFOLK REGT will relieve the 9th ESSEX.R.
in the front line of the EPEHY Sector on the night
26/27 Sept 1918.

2. INTENTION
The 1/1 CAMB.R. will relieve the 7th NORFOLK.R.
in the Support position on the same night
in accordance with details in para 3.

3. DETAIL
(a) C Coy 1/1 CAMB.R. will relieve A Coy 7th NORFOLK.R.
in the 2nd line of resistance.
HORSE POST will be relieved at 7.45 p.m.
Relief of remaining posts will commence at
8.15 p.m.

(b) B Coy 1/1 CAMB.R. will relieve B Coy 7th NORFOLKS.
in PATRICKS AVENUE in the Counter Attack
Company position.
Leading Section of B Coy will arrive in
PATRICKS AVENUE at 6.30 p.m.

(c) D Coy 1/1 CAMB.R. will relieve troops of 7th NORFOLKS
in trench running N & S through F.2 central.
D Coy will also take over post at F.2.C.2.0 (1 section)
Relief by D Coy will commence at 5.15 p.m.
and be complete by 6.0 p.m.

(d) A Coy 1/ CAM 3 R will be in reserve to the Support Batt̃ⁿ & will garrison post at F.2.c.4.3 (double L.G. section) & will be accommodated in dugouts below this trench & trench adjacent.

(e) Bⁿ H.Q. will remain in present location.

4. COUNTER ATTACK COMPANY
   B Coy will be at disposal of O.C. Front Line Batt̃ⁿ for counter attack purposes.

5. 2ⁿᵈ LINE of RESISTANCE
   C Coy will garrison posts at in 2ⁿᵈ line of resistance & will not be available for reinforcing front line.

6. SUPPORT COMPANY
   D Coy will find garrison for the 3 posts allotted to it. The remaining 2 platoons will be available for counter attack under orders of Batt̃ⁿ Commander.

7. RESERVE COMPANY
   This Coy less 1 double L.G. section for post F.2.c.4.3 will be available for counter attack under orders of Batt̃ⁿ commander.

8. SIGNAL COMMUNICATION
   B Coy will be in signal communication with O.C. Front Batt̃ⁿ (Fig.c.2.9.) & by runner to this Batt̃ⁿ.
   C Coy will be in communication by lamp with Batt̃ⁿ H.Q. via a transmitting station at E end of TETARD WOOD.

9. COOKING
   Cookers will remain in their present location & supply B & C Coys by means of food containers. No cooking in the line will be done by B & C Coys

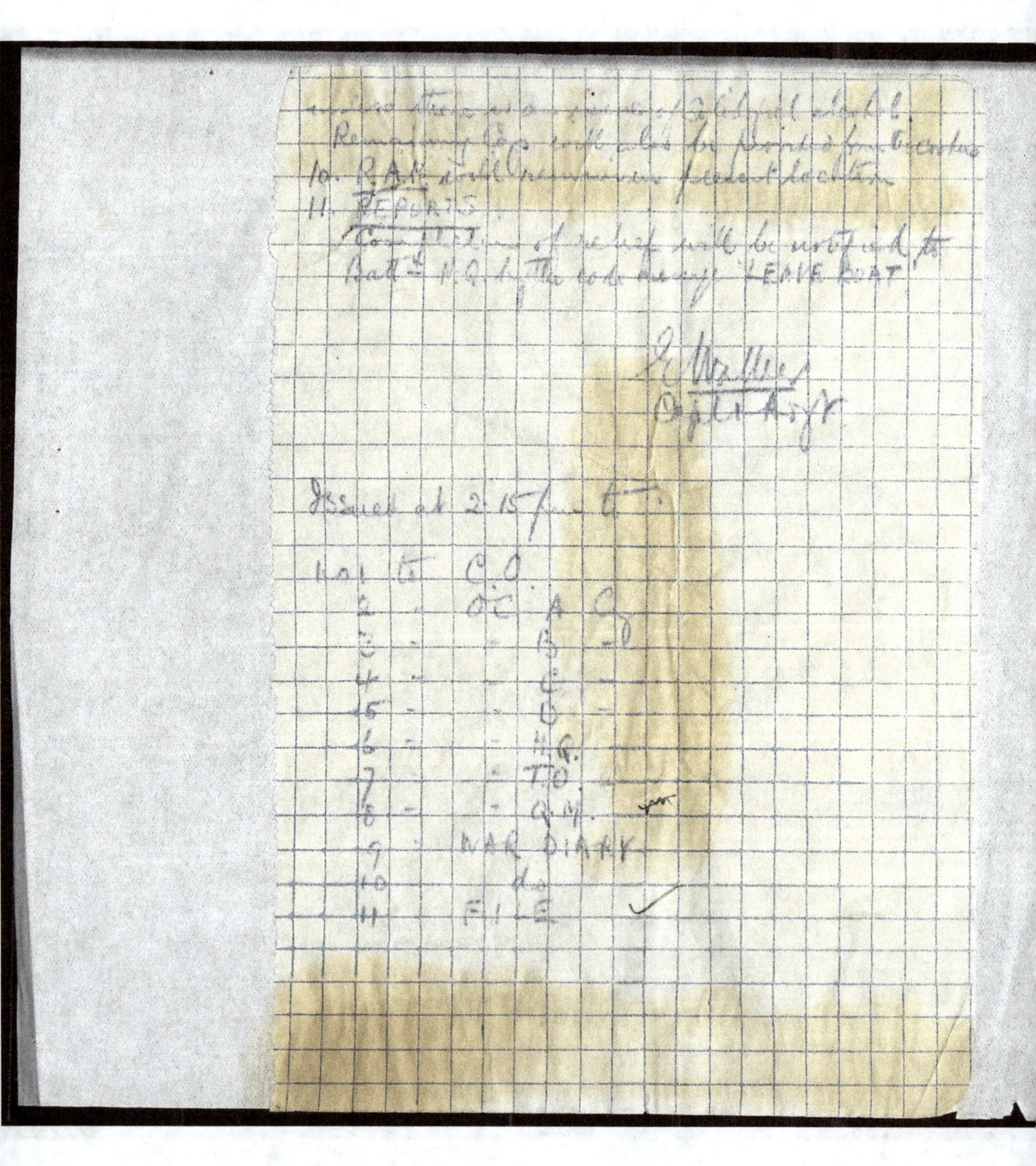

...and there was a [illegible] of [illegible] which
Remaining [illegible] will also be [illegible] for [illegible]
10. R.A.M. [illegible] in present location.
11. REPORTS.
Coy. H.Q. [illegible] of relief will be notified to
Battⁿ H.Q. by the code [illegible] LEAVE BOAT

E. Walker
Capt & Adjt

Issued at 2.15 p.m. to:

No. 1 to C.O.
2 - O.C. A Coy
3 - " B "
4 - " C "
5 - " D "
6 - H.Q.
7 - T.O.
8 - Q.M.
9 - WAR DIARY
10 - do
11 - FILE ✓

1/1st Cambridgeshire Regt.
Casualties during September 1918.

5/9/18
Lieut. D. Orbell
2nd Lt. H. W. Huckle } Killed.
" G. G. R. Nock

Lieut R. S. Crose
" F. C. Banyard } Wounded
" H. J. Unwin

25 ORs killed.
70 " wounded.
5 " missing

18/9/18.
Capt A. Johnson.
" B. H. Wallis.
Lieut G. H. Keating } Killed.
2nd Lt B. Carter
" H. W. Fuller

Capt H. D. Boyd.
2nd Lt H. F. Woot } Wounded
" J. W. Burton.
" G. G. Broom   N.Y.D.N.

19/9/18
Capt A. B. H. Dunlop M.C. Wounded. Died 20/9
Lieut. A. E. M. Coles.   Wounded

18-23/9/18. 26 ORs killed
129 ORs wounded
8 ORs missing.

24/9/18. 2 ORs wounded (Attd 35th T.M.B)

27/9/18. 2nd Lt E. Gloster (5th Suffks) wounded.
8 ORs killed.
10 ORs wounded

28/9/18. 1 OR. wounded.

29/9/18. 2 ORs killed
2 ORs wounded

1/1 Cambridgeshire Regt
September 1918.

Strength Sept 1st
29 Offrs 911 ORs.

Strength Sept 30th
28 Offrs 772 ORs.

4th Cavalry Regt

1/1st Cambridgeshire Regiment.

Reinforcements during September 1918
_____

1st   25   O.R.
2nd.   17   O.R.
3rd.   11   O.R.
8th.   13   O.R.
9th.   { Major R. G. ROYLE D.S.O. (K.O.Y.L.I.)
         { 2   O.R.

12th.   17   O.R.
13th.   { a/Capt. A.B.H. DUNLOP. M.C.
        { Lieut.   H.H.B. GRAIN M.C.
        { 2/Lt.   H.B. HART.
        {   "   H.W. WILKIN.
        {   "   H.J.A. HOOLE
        {   1   OK

14th.   { Lieut.   C.B. RIGBY   (4th Suffolks)
        { 2/Lt   H.W. BURTON.   "   "
        {   "   E.E. GROOM.   "   "
        {   "   C.S. SEMMENS   "   "
        {   "   J.V. MEYER.   "   "
        {   "   H.W. FULLER   (5th Suffolks)
        {   "   E. GLOSTER   "   "
        {   "   W.R. HARRIS.   "   "
        { 10.   O.R.

18th.   { 2/Lt A.A. GEATER
        { 29   O.R.
21st.   { Capt. C.L. TEBBUTT. M.C.
21st.   { 21   O.R.
23rd.   29   O.R.
25th.   1   OK
26th.   1   O.R.

35th Brigade.
12th Division.

1/1st BATTALION

CAMBRIDGESHIRE REGIMENT.

OCTOBER 1 9 1 8

Vol 29

35/12

War Diary
=
1/1st Kent Kyr.
=
October - 1918
=

WAR DIARY or INTELLIGENCE SUMMARY

Army Form C. 2118.

1/1 Can 6 R

Place	Date 1918	Hour	Summary of Events and Information	Remarks and references to Appendices
EPÉHY	Sep. 30		Battalion withdrawn from this Sector & bivouacked near GUYENCOURT.	
	Oct. 1		Day spent in reorganisation & refitting.	
	" 2		Battalion moved by bus to PROYART & bivouacked in road by River SOMME	
	" 3	5.25 a.m.	Battalion entrained at MÉRICOURT Station & travelled to AUBIGNY reaching there at about midnight.	
	" 4		On arrival from at AUBIGNY marched to SUBURBAN CAMP, VILLERS AU BOIS — day spent in reorganisation	Strength No. 1 offrs order 100
	" 5		Moved up by bus to MONUMENT at THELUS — marched in morning to BROWN LINE near VIMY (between	offrs order No 5 offrs order No 6
			VILLERVAL and BRULÉ. B.Co. McCLAYTON remained as Transport lines — Major RICKAYLE in command	
	" 6	9 am	Moved forward to BLACK LINE subsequently relieving 78 SOMERSET L.I. in front line between FRESNOY	offrs order No 7
			and OPPY. Battalion H.Q. in ARLEUX LOOP.	
	" 7	11.00	Battle patrols (who went forward with object of establishing forward posts in enemy front line (VILLAGE TRENCH) —	appendix No 11 offrs order No 18
			from platoons (2 of B Coy, 1 back of A & C Coys) — A Coys Platoon & 2 officers (Capt. L.H. HOPKINS, Rifles) was	
			unable to attain its objective & returned to its original trenches. C Coys platoon moved up FOOT ALLEY	
			& was driven back by enemy machine gun fire, during retirement 2 of the gun shells burst in the midst of men	
			causing casualties & confused retirement. B Coys platoons were both successful in reaching their objective but were	
			heavily engaged on all sides during afternoon & were withdrawn at night	
			to line against —	
	" 8		Patrols pushed forward during Early morning — Enemy front line found to be more active & telegraph	
	" 9		taken over by A + B Coys who pushed up a further 2000 yds towards FRESNES — RONVILLY LINE	
	" 10		C + D Coys moved forward through A + B Coys & occupied line of SUNKEN ROAD along 840 yds in front	
			of QUÉANT — DROCOURT LINE at dusk — Some M.G. obstruction	
	" 11	10.45	C + D Coys advanced to occupied portion of QUÉANT — DROCOURT LINE — A + B Coys in support on SUNKEN ROAD	
	" 12		Battalion advanced in artillery formation EAST & BEAUMONT to FLERS — HENIN LIETARD ROAD then	
			advanced between FOSSE and FOSSE 7 trans very heavily shelled. Major KOYLE wounded + it GR.	
			CLAYTON taking command on arrival Nomainent (No 5) Capt. C. L. TEBBOT being in charge until his arrival.	
	" 13		D Coys. On arrival at FLERS dug in lightly in sheltered position under cover of RAILWAY EMBANKMENT	
			Battalion in Bdg. Reserve in old line of occupied RUSSY trenches — Division's wire-cutting coy & heavy M.G. fire & day	

HENIN LIETARD ROAD

WAR DIARY
INTELLIGENCE SUMMARY

Army Form C. 2118.

1/1 CAMB R

Place	Date	Hour	Summary of Events and Information	Remarks and references to Appendices
AUBY	1918 OCT 14	0515	Batt attached to AUBY in conjunction with 1st WORCESTERS (8th DIV) on the night. Assembly was carried out successfully by Capt C BOWERS in spite of harassing fire from M-Gs. Order of ascent:— D Coy (Capt Harding-Newman) A Coy (Capt Zellatt) C Coy (Capt Hollis) B Coy (2/Lt HOORE) Attack went well ad head of LA HAUTE DEULE CANAL made good from Q26 a 2.0 to Q26 a 8.6. About 45 prisoners and enjr M-Gs were captured. Unfortunately 1st Worcesters did not clear the village on the right and fell back to line west their C/P flank resting at Q3 d 5.5 leaving the right of the battn exposed to the enemy who were in considerable strength at the eastern end of the village.	Sheet 44A S.2
		1230	2 views of the push on the right the 1st Cambs preventive was made to the left railway running through Q31 a to and a different place forced to join a push butt on the right. Very heavy hostile artillery fire throughout the afternoon & evening. The enemy adopted to attack however very well - the new gas mines proved ???? to each of the hostile barrage. The front ??? also enabled D Coy	MCC

Army Form C. 2118.

WAR DIARY
or
INTELLIGENCE SUMMARY.
(Erase heading not required.)

1/1 Cam B K

Place	Date Oct	Hour	Summary of Events and Information	Remarks and references to Appendices
AUBY	14		In the C of [illegible] to of a heavy enemy force in support of his many that of the outskirts of the village which materially arrested the advance MGC	Appendix [illegible]
do	15		of C + B Coys. In front line — Relieved at night by 7th NORFOLKS + marched to billets at DROCOURT LA FOSSE (HENIN LIETARD) — in Reserve to Brigade.	Appendix G: 5 [illegible]
DROCOURT LA FOSSE	16		Spent in re-organising + refitting. do.	
do.	17	16.00	Moved to billets in AUBY.	
	18		Moved from AUBY to RAIMBEAUCOURT — rested there during day — moved at night to billets at BOUVIGNIES.	
	19		Moved forward as Support Battalion to Brigade through COUTICHES to ORCHIES and billets for night at MANNEVILLE (C Coy in farm S. of ORCHIES).	
	20		Moved forward as Advance Guard to Brigade along the roads ORCHIES — RUE D'ORCHIES — LANDAS — SAMEON and LANDAS — LE QUENNE — GUVAKMEZ — VIEUX CONDÉ. D Coy on right + A Coy on left as Vanguard. B + C Coys. Rearguard. No opposition was met with until our Advance Guard reached the E. outskirts of LANDAS when they came under heavy fire from a party of BOSCH estimated at about 30 men. During the movement forward from LANDAS considerable M.G. was made of covering fire which greatly facilitated the advance. The advance was thus rapid + the situation was quickly cleared up — A + D Coys. Capturing 8 prisoners + 3 Machine Guns — And an outpost line was taken up on the KUMEGTIES — RUE MOKINETZ — SAMEON for the night of the 20th — 21st.	

WAR DIARY / INTELLIGENCE SUMMARY

Army Form C. 2118.

1/1 CAMB. R.

Place	Date 1916 Oct.	Hour	Summary of Events and Information	Remarks and references to Appendices
SAMEON	21		1st NORFOLKS passed through on line of outposts & Bn. concentrated in SAMEON as support Bn.	
RUE BALORY (ROSULT)	22	09.00	Battalion moved to RUE BALORY (& billets — Brigade being Divisional Reserve.	
	23		Spent in re-organizing, re-fitting & training.	
	24			
	25	09.30	Inspection by Brig. Gen. VINCENT. Major S.G. TYTE, M.C. 9th K.F. assumed command	
	26	—	Intimation made for relief of 7th ROYAL SUSSEX in front line but relief cancelled at 12.30 hrs in consequence of divisional relief.	
COUTICHES	27	09.00	Moved to billets in COUTICHES for night only	
RACHES	28	15.08	Moved to billets in RACHES arriving there about 17.00 hours.	
	29		Spent in training.	
	30			
	31			

SECRET.   Appendix No. 1   Copy No. 9
                 1/1st CAMBRIDGESHIRE REGIMENT.

                      Operation Order No.100.

Ref. Map.   In the Field.
Sheet 51.b.N.W.   8th October 1918.

───

INFORMATION.   1.   The 1/1st CAMB. REGT. will move up to the BRN
               BROWN LINE today 8:10:18. On arrival in BROWN
               LINE the Battalion will come under orders of the
               G.O.C. 61st   Infantry Brigade.

INTENTION.   2.   The 1/1st CAMB.REGT. will embus at W.30.c.8.5.
               at 1330 hours today.

DETAIL.   3. (a). The Battalion will parade at 1245 hours
               today in column of route on road in front of Q.M.STORES
               facing Main Road, in the following order:-
                    H.Q., A, B, C, D.
               Dress:- Full Marching Order. Steel helmets under
               pack straps.
               Lewis Guns will be carried.

                  (b). Officers valises and surplus mess stores etc.
               will be dumped at Q.M.Stores at 1201 hours today.

                  (c). Mess Stores, R.A.F.Stores, etc., will be
               dumped outside the Guard Tent at 1230 hours today.

                  (d). Transport. The Transport will move to
               NEUVILLE- ST - VAAST today. Further instructions
               will be issued later.

                  (e). Battle Surplus. The Battle Surplus will parade
               under Lieut. C.WARREN, at 1245 hours today, in front
               of H.Q.Mess.

REPORTS.   4.   Certificates of cleanliness of vacated billets will
               be forwarded to Battn.H.Qrs. on arrival in new area.
               Lists of trench stores taken over will be forwarded
               to Battn.H.Qrs. by 1201 hours tomorrow 9th inst.
               Arrival in new area will be forwarded to Battn. H. Qrs.
               as early as possible giving location.

          ACKNOWLEDGE.

                                   (sd). C.H. Bowers. Capt. & A/Adjt.
Copies issued at   1/1st Cambridgeshire Regiment.
to.
No.1. A Coy.
No.2. B "
No.3. C "
No.4. D "
No.5. H.Q.
No.6. Q.M.
No.7. T.O.
No.8. Lieut.C.Warren.
No.9.&10. War Diary.
No.11. File

Appendix No 2

SECRET.   Copy No 6

1/1 CAMBRIDGESHIRE REGIMENT
Operation Order No. 101.

Ref Map.   In the Field
Sheet 51. b. N.W.   5/10/18.

INFORMATION. 1. The 1/1 CAMB. R. will move to the BLACK LINE (BOW SUPPORT B.16.b.6.4 to B.4.c.7.4.).

DETAIL
2(a) "D" Coy will move via TOMMY ALLEY & hold from B.16.b.6.4 to B.10.d.1.0.
"C" Coy will move via TIRED ALLEY & CLYDE ALLEY & hold from B.10.c.8.7. to B.10.d.1.0.
"B" Coy will move via TIRED ALLEY & hold from B.10.a.7.6 to B.10.c.8.7.
"A" Coy. will move via TIRED ALLEY & hold from B.10.a.7.6 to B.4.c.7.4.
(b). Time. All Companies will move off at 0900 hours tomorrow 6th inst.
(c). All Cooking Utensils will be taken by Companies.
(d) Battn H.Q. for BLACK LINE same as for BROWN LINE.

REPORTS 3. Reports of arrival in new area will be forwarded to

---

Sheet 2   Operation Order No 101.   5/10/18

REPORTS 3. Battn HQ. as early as possible.
(cont'd)

                                C Bowes
                                Capt & a/Adjt.
                                1/1 Cambridgeshire Regiment

Copies issued at 2030 hours 5/10/18
No 1   A. Coy.
" 2   B "
" 3   C "
" 4   D "
" 5 & 6 War Diary
" 7   File

SECRET   Appendix No 3   Copy No. 6

1/1 Cambridgeshire Regiment.
Operation Order No.102

Ref. Map.
Sheet. 51. b. N.W.   In the Field
       6/10/18

INFORMATION   1. The 1/1 CAMB. R. will relieve the 7th SOMERSET. L.I. in the ARLEUX SECTOR. RIGHT SUB-SECTION tonight 6th inst.

DETAIL   2.(a) Relief. Coy will relieve as follows:-

"A" Coy 1/1 CAMB. R. will relieve "D" Coy 7th SOM.L.I.
"B"   "   "   "   "   "   "   "B"   "   "   "

Front Line Companies.

"C" Coy 1/1 CAMB. R. will relieve "A" Coy 7th SOM. L.I.

"D" 1/1 CAMB. R. will relieve "C" Coy 7th SOM. L.I.

Battn. H.Q. 1/1 CAMB. R. will relieve Battn. H.Q. 7th SOM. L.I. at B.12.a.25.70

(b) Time As given to Company Commanders.

(c) Rations As given to Company Commanders.

Sheet 2.   Operation Order No 102   6/10/18

REPORTS   3. Code Word for Relief
          Complete "NEWMAN"
          List of Trench Stores, Maps, etc,
          taken over will be forwarded
          to Battn H.Qrs by 1200 hrs.
          tomorrow 7th inst.
          Coy Commdr will forward as
          early as possible Dispositions of
          Companies & Location of
          Coy. H.Qrs.

          Copies issued at 12.05 hrs 6/8/18
          No 1. A. Coy.
          " 2. B. "   C Bowes
          " 3. C. "   Capt & Adjt
          " 4. D. "   1/1 Cambridgeshire Regt
          " 5&6 War Diary.
          " 7 File.

SECRET Appendix No 4 Copy No. 6.

1/1 CAMBRIDGESHIRE REGIMENT
Operation Order No 103.

Ref. Map.   In the Field
Sheet 51. b. N.W. & 44. A. S.W.   6/10/18

INFORMATION 1. Tomorrow, the 24th Inf. Bde.
on the right, will attack &
capture CHAPEL TRENCH, and
establish Platoon Posts at the
following points:—
(a). C.8.c.03.50 (Junction of
COW LANE & CHAPEL TRENCH).
(b). C.7.d.88.62. (Junction of COKE
& CHAPEL TRENCHES).
(c). C.7.b.45.05. (Junction of
Truck & CHAPEL TRENCH.)

INTENTION   2.(a) From ZERO to ZERO plus
8, the Artillery will place a
barrage on CONNIE & VILLAGE
TRENCHES from C.1.d.85.10. to
U.25.d.25.25.
At ZERO plus 8, the Artillery
will lift on to CRADDOCK &
RUPERT TRENCHES from C.1.d.90.40
to U.25.d.77.80, where it will
remain until ZERO plus 12

Contd

Sheet 2.	Operation Order No 103 6/10/18
INTENTION. (Cont'd)	(b) Under cover of this barrage the 1/1 Camb. R. will send forward Battle Patrols towards CONNIE & VILLAGE TRENCHES, and endeavour to establish Platoon Posts at the following points:- C.1.d.72.26 (Junction of CRADDOCK & CONNIE TRENCHES. C.1.d.55.80. C.1.b.5.4. (Junction of FOOT ALLEY & VILLAGE TRENCH). U.25.d.25.40. (Junction of UNFIT & VILLAGE TRENCHES).
DETAIL	3.(1). "B" Coy. will establish Platoon Post at C.1.d.72.26 (Junction of CRADDOCK & CONNIE TRENCHES) and C.1.d.55.80. (2). "C" Coy. will establish Platoon Post at C.1.b.5.4 (Junction of FOOT ALLEY & VILLAGE TRENCH.) (3). "A" Coy. will establish Platoon Post at U.25.d.25.40.(Junction of UNFIT & VILLAGE TRENCHES.

Cont

Sheet 3.   Operation Order No 103   6/10/18.

DETAIL.
(Cont.)

(4). One Platoon of "B" Coy will move forward from CADDY TRENCH up the C.T. 300× S. of FOOT ALLEY & work up CONNIE TRENCH to C.1.d.55.30 and establish Platoon Post.

(5). One Platoon of "B" Coy. will move due EAST from CADDY TRENCH at about C.1.2.9.2. & on reaching junction of CRADDOCK & CONNIE Trenches (C.1.d.72.26.) will establish Platoon Post.

(6). One Platoon of "C" Coy will move up FOOT ALLEY and establish post at junction of FOOT ALLEY and VILLAGE TRENCHES (C.1.b.5.4.)

(7). The Platoon of "A" Coy at C.1.a.9.8. will move up UNFIT TRENCH & establish the post at junction of UNFIT & VILLAGE TRENCHES (U.25.d.25.40.)

(8). Platoons which are to move forward will be in position at least half an hour before ZERO & will move at ZERO keeping as close to the barrage as possible. If posts are successfully established intermediate portions of VILLAGE

Cont.

Sheet 2.   Operation Order No 103.   6/10/18

DETAIL   (7 cont) & CONNIE TRENCHES will be
(cont.)   patrolled carefully.
         (8) ZERO HOUR. ZERO HOUR will
         by 11.00 hours 7th October 1918.

REPORTS 4. Reports as to progress will
         be forwarded as early as possible
         to Battn. H.Qrs.

Copies issued at 02.20 hrs 7/10/18
No 1.   A. Coy
 " 2.   B. "
 " 3.   C. "
 " 4.   D. "   C Bowers
 " 5 & 6 War Diary   Capt & a/Adjt.
 " 7   File   1/1 Cambridgeshire
                                           Regiment

SECRET   Appendix No 5.   Copy No 9

1/1st Cambridgeshire Regiment
Operation Order No.104.

Ref. Map.   In the Field.
Sheet 44A S.E. & S.W.   15/10/18

INFORMATION. 1. The 7th NORFOLK. R. will relieve the 9th ESSEX R and 1/1 CAMB. R in the Front System of the Right Brigade Sector tonight 15th Oct.

INTENTION 2. On relief the 1/1 CAMB. R. will move to LENIN-LIETARD & be in Brigade Reserve.

DETAIL. 3. (a) *Guides.* Guides for Right & Left Company will report to Battn H.Q. at 17.50 hrs today.

(b) *Relief.* Two Coys 7th NORFOLKS will relieve Three Coys 1/1 CAMB R (B & C. Coy treated as one Coy) in the Front System tonight. On relief Coys will proceed to Battn H.Q. where they will be met by their C.S.M.s who will guide them to new area.

(c) *Lewis Guns.* These will be loaded on Limber at Battn H.Q.

cont

Sheet 2.   Operation Order No 104   15/10/18.

DETAIL (cont.)

3. (d). Packs. These will be dumped at Company billets in new area.
   (e) Mess Stores, Dixies, etc., are being taken to new area this afternoon.

REPORTS

4 (1) Relief Complete will be sent to Battn H.Q. Code Word Name of Company Commander.
   (2) Arrival in Billets will be forwarded to Battn H.Q. with Location.
   Location of Battn H.Q. will be notified later.

Copies issued at 14.37 hrs 15/10/18
No 1   A Coy
 " 2   B "
 " 3   C "
 " 4   D "
 " 5   HQ
 " 6   Q.M. & T.O.
 " 7 & 8 War Diary
 " 9   File

C. Dowell
Capt a/Adjt
1/1 Cambridgeshire Regt

Battn H.Q. U. 35. c. 5. 6
Coys in Billets in Houses round

1/1st Cambridgeshire Regiment
Casualties for October 1918

Appendix No 7

4/10/18	Capt L. H. Hopkins (1/1st Hunts Cyc) Killed.
	Lieut. J. A. McNish do Missing
	8 ORs Killed
	18 " Wounded
	11 " Missing
9/10/18.	1 " Wounded.
10/10/18.	2nd Lt. W.R. Harris. Died in Hos.
	1 OR. Killed
	8 " Wounded
11/10/18.	Major R. G. Royle. D.S.O. Wounded.
	3 OR. Wounded
12/10/18.	1 OR. Wounded.
13/10/18.	2nd Lt. J. V. Meyer (4th Suffks). Wounded & Prisr
	" C. S. Semmens. " Wounded/at duty.
14/10/18.	2nd Lt H.W. Wilkin. Wounded.
	" R. A. Robinson (1/1st Hunts Cyc) do
	Lt. S. B. Bowditch do do
	2nd Lt. G. W. Linsey do
	8 OR. Killed.
	45 OR. Wounded
	1 OR. Missing.
15/10/18	4 OR. Wounded
20/10/18.	1 OR. Killed.
22/10/18.	1 OR. Killed
	4 OR. Wounded.
24/10/18.	1 OR. Killed.

1/1st Cambridgeshire Regiment
Reinforcements for October 1918.

Appendix No 6.

Officers

14/10/18.	Lieut. J. A. Hardman	
"	G. O. Wallis-Palmer	
"	C. F. Steward	(Suffk Regt)
"	F. J. Harvey	do.
	2nd/Lt. A. H. H. Sykes	do.
"	J. G. Hannan	(1/1st Hunts Cyc)
"	A. F. Wilkins	
"	J. F. Suttle	
19/10/18.	2nd Lt. C. Pollard	
"	A. Stone	(Suffk Regt)
"	H. C. Holborn	do.
"	W. Hodges	do.
25/10/18.	Capt S. G. Tyte. M.C.	(9th Bn R. Fusiliers)

ORs

4/10/18.	1.
7/10/18.	17.
9/10/18.	20.
10/10/18	3.
14/10/18.	7.
16/10/18.	8.
21/10/18.	11.
26/10/18.	23.
27/10/18.	2.
28/10/18	8.

Appendix
No 2.

1/1st Cambridgeshire Regiment.

Effective Fighting Strength
of the Battalion on

1/10/18   32 Officers   768 O.R.

31/10/18   31 Officers   732 O.R.

35th Brigade.
12th Division.

1/1st BATTALION

CAMBRIDGESHIRE REGIMENT.

NOVEMBER 1918

Vol 30

War Diary

1/1st Cambridge Regt.

November 1918

Army Form C. 2118.

WAR DIARY
or
INTELLIGENCE SUMMARY

(Erase heading not required.)

1/1 CAMB. R.E.

Place	Date Nov. 1918	Hour	Summary of Events and Information	Remarks and references to Appendices
RACHES	1-4	—	Divisional out of line — Battalion billets at RACHES — day spent in training — Major S. G. TYTE M.C. assumed command of Battalion during absence on leave of Lt Col. M.C. CLAYTON D.S.O.	App.I 20105
LE HENNOY	5	—	Moved to billets at LE HENNOY	
"	7-8	—	Spent in training	
"	9	08.30	Marched to BEUVRY where Bn. entrained — detrained at ST AMAND marched to ODOMEZ — in billets at ODOMEZ for night.	App.III 20104
ODOMEZ	10	10.30	Battalion marches to HERGNIES — working parties under C.R.E. — moved later to billets	App.III 20106
HERGNIES	11	—	working parties under C.R.E.	
BONSECOURS	12	—	Battalion marches to BONSECOURS stopping en route to repair CONDÉ – BONSECOURS ROAD turning into billets about 15.30 hrs.	App.IV 20109
	13-15		Spent in training, working parties under C.R.E.	
	16		Training — Lt Col. M.C. CLAYTON D.S.O. returned from leave & resumed command.	
	17		Brigade Church Parade on BONSECOURS FOOTBALL GROUND — Thanksgiving service.	
	18/19 20		Spent in training	
	21		Inspection of Battalion on Football Ground by Brig Gen. B. VINCENT CMG GOC 35th Inf Bde.	
	22-24		Spent in training	
ST AMAND	25		Marched to ST AMAND where billets for night.	

Army Form C. 2118.

WAR DIARY
or
INTELLIGENCE SUMMARY.
(Erase heading not required.)

(2) 1/1 CAMB. R.

Instructions regarding War Diaries and Intelligence Summaries are contained in F. S. Regs., Part II. and the Staff Manual respectively. Title pages will be prepared in manuscript.

Place	Date 1914	Hour	Summary of Events and Information	Remarks and references to Appendices
SOMAIN	Nov. 26		Battalion marched to SOMAIN — in billets	Appx OS.111.
		17-30	Spent in training	
			Effective strength at beginning of month Officers 31 Other Ranks 732	
			" " " end of month 47 778	

SECRET.   Copy No. 10

1/1st CAMBRIDGESHIRE REGIMENT.

Operation Order No.106.

Ref. Maps.   In the Field.
Sheets 44A and 44 1:40,000.   4th November 1918.

INFORMATION. 1. The 1/1 Camb.R. will move to the LANDAS Area to-morrow.

DETAIL. 2. (a). <u>Starting Point.</u> Junction of road and track R.21.c.9.3.
(b) <u>Time.</u> C Company will pass the starting point at 08.31 hours.
(c). <u>Order of March.</u> C, D, Drums, A, B, H.Q. Transport.
A distance of 500 yards will be maintained between Battalions and 200 yards between Companies and Transport.
(d). <u>Route.</u> Junction of road and track R.21.c.9.3. - FLINES - COUTRICHES - ORCHIES - RUE D'ORCHIES - LANDAS.
(e). <u>Dress</u> Full marching order. Soft caps and leather jerkins will be worn.
Officers in marching order.
(f). <u>Blankets</u> will be rolled in bundles of 10 labelled and clearly marked by platoons.
These will be stacked at Q.M.Stores by 07.00 hours.
Officers valises will be stacked at Q.M.Stores at the same time.
(g). <u>Limbers</u> will report to Companies to collect Lewis Guns and Mess stores at 07.30 hours.
(h). <u>Cookers</u> with mens dinners will accompany the Transport.
(i). C.Q.M.S.s with bicycles will report to 2nd.Lt.H.B.HART, at Battn. H.Qrs. at 06.45 hours.

REPORTS. 3. Arrival in billets and location of Company Headquarters will be forwarded to Battn.H.Q. on arrival.
Map reference of A.A.Lewis Gun Posts will be forwarded to Battn.H.Qrs as early as possible.

The Commanding Officer directs that the inspection before the march will be carried out just as thoroughly as for an inspection parade.
No sandbags will be carried on the line of march.

(sd). C.H. Hollis. Capt. & A/Adjt.
1/1st Cambridgeshire Regiment.

Copies issued at 21.50.hrs.
No.1. A Company.
 2 B   "
 3 C   "
 4 D   "
 5 H.Q.
 6 Q.M.
 7 T.O.
 8 2nd.Lt.H.B.HART.
 9 War Diary.
10.   "   "
11 File.

SECRET.   Copy No. 10

1/1st CAMBRIDGESHIRE REGIMENT.

Ref.Maps.   Operation Order.No.107.   In the Field.
Sheet 44. 1:40,000.   9th November 1918.

INFORMATION. 1.   The 1/1st Camb.R. will move by bus to ODOMEZ today. 9th November 1918.

INTENTION. 2.   The Battalion will embus at 08.00 hours on the BEUVRY - ST AMAND Road. Head of column at BEUVRY Church.

DETAIL. 3.(a).**Starting point.** Head of column at road junction H.27.d.2.1.
(b).**Time.** The battalion will be formed up ready to move off, at road junction by 07.30 hours.
(c).**Order of march** B, D, Drums, A, C, H.Q.,
(d).**Dress.** Full marching order. Leather Jerkins will be worn. Packs will be slung. All shovels at at present in possession of Companies A and C Coys will be handed in to Transport by 06.30 hours. B and D Coys will draw all shovels available and 24 picks per Coy. from Transport Lines at 06.30 hours.
These will be carried in the lorries.
(e).**Embussing.** On arrival at embussing point the Battalion will form up in parties of 25, starting from the head of the column.
(f).**Reveille.** 04.30 hours.
(g).**Breakfast.** 05.00 hours.
(h).**Dixies.** Enough dixies to make tea and a hot meal for the men on arrival in new area will be taken on the lorries.
(i).**Mess stores.** Enough mess stores for a meal on arrival in new area will be taken in sand bags, remainder of mess stores will be stacked outside Company Headquarters by 06.45 hours.
(j).**Valises.** Officers valises will be stacked outside Company H.Q, by 05.45 hours.
(k).**Blankets.** Blankets will be rolled in bundles of 10 labelled and clearly marked by platoons and stacked at Q.M.Stores by 05.30 hours.
(l).**Limbers** will report to Companies to collect Lewis Guns, Mess stores and Officers valises at 0645 hours
(m).**Billetting Party.** 2nd.Lieut. H.B.HART. and the 5 C.Q.M.S.s will proceed with the battalion, they will meet the Staff Captain at ODOMEZ Church at 10.30 hours.

REPORTS. 4.   Location of Company Headquarters will be forwarded to Battalion Headquarters on arrival in billets.

O.s C Coys will render to Battalion Headquarters a certificate stating that the billets occupied by their Coys were left in a clean and sanitary condition.

(sd). C.H. Hollis. Capt. & A/Adjt.
Copies issued at 03.00 hours.   1/1st Cambridgeshire Regiment.
No.1. A Company.
  2. B   "
  3. C   "
  4. D   "
  5. H.Q.
  6. Q.M.
  7. T.O.
  8. 2nd.Lt.H.B.HART.
  9. War Diary.
 10.   "   "
 11. File.

SECRET.   Copy No. 9

1/1st CAMBRIDGESHIRE REGIMENT.

Ref. Map.   Operation Order No.108.   In the Field.
Sheet.44. 1:40,000.   10th November 1918.

=:=

INFORMATION.   1.   The 1/1 Camb.R. will move to HERGNIES today 10th November 1918.

DETAIL.   2.(a). Starting Point. Head of column at road junction Q.3.d.3=9. at 10.30 hours.
Companies will pass the starting point in the following order:- Drums, H.Q, A, B, C, D, Transport.
   (b). Route. Q.3.d.3.9. - Q.3.b.9.7. - K.33.c.1.3. - thence via Pontoon Bridge to HERGNIES.
   (c). Dress Full Marching Order. Leather Jerkins and steel helmets will be worn.
   (d). Tools. All picks and shovels at present in charge of Companies will be carried on the line of march
   (e). Reveille. at 07.00 hours.
   (f). Breakfast at 07.45 hours.
   (g). Valises. and Mess stores. Limbers will report to Companies to collect valises, mess stores and Lewis Guns at 09.00 hours.
   (h). Blankets. Blankets will be rolled in bundles of 10, clearly marked by Platoons and stacked at Q.M.Stores at 07.30 hours.
   (i). Billetting Party. 5 Q.Q.M.S.s with bicycles will report to 2nd.Lieut. H.B. HART, at Battn.H.Q. at 07.45 hours.
One N.C.O. per Company,H.Qrs and Transport will report to Battn.H.Q. at 10.00 hours.
These will act as Guides for the 7th Bn.NORFOLK.REGT. who are taking over the billets occupied by this Battalion.
   (j). Working Parties. All parties proceeding to work under the 89th Field Coy.R.E. will wear Full Marching Order. Packs will be dumped in HERGNIES and one man put in charge under Company arrangements, before parties proceed to work.

REPORTS.   3.   Location of Company Headquarters will be forwarded to Battalion Headquarters on arrival in billets.
O.s C Coys will render a certificate stating that the billets were left in a clean and sanitary condition, to the Adjutant at the starting point.

                              (sd). C.H. Hollis. Capt. & A/Adjt.
                                 1/1st Cambridgeshire Regiment.

Copies issued at 01.30 hours.
No.1. A Company.
  2. B   "
  3. C   "
  4. D   "
  5. H.Q.
  6. Q.M.
  7. M.O.
  8. 2nd.Lieut. H.B. HART.
  9. War Diary.
 10.   "   "
 11. File.

SECRET.   Copy No. 11

                    1/1st CAMBRIDGESHIRE REGIMENT.

Ref. Map.   Operation Order No.109.   In the Field.
Sheet 44. 1:40,000.   12th Nov. 1918.
=:

INFORMATION.   1.   The 1/1 Camb.R. will move to the
                     BONSECOURT Area today 12/11/18.

DETAIL.   2.(a).Parade. The Battalion minus working parties
                     will parade outside Battalion Headquarters at
                     10.15 hours.
                     Lieut. F.J.HARVEY, will be in charge of the parade.
                     One Officer will be left behind from each Company
                     to supervise the cleaning of billets, dumping
                     of blankets etc.
                     They will report to Lieut. F.J.HARVEY, with their
                     Company Details at 10.15 hours.
                       (b).Dress:- Full marching order. Soft caps and
                     Leather Jerkins will be worn.
                       (c).Order of march:- Drums, H.Q, A, B, C, D Coys
                     Transport.
                       (d).Route:- Batn. H.Q. - Cross roads K.24.a.8.6
                     - Road junction K.14.b.2.4. - BONSECOURT.
                       (e) Working parties. Working parties will proceed
                     to their tasks in Full marching order. Leather
                     Jerkins and soft caps will be worn.
                     After completion of tasks they will march to
                     BONSECOURT where guides will meet them.
                     Packs will be dumped at a point where battalion meets
                     R.E.Guides, under arrangements to be made by
                     Capt. E.H.BOWERS.
                       (f).Blankets, valises, mess stores and Lewis Guns.
                     Blankets will be rolled in bundles of 10 and clearly
                     marked by platoons.
                     Officers valises, mess stores and lewis guns will be
                     stacked outside Company Headquarters by 08.00 hours.
                     The Transport Officer will arrange to collect these
                     and convey them to the Q.M.Stores.
                       (g).Billetting party. 5 C.Q.M.S.s will report to
                     2nd.Lieut. H.B.HART at Battalion Headquarters at
                     08.45 hours with bicycles.

REPORTS.   3.   Location of Company Headquarters will be
                     forwarded to Battalion Headquarters on arrival in
                     billets.

                     O.s C Coys will render a certificate that all billets
                     were left in a clean and sanitary condition.

                                       (sd). C.H. Hollis. Capt. & A/Adjt.
                                             1/1st Cambridgeshire Regiment.

Copies issued at 04.30 hours.
   No.1. A Company.
      2 B   "
      3 C   "
      4 D   "
      5 H.Q.
      6 Q.M.
      7 T.O.
      8 Lieut.F.J.HARVEY.
      9 2nd.Lieut. H.B.HART.
     10. War Diary.
     11. Bde. "
     12. File.

SECRET.   Copy No. 8

1/1st CAMBRIDGESHIRE REGIMENT.

Operation Order No. 110.

Ref. Maps Sheet 44. 1/40,000. &   In the Field.
TOURNAI & VALENCIENNES. 1/100,000.   24th November 1918.

INFORMATION. 1.   The 1/1st Cambridgeshire Regiment will move to ST AMAND on November 25th 1918.

DETAIL.   2. (a). Parade.   The Battalion will parade in rear of Billets in close column of Coys at 09.05 hours.
            (b). Dress.   Full Marching Order, soft caps and Leather Jerkins will be worn.
            (c). Order of March.   Drums. C, D, H.Q., A, B, Transport.
            (d). Route.   L.16.b.40.95 - HERGNIES - K.33.a.9.6. - Q.1.b.8.7. - OUBRAY - ST AMAND.
The following distances will be maintained on the march:-
    100 yards between Coys and Transport.
    50 Yards between each section of 12 Vehicles.
            (e). Stores. Blankets. Valises. Mess stores.
Blankets will be rolled in bundles of 10 and be clearly marked by Platoons and will be stacked in the Guard Room by 08.00 hours.
Mess Cart will report to Coys at 08.15 hours to collect one mess box.   Remaining Coy Mess Stores will be taken to the Q.M.Stores by 08.15 hours.
Officers valises will be stacked at Q.M.Stores by 07.30 hours.

REPORTS.   3.   Location of Coy. H.Q. will be forwarded to Battalion Headquarters on arrival in billets.

O.C. Coys will render a certificate that billets were left in a clean and sanitary condition to the Adjutant non parade.

No sandbags or parcels will be carried on the march.

                              (sd). C.H. Hollis.
                                    Capt. & A/Adjt.
Copies issued at 19.45 hours.   1/1st Cambridgeshire Regiment.
No. 1. A Company.
    2 B   "
    3 C   "
    4 D   "
    5 H.Q.
    6. Q.M.
    7 T.O.
    8 & 9 War Diary.
    10. File.

SECRET.   Copy No.

                    1/1st Cambridgeshire Regiment.
                    ─────────────────────────────

                        Operation Order No. 111.   In the Field,
Ref. Map. VALENCIENNES. 1/100,000   25th November 1918.
:=:

INFORMATION.   (1). The 35th Inf. Bde. will move to SOMAIN
                      on November, 26th 1918.

INTENTION.   (2). The 1/1st Camb. Regt. will move by March Route.

DETAIL.   (3). (a) PARADE. The Battalion will parade on
                          ground in front of Billets in close column of
                          Companies at 08.30 hours.
                      (b) Dress. Full Marching Order, soft caps
                          and leather jerkins will be worn.
                      (c) Order of March. D. H.Q. A. B. Drums. C. and
                          Transport.
                      (d) Route. Bridge South of ST. AMAND where
                          Road crosses River SCARPE,- RUE DUMONTEL-
                          GRAND BRAY - WALLERS - HELESMES - ERRE -
                          SOMAIN.
                          The following distances will be maintained
                          on the march :-
                              100 yards between Coys & Transport.
                              50 Yards between each section of 12
                              vehicles.
                      (e) Stores, Blankets, Mess Stores, Valises etc
                          Blankets will be rolled in bundles of 10
                          and clearly marked by Platoons and will be
                          stacked at Q.M.Stores at 07.30 hours.
                          Mess Cart will report to Coys. at 07.45 hours
                          to collect one mess box. Remaining Coy. Mess
                          Stores will be taken to the Q.M. Stores by
                          07.45 hours.
                          Officers' valises will be stacked at Q.M
                          Stores by 07.30 hours.

REPORTS.   (5). Location of Coy. H.Q. will be forwarded to
                      Battn. H.Q. on arrival in Billets.

                      O.C. Coys. will render a certificate that
                      Billets were left in a clean and sanitary
                      condition to the Adjutant on parade.

                      No sand-bags or parcels will be carried on
                      the march.

                                        (sd) C.H.Hollis, Capt. A/Adjt.
Copies issued at   Hours.   1/1st Cambridgeshire Regiment.
No.1. A Coy.
   2. B "
   3. C "
   4. D "
   5. H.Q.
   6. Q.M.
   7. T.O.
   8 & 9 War Diary.
   10. File.

1/1st Cambridgeshire Regt.

Reinforcements during November 1918.

1/11/18.	14 ORs.
2/11/18.	2nd Lt. J. Ogle. (H.A.C.)
	6 ORs.
4/11/18.	2nd Lt. C. Blake Frost (H.A.C.)
6/11/18.	2nd Lt. C.S. D'Morgan. (H.A.C.)
	5 ORs.
8/11/18.	9 ORs.
10/11/18.	4 ORs.
11/11/18.	5 ORs
13/11/18.	Lieut. F.O.P. Harrison (ASC)
14/11/18.	1 OR.
15/11/18.	2nd Lt H.J.A. Hoole.
16/11/18.	Lieut. A.A. Rayson.
	Capt. C.L. Tebbutt. M.C.
18/11/18.	13 ORs.
24/11/18.	3 ORs.
28/11/18.	Capt A.H. Carrette.
	" F. Clayton
	" B.G. Quin. M.C.
	Lieut C.G. Burns.
	" R.L. Brice
	" C.C. Cope
	" J. Le G. Lacy.
	" C.G. Myer
	" W.H. Selbie
	" J.M.D. English.
	2nd/Lt C.W. Sale
	57 ORs.

1/1st Cambridgeshire Regt.
Casualties during November
1918

15/11/18	1 OR died of sickness
18/11/18	1 OR ditto.

War Diary
1/1st Cumb Regt.
November 1918.

1st Cambridgeshire Regt.

Reinforcements during December 1918.

2/12/18.	5 ORs.
6/12/18.	Lieut. S. C. Knight. (6th Suffolks)
	10 ORs
10/12/18.	2 ORs.
11/12/18.	3 ORs.
12/12/18	5 ORs
13/12/18	1 OR
14/12/18	1 OR
17/12/18	6 ORs.
21/12/18.	4 ORs.
23/12/18.	3 ORs.
24/12/18.	Capt. E. Walker M.C. (Rejoined from Adjutants' Sch. Cambridge.)

Alan Dean
Vit Count Rd
Dec 1918

35th Brigade.
12th Division.

1/1st CAMBRIDGESHIRE REGIMENT

DECEMBER 1918

War Dept

December 1918

Combs Rept

Army Form C. 2118.

WAR DIARY
or
INTELLIGENCE SUMMARY.
(Erase heading not required.)

1st CAMB. RGT.

Place	Date	Hour	Summary of Events and Information	Remarks and references to Appendices
SOMAIN	1-12-18		Battalion Parade for Field Training	
"	2-12-18		Brigade Route March	
"	3-12-18		Battalion Parade for Ceremonial. Lre- A.E.M. Cito. M.C. Cpl. J.B. Clulow M.C. awarded Bar to Military Cross. 326037 Sergt. F.S. Blamire awarded D.C.M.	
"	4-12-18		Battalion Parade for Brigade Ceremonial Drill.	
"	5-12-18		Companies engaged in Salvage work at VILLERS CAMPEAU	
"	6-12-18		Companies engaged in Salvage work at VILLERS CAMPEAU. Capt- T.H.H. Harding-Newman of this Battalion to mobilization Officer. Lieut S.C. Knight S. (6th Suffolk Regt) returned for duty.	
"	7-12-18		Battalion Parade for Church Service	
"	8-12-18		Battalion Parade for Brigade Ceremonial and presentation of medal ribbons by Maj.General Higginson D.S.O	
"	9-12-18		Brigade Route March	
"	10-12-18		Battalion Parade for Ceremonial Drill. 326203 Sgt- Lilley H. 326952 Cpl. Coulson F. 325258 Pt. Wordham S. 326056 Pt. Clarke G.R. 326540 Cpl. Coulson M Molt. 326025 Pt. Wordley S. 415 70. Yeff. Booth W.F. 325227 Yeff. Katon J.H. 325229 Pt. Harris J.F. 326901 Pt. Toulson AN 329138 Pt Newbury B. 326273 Pt Smith C.	

WAR DIARY
or
INTELLIGENCE SUMMARY.

1st CAMB. REGT

Army Form C. 2118.

Place	Date	Hour	Summary of Events and Information	Remarks and references to Appendices
SOMAIN	10-12-18		326527 Pte Southgate F. awarded the Military Medal	
"	11-12-18		Battalion Parade. Capt. T.H.H. Harding-Newman awarded Military Cross	
"			10946 C.S.M. W.C. Parry M.M. awarded D.C.M.	
"	12-12-18		Battalion Parade. Ceremonial Drill. 8 Col Officers Demobilized.	
"	13-12-18		Battalion Parade to receive the Colours	
"	14-12-18		Battalion Parade. Church Service	
"	15-12-18		Battalion Parade. Ceremonial Drill	
"	16-17-18		Battalion Parade for Brigade Route March. 325014 C.Q.M.S Mansfield J.S. awarded D.C.M	
"	17-12-18		Coys engaged in Salvage work at VILLERS CAMPEAU CHATEAU	
"	18-12-18		A. B. D. Coys engaged in Salvage work at VILLERS CAMPEAU CHATEAU. B Coy on guard at SOMAIN Station.	
"	19-12-18		Battalion Parade for Field Training	
"	20-12-18		Company training with Coy Commanders	MM
"	21-12-18		Battalion Parade for Church Service. 21 O/R Demobilized	
"	22-12-18		Battalion Parade for Battalion Training	

Army Form C. 2118.

WAR DIARY
INTELLIGENCE SUMMARY
(Erase heading not required.)

1st CAMB REGT

Place	Date	Hour	Summary of Events and Information	Remarks and references to Appendices
SOMAIN	23-12-18		Battalion Parade and Company Training	
"	24-12-18		No. 9 Section Cpl. E. Walker M.C. reported back from Cambridge Course and took over the duties of his Section.	
"	25-12-18		Battalion Parade for Church Service. Ceremonial Parade for the award of 12.0 Leave for presentation of Medal ribbons by Brigadier General Vincent C.M.G.	
"	26-12-18		No. Parade. Yr. H.M.B. Irwin M.C. acted S.O.P. Demobilized Company Training under Coy Commanders	
"	27-12-18		Company Training under Coy Commanders	
"	28-12-18		Company moved Coy Comdrs. 2i/c. & Junior Leery M.C. and 17 o/r. Demobilized	
"	29-12-18		Battalion Parade for Church Service	
"	30-12-18		Company Training under Coy Commanders	
"	31-12-18		Company Training under Coy Commanders	

Effective strength 1/12/18. 41 Off. to 743 O.R.
31/12/18. 46 " 744 O.R.

M.C.O. Elliott
Cmdg 1st...

War Diary
January 1917

1/1st Bn
Cambridgeshire Regt

1/1 CAMBRIDGESHIRE REGT.

Army Form C. 2118.

WAR DIARY
or
INTELLIGENCE SUMMARY.
(Erase heading not required.)

Instructions regarding War Diaries and Intelligence Summaries are contained in F. S. Regs., Part II. and the Staff Manual respectively. Title pages will be prepared in manuscript.

Place	Date	Hour	Summary of Events and Information	Remarks and references to Appendices
SOMAIN	1-1-19		The advent of the New Year was celebrated by the Batt" on the Square at SOMAIN. The Drums played for ½ an hour before midnight, and a display of rockets was organised by CAPT. C.L. TEBBUTT. M.C. – There were no parades during the day – Football B.Cy.2 – D.Cy.2	
"	2-1-19		Company Training was carried out in the morning – C. Coy went engaged in salvage at VILLERS. CAMPEAU.	
"	3-1-19		Company Training in the morning + Educational class – Practice was also carried out for the Divisional Boxing Contest & Crosscountry Run. – The Batt"s were allotted to the Batt"s – The Regimental Censorship of letters was abolished – Company football. Transport v D.M.Wrs 4 – A.Cy nil. The following mention in despatches (8th Nov 1918) were published.	

LIEUT. COL. E.T. SAINT. D.S.O. 1st CAMB.R. (since died of wounds 29/8/18).

MAJOR. M.C. CLAYTON. D.S.O. "

LIEUT. & Q.M. B. POOLEY. "

3-5097 Sgt. BURR. S.A. "

3-262-1/3 " WARREN. R.W. "

1/1 CAMBRIDGESHIRE REGT.

Army Form C. 2118.

WAR DIARY
or
INTELLIGENCE SUMMARY.

(Erase heading not required.)

Place	Date	Hour	Summary of Events and Information	Remarks and references to Appendices
SOMAIN	4/1/19		Company Training & Educational Classes as usual - A Coy was working on the Coal Dump SOMAIN during the morning.	
"	5/1/19		There was a Special United Thanksgiving Service in the Brigade Concert Hall at 1100 hrs.	
"	6/1/19		Company Training & Educational Class as usual.	
"	7/1/19		Company Training & Educational Class. B. Coy were employed in the morning in work on the new Divl. Reception Camp	
"	8/1/19		Batt'n Training including a Route March & movement in Artillery formation across country. First night of the Divisional Boxing Contest at AUBERCHICOURT.	
AUBERCHICOURT			The Batt'n had one entry in each of the two eights. Footballs A Coy v 9th ESSEX R. 3. - A Coy 1/1 CAMB R. NIL. A Free Cinema performance was given to the Batt'n by the Y.M.C.A in the evening	
PECQUENCOURT	9/1/19		The Batt'n moved to billets at PECQUENCOURT under MAJOR. S.G. TYTE. M.C. for Salvage Work - A nucleus was left in SOMAIN. "Old billets"	Appendix No 13 Op. Order 112.
"	10/1/19		Engaged on Salvage work at PECQUENCOURT.	
"	11/1/19		Last night of the Divisional Boxing Contest at AUBERCHICOURT.	

1/1 CAMBRIDGESHIRE REGT.

Army Form C. 2118.

WAR DIARY
or
INTELLIGENCE SUMMARY.
(Erase heading not required.)

Place	Date	Hour	Summary of Events and Information	Remarks and references to Appendices
	11/4/19		Results 1/1 Camb. R. 2nd team 3rd in the Division with 23½ points	
			C.S.M. ROZIER. P. 'B' Coy Heavyweight champion of the Division	
			Pte WALLIS. C.P. 'B' Coy Middleweight champion of the Division	
			L/Cpl BATES. W. 'D' Coy Runner-up in the Lightweight championship.	
SOMAIN	12/4/19		The Battn returned to billets at SOMAIN.	
	13/4/19		Company training under Coy Commanders. Brazaban Class.	
AUBERCHICOURT			The Divisional Cross Country Run was held near AUBERCHICOURT	
	14/4/19		The 1/1 Camb. R. team, trained by 2/Lt. J. OGLE got 32 out of 50 men home	
			Company training & Education Class.	
SOMAIN	15/4/19		The Battn relieved the 9th Essex. R. on the SOMAIN. STA. GUARD at	Appendix No 2 Opn Order No 1/24
			10 o'clock. - The guard was found by 2 Companies & relieved by the other	
			2 Companies daily. Strength of the guard 4 Offrs & 125 O.R.'s	
	16/4/19		SOMAIN. STA. GUARD. -	
	17/4/19		SOMAIN. STA. GUARD. - The authority for the wearing of the ribbons of	
			the 1914-15 STAR was received. About 220 all ranks of the Battn are now	
			entitled to this decoration. - Divisional Tug of War competition.	
			1/1 CAMB. R. 2 pulls 9th Essex. R. 1 pull.	

1/1 CAMBRIDGESHIRE REGT

Army Form C. 2118.

WAR DIARY
or
INTELLIGENCE SUMMARY.
(Erase heading not required.)

Instructions regarding War Diaries and Intelligence Summaries are contained in F. S. Regs., Part II. and the Staff Manual respectively. Title pages will be prepared in manuscript.

Place	Date	Hour	Summary of Events and Information	Remarks and references to Appendices
SOMAIN	18/1/19		SOMAIN STA. GUARD. — Football. 9th ESSEX R. 4 goals — 1/1 CAMB.R. nil	
	19/1/19		SOMAIN STA. GUARD — Rugby Football. 1st CAMB.R. nil — 9th R.F. nil. Divisional Insp of War. Competition. 1st CAMB R. 2 pulls — 7th NORFOLKS nil	
	26/1/19		SOMAIN STA. GUARD	
	21/1/19		The Divisional Race Meeting was held near AUBERCHICOURT. The Batt Tug of War team trained by Sergt Wm POOLE got into the Finals of the Divisional Competition but were beats by the R.F.A.
	22/1/19		SOMAIN STA. GUARD. — The following award were published (18/1/19) 325014 Q.M.1. J.S. MAYSFIELD. D.C.M. } Meritorious Service Medal. 321674 C.Q.M.S. J.P. KNOLL.	
	23/1/19		SOMAIN. STA. GUARD.	
	24/1/19		The Batt n was relieved from SOMAIN STA. GUARD. at 10.00 hrs by the 7th E NORFOLK R.	
	25/1/19		Inspection of equipment by the C.O. — The Batt 2 took over the D.A.D.O.S guard for 1 week.	
	26/1/19		Voluntary Church Service.	
	27/1/19		The Batt n found the Guard for 12th Div 2nd H.Q. at MASNY — Company training. Educational class.	
	28/1/19		Company training & Educational Classes (about 50 now attending).	

1/1 CAMBRIDGESHIRE. REGT.

Army Form C. 2118.

WAR DIARY
or
INTELLIGENCE SUMMARY.
(Erase heading not required.)

Place	Date	Hour	Summary of Events and Information	Remarks and references to Appendices
SOMAIN	29/1/19		Company training under Coy Commanders. Education Class.	
	30/1/19		"	
	31/1/19		A party of 3 Officers & 70 O.R.'s proceeded to LILLE by lorry. Rehearsal for the presentation of Colours to the other Regiments of the Brigade on Brigade Parade ground	Appendix 3. Generals during January. Appendix 4. Reinforcements during January.
			Effective Strength 1/1/19 44 Officers & 728 O.R's.	
			" 31/1/19 39 " & 587 "	

1st Cambridgeshire Regiment.   Copy No. 10

Operation Order No 112.

Ref. Maps: 44 S.W. 1/20,000. 51ᵃ N.W 1/20,000.   Appendix No 1.   8.1.19.
                                                                                                       In the Field

INFORMATION. (1) The 1st Cambridgeshire Regt will proceed to PECQUENCOURT on the 9th inst. for salvage work & will be billeted in PECQUENCOURT, returning to billets in SOMAIN after doing two days salvage work.

INSTRUCTIONS. (2) (a) The Battn will parade at 10.00 hrs. on Battn. Parade Ground.
Markers will report to the R.S.M at 09.55 hrs.
The Drums will accompany the Battalion.
Dress:- Full Marching Order. ~~Blankets~~ Steel Helmets & SBRs will not be carried.

(b) Route :- VILLERS CAMPEAU - BRUILLE - PECQUENCOURT.

(c) Two officers per company, only, in addition to the Coy Commander will proceed with Battn

(d) The following personnel will be left by each company at SOMAIN :-
2 N.C.Os.   1 OR per billet.   1 Coy Cook.
& 'B' Coy H.Q. Guard.
H Q details as per instructions issued to OC "H.Q".

(e) ~~Blankets~~ Steel helmets, SBRs & Coy Lewis Guns will be stored in SOMAIN under company arrangements.

(f) Transport. S.A.A limbers & Officers' chargers will accompany the Battn.

(g) Cookers. The four Coy. cookers will proceed with the Battn. & a hot meal will be served on arrival at PECQUENCOURT.

(h) Officers' Valises & Mess Stores will be collected by limber from the Coys' H.Q. at 09.30 hrs.

(i) R.A.P. The M.O & 1 OR will accompany the Battn

(j) Blankets will be rolled in bundles of 10, clearly labelled & dumped at Coys' H Q by 09.00 hrs. T.O will arrange to convey blankets to PECQUENCOURT.

ACKNOWLEDGE (3).

Copies issued at   to
No 1. C.O.   No 7. OC "H.Q"
- 2 Maj Lyle M.C.   - 8. T.O.
- 3. OC "A" Coy   - 9. Q.M
- 4. "B" "   - 10. War.
- 5. "C" "   - 11. Diary.
- 6. "D" "   - 12. File.

(sd) E. WALKER, Capt & Adjt
1st Cambridgeshire Regt.

1st Cambridgeshire Regiment   Copy No. 19.
Operation Order. No 114.   14.1.19.
                 Appendix No 2.   In the Field

INFORMATION. 1. The 1st. CAMB.R will provide the SOMAIN. STATION GUARD from 15/1/19 to 19/1/19 and will relieve the present guard of the 9th ESSEX. R at 10.00 hrs on 15/1/19. The guard will be relieved daily at 10.00 hrs.

INSTRUCTIONS. 2. (a) The guard will be constituted as follows:-
Mounting on 15/1/19 & 17/1/19.
CAPT. C.L. TEBBUTT. M.C (in Command).
3 Offrs and 60. O.Rs of "A" Coy.
             40. O.Rs of "C" Coy.
Mounting on 16/1/19 & 18/1/19.
CAPT. B.G. QUIN. M.C. (in Command).
2 Offrs and 60. O.Rs of "D" Coy.
1 Offr and 40. O.Rs of "B" Coy.
(Numbers of O.Rs are exclusive of cooks).

(b). The relieving guards will parade on the Square daily at 09.15 hrs.
DRESS:- Full Marching Order.

(c). Officers i/c guards will arrange details of relief on the day previous to mounting.

(d). Cooking: "A" Coy cooker will accompany the guard on the 15th & 17th inst. "D" Coy cooker on the 16th & 18th inst.

(e) Rations:- Dry rations for the tour of duty will be carried on the man. Meat rations will be conveyed on the cookers.

(f) Blankets:- T.O will arrange for the conveyance of blankets to the Station. These will be rolled in bundles of 10 & dumped at Coy. H.Q. daily by 09.00 hrs.

ACKNOWLEDGE. (3)

Copies issued by runner at 13.00 hrs to:-
No. 1. C.O.
  " 2. CAPT. C.L. TEBBUTT. M.C.
  " 3. CAPT. B.G. QUIN. M.C.
  " 4. O.C. "B" COY.
  " 5. O.C. "C" COY.
  " 6. T.O.
  " 7. Q.M.
  " 8. 9th ESSEX. R.
  " 9 & 10. War Diary. ✓
  " 11. File.

(sd) E. WALKER. Capt & Adjt
            1st Cambridgeshire Regt.

1st Cambridgeshire Regiment
Decreases During January 1919

Appendix 3.

2.1.19	2 ORs	Demobilised
2.1.19	1 OR	Evac (Sick)
3.1.19	2 ORs	Demobilised
4.1.19	3 ORs	"
5.1.19	4 ORs	"
6.1.19	2 ORs	"
9.1.19	2 ORs	"
10.1.19	6 ORs	"
11.1.19	1 OR	"
11.1.19	4 ORs	To Eng (Reg Soldiers)
12.1.19	25 ORs	Demobilised
12.1.19	2 ORs	Watford Details
13.1.19	2 ORs	Struck off Str
14.1.19	2 ORs	Evac (Sick)
15.1.19	5 ORs	Demobilised
17.1.19	Lieut. F.O.P. Harrison	(To Eng)
17.1.19	1 OR	Demobilised
18.1.19	5 ORs	"
19.1.19	7 ORs	"
20.1.19	5 ORs	To Eng (Reg Soldiers)
20.1.19	13 ORs	Demobilised
21.1.19	12 ORs	"
22.1.19	11 ORs	"
23.1.19	5 ORs	"
25.1.19	21 ORs	"
25.1.19	1 OR	To Eng (Reg Soldier)
26.1.19	8 ORs	Demobilised
27.1.19	Capt. F. Clayton	"
27.1.19	9 ORs	"
28.1.19	Lt & Q.M. B. Pooley	"
28.1.19	14 ORs	"
29.1.19	Lt F.M. Bond	"
29.1.19	2nd Lt E.W. Bale	"
29.1.19	13 ORs	"
29.1.19	1 OR	Evac (Sick)

Lieut Col
Commdg 1st Camb Regt

Wm Dey
1/1st Bn Cambridgeshire
Regt

February 1919

Army Form C. 2118.

1/1 CAMBRIDGESHIRE Regt.

WAR DIARY
or
INTELLIGENCE SUMMARY.
(Erase heading not required.)

Instructions regarding War Diaries and Intelligence Summaries are contained in F.S. Regs., Part II. and the Staff Manual respectively. Title pages will be prepared in manuscript.

Place	Date	Hour	Summary of Events and Information	Remarks and references to Appendices
SOMAIN	1-2-19		Companies engaged in Company Training. 11 O/R Demobilized	
"	2-2-19		Battalion Parade for Divine Service. Lt. SEMMENS and 11 O/R Demobilized	
"	3-2-19		Battalion Parade for Ceremonial Drill. Lt C.L. MYER and 12 O/R Demobilized	
"	4-2-19		Battalion Parade for Presentation of Colours by H.R.H. the Prince of Wales to the 7th Bn. NORFOLK Regt. 9th Bn. ESSEX Regt. and 6th Bn. NORTHANTS Regt.	
"	5-2-19		Companies engaged in Company Training	
"	6-2-19		Companies engaged in Company Training	
"	7-2-19		Companies engaged in Company Training. Lt. A.A. PAYSON and 14 O/R Demobilized	
"	8-2-19		Companies engaged in Company Training 17 O/R Demobilized	
"	9-2-19		Battalion Parade for Divine Service. 14 O/R Demobilized A & C Coys on Sorrow Station Guard	
"	10-2-19		6 O/R Demobilized	
"	11-2-19		B & D Coys on SOMAIN Station Guard. 15 O/R Demobilized	
"	12-2-19		A & C Coys " " " " "	
"	13-2-19		B & D " " " " " 4 O/R Demobilized	
"	14-2-19		A & C " " " " " 5 O/R "	
"	15-2-19		B & D " " " " " 5 O/R "	
"	16-2-19		A & C " " " " " 7 O/R "	
"	17-2-19		Battalion Parade for Route March	
"	18-2-19		Companies engaged in Reorganisation	

1/1 CAMBRIDGESHIRE Regt.

WAR DIARY
or
INTELLIGENCE SUMMARY

Army Form C. 2118.

Place	Date	Hour	Summary of Events and Information	Remarks and references to Appendices
SOMAIN	19-7-19		Companies engaged in Company Training	
	20-7-19		A B C D Coys on SOMAIN Station Guard & G.R. Demobilised	
	21-7-19		Companies engaged in Company Training 8 O.R. Demobilised	
	22-7-19		Battalion Parade for Route March 7 O.R. "	
	23-7-19		A B C D Coys on SOMAIN Station Guard 33 O.R. "	
	24-7-19		Parade of all men returnable for Demobilisation for C.O.I. Inspection. 23 O.R. Demobilised	
	25-7-19		Battalion Musketry Parade. Draft of 2 officers (Capt. R.N. CARETT & Lt. BRUCE) & 29. O.R. 1/4 (CAMB) Bat. SUFFOLK Regt.	
	26-7-19		Companies engaged in Company Training	
	27-7-19		No Parades	
	28-7-19		Battalion reorganised into one Company	

[signature]
Lt Col
Commander

War Diary
1/1ᵗʰ Camb Regt
Feby 1915

1st Cambridgeshire Regiment

		OFF.	ORs
Effective Strength of Unit. February 1st 1919.		39	602.
Effective Strength of Unit February 28th 1919.		32.	196.

Demobilized

	OFF	O.Rs
	2.	240
Draft to 11th Suffolk Regiment.	OFF 2.	O.Rs 128

[signature]
Lt. Col.
Comdg. 1st Cambridgeshire Regt.

War Diary Vol 34

11st. Cambridgeshire Regiment

From 1/3/19 To 31/3/19

Army Form C. 2118.

WAR DIARY
or
INTELLIGENCE SUMMARY.
(Erase heading not required.)

Place	Date	Hour	Summary of Events and Information	Remarks and references to Appendices
SOMAIN.	MARCH, 1919			
	1		Summer Time commenced. (Div Order No 3018 — Summer time will come into use on 1st March, 1919. At 23.00 hours (Winter time) on that date all clocks will be put forward one hour). Battalion Parade for Divine Service at 10.45 hours	
	2.			
	3,4,5,6,7,8		No parade — All men in the Battalion employed	
	9th		Battalion Parade for Divine Service	
	10,11,12		No parade	
	13		Parade of drafts of returnable men proceeding to join the 11th (Cmb Battn) Suffolk Regt. for Commanding Officers inspection. This draft of 15 O.R. entrained at SOMAIN station at 01.55 hours to join	O.i/c Operation Order No 1117 of 13.3.19
	14			

Army Form C. 2118.

WAR DIARY
OR
INTELLIGENCE SUMMARY.
(Erase heading not required.)

Instructions regarding War Diaries and Intelligence Summaries are contained in F. S. Regs., Part II. and the Staff Manual respectively. Title pages will be prepared in manuscript.

Place	Date	Hour	Summary of Events and Information	Remarks and references to Appendices
SOMAIN			11th (Camb) Battn SUFFOLK REGT.	
	15		No parades	
	16		Battalion Church Parade	
	17 }		No parade	
	18 }			
	19		Parade of the Battalion Baths at 14.00 down for Commanding Officer's inspection	
	20		3 Officers and 15 O.R. proceeded on 2 days leave to LILLE	Recommendations
	21 }		No parades	
	22 }			
	23		Battalion Church Parade	
	24		1 Officer and 16 O.R. proceeded on 2 days leave to LILLE	
	25 }		No parade	
	26 }			
	27		Another party of 1 Officer and 15 O.R. of the Battalion Cadre proceeded to LILLE	
	28 }		No parades	
	29 }			
	30 }			
	31 }			

Lieut. Col:
Comdg. 1st Bn. Cambridgeshire Regt.

Appendix
No I

1st CAMBRIDGESHIRE REGIMENT.   Copy No.

Operation Order No.117.

SOMAIN.   13th March 1919.
-:-

1.   The draft of 12 other ranks of this Battalion who
are retainable for the Army of Occupation, under Army Order
(IV of 1919, will proceed to join the 11th.(Cambs) Battn.
SUFFOLK REGIMENT on 14th March 1919.   01.15
The draft will entrain at SOMAIN Station at 02.xx hours on
14th. March.1919.

2.   The draft will be under the command of No.241281
Corpl. CLARKE. W.F.

3.   The Draft will parade on the Square at 01.30 hours.
Dress:- Full Marching Order. Overcoats and Jerkins will be
worn. 3 Blankets will be rolled and carried on the Pack.

4.   RATIONS. One day's rations will be carried.

5.   MEALS. A hot meal will be served to the draft
at 01.00 hours.

ACKNOWLEDGE.

                            (sd). E. WALKER. Capt. & Adjt.
                                  1st Cambridgeshire Regiment.

Copies issued to
No.1. C.O.
" 2. O.C. Company.
" 3. Q.M.
" 4. Corpl.Clarke. W.F.
" 5. War Diary.
" 6.   "   "
" 7. File.

Appendix No 2

1st Cambridgeshire Regiment

Decrease in Strength during month of March 1919

1-3-19	8 O.Rs.	Demobilised
2-3-19	6 O.Rs.	do
	Lieut A. M. Lison	Stt off Strength, Ordered Medical Board whilst on Leave
4-3-19	Lieut F. J. Harvey	Transferred to 41st P. of W. Coy
"	F. J. Suttle	— 233rd — do —
"	W. B. Rebbie	— 100th — do —
	2nd Lt H. J. A. Hoole	— 108th — do —
3-3-19	2nd Lt H. B. Hart	To England (sick)
6-3-19	28 O.Rs.	Demobilised
7-3-19	15 O.Rs.	Demobilised
14-3-19	15 O.Rs.	Demobilised
9-3-19	Lieut J. A. Hardman	Demobilised
17-3-19	" J. M. D. English	Demobilised on Leave
24-3-19	3 O.Rs.	Demobilised
25-3-19	2 O.Rs.	do
26-3-19	4 O.Rs.	do
27-3-19	7 O.Rs.	do
	Lieut E. Pollard	Demobilised
26-3-19	1 O.R.	Transferred to 11th Bn. Suffolk Regt
31-3-19	6 O.Rs.	Demobilised

1-4-19 For O.C. 1st Cambridgeshire Regiment

Major

Appendix No 2

Appendix No 3.

1st Cambridgeshire Regiment.

Strength.

	Officers.	O.R.
1 - 3 - 19.	32	196
31 - 3 - 19.	19	77

Major.
Lieut. Col:
Comdg. 1st Bn. Cambridgeshire Regt.

War Diary
of
1/1st Bn. Cambridgeshire Regt.

April 1919

Army Form C. 2118.

1st Bn. Cambridgeshire Regt.

WAR DIARY
or
INTELLIGENCE SUMMARY.
(Erase heading not required.)

Place	Date	Hour	Summary of Events and Information	Remarks and references to Appendices
SOMAIN	2/4/19		Inspection of the Cadre by the Commanding Officer.	
	4/4/19	6 pm	1 Officer & 7 men on SOMAIN STATION GUARD.	
			Church parade in the Cinema Hall.	
	6 pm			
	10 pm		Inspection of the Cadre by the Commanding Officer.	
	13 pm		Church parade in the Cinema Hall.	
	14 pm		Capt C.L. TEBBUTT M.C. assumed command of the Battn in the absence of the Commanding Officer on leave	
	16 pm		Inspection of the Cadre by the Commanding Officer	
	18 pm		Good Friday – Church Parade in the Cinema Hall.	
	19/4		Easter – Party to LILLE for the day by lorry	
	20 pm		Easter day. Church parade in the Cinema Hall. Football match at finish SOMAIN. Won by 3 % Camb	
	25 pm		Inspection of the Cadre by the Commanding Officer.	
	27 pm		Church Parade in the Cinema Hall	Appendix I (December) Appendix II Strength

C L Tebbutt
Captain
Commdg 1st Cambridgeshire Regiment

1st CAMBRIDGESHIRE REGIMENT.

Appendix I

Decreases during the month of APRIL 1919.

17:3:19.	Lieut, I.M.D. English. Demobilized.
28:3:19.	1 Other rank transferred to 11th Bn. Suffolk Regiment.
31:3:19.	6 " " Demobilized.
31:3:19.	Lieut, G.O. Wallis-Palmer. Demobilized.
3:4:19.	Captain, H.C. Banting. do.
3:4:19.	3 Other ranks do.
10:4:19.	2 Other ranks re-posted to 9th Bn. Essex Regiment.
9:4:19.	Major, S.G. Tyte, M.C. Demobilized.
14:4:19.	4 Other ranks transferred to 11th Bn. Suffolk Regiment.
16:4:19.	Lieut, C.C. Cope.)
	A/Capt, C. Warren .) Demobilized.
19:4:19.	Lieut, C.J. Webb. do.
22:4:19.	4 Other ranks transferred to 11th Bn Suffolk Regiment.
21:4:19.	1 Other ranks demobilized.
24:4:19.	Lieut, S.C. Knight and 4 Other ranks demobilized.

C L Tebbutt

30:4:19.

Captain,
Commdg. 1st Cambridgeshire Regiment.

Appendix II

1st CAMBRIDGESHIRE REGIMENT.
****

<u>S T R E N G T H.</u>   Officers.   Other ranks.

    1:4:19.   16.   75.

   30:4:19.   11.   48.

   30:4:19.   *C. Tebbutt*

                              Captain,
                   Commdg. 1st Cambridgeshire Regiment.

1/1st Bⁿ Cambridgeshire Regt.

Army Form C. 2118.

WAR DIARY
or
INTELLIGENCE SUMMARY.
(Erase heading not required.)

Vol 36

Place	Date	Hour	Summary of Events and Information	Remarks and references to Appendices
SOMAIN	1/5/19		Battⁿ still stationed at SOMAIN.	Cased
"	4/5/19		Battⁿ rec'd that the Cadre moves forward to England on the 6ᵗʰ May.	Operation Order 118
"	5/5/19		Day spent in loading stores & vehicles parked in the afternoon at the SOMAIN GUN PARK SIDING.	Appendix 421.
"	6/5/19		Vehicles loaded on the trains at the Gun Park Siding during the morning. Cadre paraded at 1700 hrs with the Drums - and marched (Colours cased) to the Station. Lt. Col. M.C. CLAYTON, D.S.O. returned from leave in the morning & resumed Command of the Battⁿ. The Cadre entrained at Somain Station & left there about 1930 hrs. Halts took place for an hour during which a hot meal was attained at MONTIGNY. Travelled during the night via DOUAI, LILLE, ARMENTIERES,	
DUNKERQUE	7/5/19		BAILLEUL & MERRIS where breakfast was obtained at the Halts enroute. Thence through CASSEL & BERGUES to DUNKERQUE arriving there at about 0900 hrs. Accommodated at HOSPL. CAMP. - Transport officers went to the Ferry during the afternoon.	
"	8/5/19		Baths & clean clothes during the morning - Moved to No2 EMBARKATION CAMP.	M.C.

Army Form C. 2118.

WAR DIARY
or
INTELLIGENCE SUMMARY.
(Erase heading not required.)

Place	Date	Hour	Summary of Events and Information	Remarks and references to Appendices
DUNKERQUE	7-5-19		Transport & Stores loaded on S.S. CLUTHA.	
	10.5.19.		Cadre Paraded at 14.30 hours & embarked on the Russian Steamer MICHAEL SIDIROV at 16.30 hours.	

Strength
6 Officers
46 O.R.

[signature]
Comdg. 1st Bn. Cambridgeshire Regt.

Sheet 2. Operation Order No. 118.

No. 11. SURPLUS PERSONNEL. Special orders will be issued later as to disposal of Personnel surplus to the Cadre.

No. 12. BILLETS. All Billets will be inspected at 15.00 hours and will be left scrupulously clean.

ACKNOWLEDGE.
                                        (Sgd) E. WALKER, Captain & Adjutant.
                                               1st Cambridgeshire Regiment.

Copies issued as under:-
No.1.   C.O.
No. 2.   O.C. Company.
No. 3.   Capt. T.H.H. Harding-Newman. M.C.
No. 4.   "   C.H. Bowers.
No. 5.   "   C.H. Hollis.
No. 6.   2nd. Lieut. A. Stone.
No. 7.   "   "   W. Hodges.
No. 8.   C.S.M. Mansfield. J.S. D.C.M.
No. 9.   R.Q.M.S.
Nos 10 & 11 War Diary.
No.12   File.